Arbitrary and Capricious

The Supreme Court, the Constitution, and the Death Penalty

MICHAEL A. FOLEY

PRAEGER

Westport, Connecticut
London

Library of Congress Cataloging-in-Publication Data

Foley, Michael A.
 Arbitrary and capricious : the Supreme Court, the Constitution, and the death penalty /
Michael A. Foley.
  p. cm.
 Includes bibliographical references and index.
 ISBN 0–275–97587–8 (alk. paper)
  1. Capital punishment—United States—History. 2. Due process of law—United
States—History. 3. Equality before the law—United States—History. 4. Capital
punishment—United States. I. Title.
 KF9227.C2F65 2003
 345.73'0773—dc21   2003042853

British Library Cataloguing in Publication Data is available.

Library of Congress Catalog Card Number: 2003042853
ISBN: 0–275–97587–8

First published in 2003

Praeger Publishers, 88 Post Road West, Westport, CT 06881
An imprint of Greenwood Publishing Group, Inc.
www.praeger.com

Printed in the United States of America

The paper used in this book complies with the
Permanent Paper Standard issued by the National
Information Standards Organization (Z39.48–1984).

10 9 8 7 6 5 4 3 2 1

For my parents,
Marion and Reba Foley

Contents

Acknowledgments

Without the assistance of the following people, this book would not have been possible. First, in the early stages of this book I was fortunate enough to have two honors students from my honors course in Philosophical Perspectives on Punishment who took considerable time from their hectic schedules to read several chapters closely, carefully, and critically. Jennifer Jancola and Katie McElhenney offered invaluable advice and suggestions on how to make the presentation clearer and more coherent. They have graduated, and I miss the opportunity to have them serve as critics on my next project.

Second, two colleagues read the entire manuscript and provided insights on structure, style, and substance that kept me focused on the thesis and its development. Dr. William Conlogue, Associate Professor and Chair, Department of English, Marywood University, and Dr. William Mohan, Full Professor and former Chair, Department of Philosophy, Marywood University, offered timely advice and raised important questions in a manner that was critical yet supportive. I cannot thank them enough for the time they spent reading my manuscript.

The book is better thanks to the helpful suggestions of these readers. I remain solely responsible for the book's shortcomings.

Third, I want to thank several people at Marywood University for the financial support they provided in the four years I worked on the manuscript. The Faculty Development Committee never hesitated in granting my requests for research money to travel to Washington, D.C. I cannot thank the members of that committee individually since terms of service expire and new members are elected. I have also had the support of my deans. Dr. Janet Reohr was the Dean of the Undergraduate School for the first three years of the project. She constantly encouraged my research and writing. Dr. John Alessio became Dean of the Undergraduate School in the fall of 2000, and immediately expressed interest in and support for the project. In addition, without the support of Marywood's administration, there would be no Faculty Development Committee. Sister Patricia Ann Matthews, Marywood's Vice President for Academic Affairs, works diligently to maintain faculty development funds for research. Sister Mary Reap, Marywood's President, maintains support for the sabbaticals that are essential to complete one's writing and research. As a faculty member in the Undergraduate School, where excellence in teaching is, and should be, the priority, and where many of us teach from 90 to 120 students/semester, I can state categorically that without the support of these people, those of us on the undergraduate faculty would be unable to maintain a critical level of research. I want to thank Sister Mary and Sister Patricia as well for their work to maintain faculty access to computers, to the Internet, and to on-line databases. Indeed, without the Internet, I could not have written this book. That I could sit in my office and do research throughout the country continues to astound me. I went to Washington, D.C., on several occasions to use the Library of Congress. Thanks to Marywood and the Internet, I had already done my research on-line and knew exactly what books and articles I needed to obtain.

I want to thank the library and academic computing staffs for their considerable help. The people in these two areas are always eager to assist in any way they can. The library staff has responded quickly and efficiently to my request for interlibrary book loans and articles. They do not even chastise me when I send them requests with incomplete information. The academic computing staff offers numerous workshops that provide helpful hints on getting the most from one's computer and its software. In addition, they have been there to answer my silly and naive questions about computers and software. Specifically, Kay McClintock and Karen Boland have always responded with alacrity to my questions and confusions.

Last, and certainly not least, I want to thank my wife, "Sue B.," for her support of my research and writing. Thanks, "Sue B."

CHAPTER 1

The Supreme Court and the Punishment Dilemma

But all punishment is mischief: all punishment in itself is evil.
Jeremy Bentham, *The Principles of Morals and Legislation*

The instinct for retribution is part of the nature of man, and channeling that instinct in the administration of criminal justice serves an important purpose in promoting the stability of a society governed by law. When people begin to believe that organized society is unwilling or unable to impose on criminal offenders the punishment they "deserve," then there are sown the seeds of anarchy—of self-help, vigilante justice, and lynch law.
Justice Potter Stewart, *Furman v. Georgia*

Men are not hang'd for stealing Horses, but that Horses may not be stolen.
George Savile

GENERAL BACKGROUND

The Supreme Court began to scrutinize the constitutionality of the death penalty in 1878 in *Wilkerson v. Utah*.[1] In *Wilkerson*, the Justices unanimously held that death by firing squad did not violate the Eighth Amendment's prohibition of cruel and unusual punishment. It would be another twelve years before the Court would hear a second capital case, *In re Kemmler*.[2] The Court, in *Kemmler*, and again unanimously, held that the use of the electric chair was constitutional.

The Court's decisions in these cases came as little or no surprise, in part because society in general had no moral or legal scruples about capital punishment. However, in the 1960s people would challenge that general truth. Indeed, in some polls in the 1960s, more Americans found the death penalty immoral, if not unconstitutional.[3] Then, in a shocking and unpredictable 1972 Court case, *Furman v. Georgia*,[4] the Supreme Court, in a 5–4 vote, held that the death penalty, as then administered, violated the Eighth Amendment's cruel and unusual punishment clause, not because the death penalty in and of itself was unconstitutional, but because there were no clear, coherent, and consistent methods for imposing the death penalty on a person convicted of a capital crime. People convicted of a capital offense received different sentences, one of which could be the death penalty. In other words, the methods used to distinguish between those guilty capital defendants who deserved the death penalty and those who did not were inconsistent and haphazard. In short, no clear and coherent method existed that guaranteed capital defendants "equal justice under law."[5] Stated constitutionally, because no consistent and coherent criteria existed that guided juries and judges in their deliberations on the "just" punishment, capital defendants were denied, under the Fourteenth Amendment, their fundamental constitutional rights of "due process of law" or the "equal protection of the laws."[6]

From 1878 to 1972, the Supreme Court deferred consistently and willingly to states' rights concerning both criminal justice and the death penalty. For most of those years, the prevailing view of the Court was that the language of the Fifth and Eighth Amendments constitutionally sanctioned capital punishment clearly and unambiguously. There was little opposition to the death penalty and, at times, no opposition at all among the justices. A literal reading of the Fifth Amendment, after all, states, directly and seemingly unambiguously, that "[n]o person shall be held to answer for a capital . . . crime," "be twice put in jeopardy of life," or "be deprived of life . . . without due process of law." Why, one could ask, would the Fifth Amendment refer explicitly to the conditions that must be met for a life to be taken if it was not constitutional to take it? And if life can be taken, assuming due process of law standards have been met, how can people argue that the death penalty is unconstitutional? No interpretation of the Bill of Rights can make a case that the Eighth Amendment nullifies the Fifth Amendment's conditions for depriving a person of his or her life.[7] Nonetheless, the major assault on the death penalty historically has been based on the Eighth Amendment: "Excessive bail shall not be required, nor excessive fines imposed, nor cruel and unusual punishments inflicted."[8] Is the death penalty unconstitutional because it is cruel and unusual? Two points must be noted in this context.

First, the federal government and the individual state governments have the constitutional right to use the death penalty if they so desire. There is no constitutional requirement that states must use the death penalty. Currently, thirty-eight states, the federal government, and the military have provisions for the use of the death penalty.

Second, there are no specific constitutional limitations on when the death penalty can be employed. For example, the death penalty has been used as a punishment for murder, rape, treason, sodomy, arson and theft, among others. Pennsylvania was the first state to abolish the death penalty (in 1789) for all criminal offenses except first-degree murder. The Supreme Court has now placed limits on the use of the death penalty. For example, mandatory death sentences (i.e., an automatic sentence of death for murder)[9] and a sentence of death for rape[10] have been declared unconstitutional. But these are recent limitations—not limitations specifically defined as cruel and unusual punishments. Changes in the Supreme Court's scrutiny of the use of the death penalty began when the Court started to apply the Bill of Rights to the states based on the concept of *selective incorporation*. Although scholarly debate on the meaning, legitimacy, and scope of selective incorporation remains divided, there is no question but that the practice of selective incorporation has become entrenched in the Court's philosophy regarding the limits of state power as it affects citizens' rights as guaranteed by the Bill of Rights.

The selective incorporation doctrine has been defined as "the process by which certain of the guarantees expressed in the *Bill of Rights* become applicable to the states through the **Fourteenth Amendment.** . . . Under the selective incorporation approach, select guarantees in the Bill of Rights and their related case law are applied to the states."[11] In their book on the Bill of Rights, Ellen Alderman and Caroline Kennedy explain the doctrine as follows:

So it was not until the Thirteenth, Fourteenth, and Fifteenth amendments were enacted, after the Civil War, that the federal Constitution began to protect individuals against the states. The Fourteenth Amendment has been the principle means by which this protection has been accomplished. It reads, in part, "No *State* shall . . . deprive any person of life, liberty, or property, without due process of law." The Supreme Court has interpreted this guarantee of liberty to embrace the fundamental liberties in the Bill of Rights, meaning that state governments must observe and protect them to the same extent as the federal government. In legal parlance, this process is called incorporation. The amendments in the Bill of Rights are said to be incorporated against the states through the due process clause of the Fourteenth Amendment. There has been an ongoing debate on the Supreme Court about the scope of incorporation, and whether the entire Bill of Rights, or only some of its guarantees, should be incorporated against the states.[12]

The importance of the selective incorporation doctrine as it applies to criminal justice issues cannot be overstated. Accordingly, a brief explanation of selective incorporation and how it has affected constitutional interpretation of criminal rights is necessary.

Originally, the guarantees of the Bill of Rights applied only to the federal government's limits over individual liberty. The language of the First Amendment offers the clearest statement about such limits. The first five words of that Amendment are, "Congress shall make no law."[13] The constitutional guarantees of the first eight amendments can be read as limited to "Congress." For example, the First Amendment prohibited Congress from "abridging the freedom of speech," not individual states; the Fourth Amendment prohibited Congress from passing laws that would permit the federal government to randomly conduct "unreasonable searches and seizures," not individual states; the Eighth Amendment prohibited Congress from imposing "cruel and unusual punishments," not individual states. Thus, states were not precluded from abridging the freedoms guaranteed to the individual against the federal government. Many states had their own guarantees safeguarding individual rights, but individuals did not have the same securities against their respective state governments as they did against the federal government. The Fourteenth Amendment would change that reality.

Section 1 of the Fourteenth Amendment established the means by which the Supreme Court would selectively apply (selective incorporation) the individual guarantees of the Bill of Rights to the separate states. The first sentence of that section reinforces the federal nature of constitutional democracy in the United States, namely, U.S. citizens "are citizens of the United States and of the State wherein they reside."[14] The second sentence of that section suggests that the rights guaranteed to the people by the Bill of Rights against the federal government apply to state governments as well. That sentence reads: "No State shall make or enforce any law which shall abridge the privileges or immunities of citizens of the United States; nor shall any State deprive any person of life, liberty, or property, without due process of law; nor deny to any person within its jurisdiction the equal protection of the laws."[15] One clause in that sentence is particularly relevant to criminal justice issues, namely, states cannot "deprive any person of life, liberty, or property, without due process of law." That clause extends the Fifth Amendment guarantee individuals have against the federal government to state governments. Stated alternatively, that clause "incorporates" a Fifth Amendment right into a right against both state and federal governments. States can no longer *legitimately*, that is, *constitutionally*, deny any citizen life, liberty, or property, without due process of law.[16] However, that states must guarantee "due process of law" to all persons strongly suggests that some, if not all, liberties and securities of the Bill of Rights now applies to the states as well. Constitutional debate about what the framers of the Fourteenth Amendment intended remains contentious. But the practice of "selective incorporation," despite ongoing scholarly debate, has become a mainstay of constitutional decision making. The impact of selective incorporation has been significant and substantive. Many of the following cases demonstrate how the Fourteenth Amendment, and the doctrine of selective incorporation, has transformed criminal justice law. One highly significant case illustrates the idea of selective incorporation.

States, as noted, had the right to define their criminal laws, including, among other things, defendant rights. One such right that is now taken for granted is the Sixth Amendment right to counsel. Prior to 1963, with few exceptions,[17] states were not required to appoint counsel in criminal trials to defendants who could not afford counsel.[18] Without counsel, however, defendants were at a distinct disadvantage not only as to the outcome of a case but also in terms of knowing their constitutional rights. In 1963 the Supreme Court held, unanimously, in *Gideon v. Wainwright*,[19] that all defendants charged with serious felonies had to be represented by counsel, and that if the defendant could not afford counsel, the state had to appoint counsel. As a result of *Gideon*, a defendant's Sixth Amendment right to legal representation now applies, by incorporation, to the states. Since *Gideon*, the right to counsel has been expanded to include the right to counsel at all stages of police interrogation. Without the Fourteenth Amendment and the Supreme Court's interpretation of it few, if any, of the Bill of Rights would apply against the states.[20]

Most, but not all, of the rights guaranteed by the Bill of Rights have been "incorporated" to apply against the states.[21] Specifically we will see Supreme Court Justices trying to walk a thin line between the rights of the states to define their criminal law and the Supreme Court's responsibility to assure all people their constitutional rights as guaranteed by the Bill of Rights. Capital punishment constitutes one of those states' rights that the Supreme Court must address both in terms of a person's fundamental rights (for our purpose, more specifically, the Eighth Amendment's prohibition against cruel and unusual punishment) and the rights of states to define not only what constitutes a crime but also to determine what they maintain constitutes an appropriate punishment.

Literal interpretations of the Fifth and Eighth Amendments, along with "selective incorporation," constitute key factors in the adjudication of most of the cases examined throughout this book. There is, however, another element that plays out in Supreme Court death penalty decisions, namely, arguments about what justifies punishment in general and the death penalty in particular. Those justifying arguments will direct the Justices' thinking as they apply the Constitution to criminal laws and punishments. It is therefore necessary to examine briefly those justifications.

Jeremy Bentham's oft-quoted remark that "all punishment in itself is evil" identifies the philosophical concern with punishment as primarily one of justification. More specifically, Bentham claims that punishment, "if it ought at all to be admitted, it ought only to be admitted in as far as it promises to exclude some greater evil."[22] Any punishment, including something as seemingly innocuous as a one-hour detention, requires justification because punishment is pain and no one has a right to inflict pain on another person without some fairly substantial moral justification. The two major justifications for punishment in general and the death penalty in particular are reflected in the opening quotes from Justice Potter Stewart and George Savile. Justice Stewart's statement that opens this chapter reflects a *retributive* justification for punishment. Retributive theory holds that people are punished because they have broken a law. George Savile's statement that follows Stewart's reflects a *deterrent* justification for punishment. Deterrence theory holds that people are punished to deter further criminal conduct. Since retributivism and deterrence are at the heart of many of the Supreme Court Justices' ruminations on the justifications of punishment in constitutional adjudication on the death penalty, it is necessary to understand these distinct philosophical justifications for punishment.

The retributive justification for punishment claims, overall, that punishment is justified because the guilty must pay for their crime, their wrongdoing. If someone commits a crime or a moral outrage, that person, from a retributivist's perspective, must be punished or morally disparaged. In addition, the punishment must fit the crime. A retributivist, for example, could argue that the death penalty (the punishment) fits first-degree murder (the crime). Retributivists, in general, maintain that punishment balances the scales of justice or that punishment rights a wrong. The public attitude, for example, that "criminals get what they deserve," is retributive in nature. A retributive philosophy looks to the past to determine a person's (criminal's) "just desert." It is a *nonconsequential* philosophy in that what occurs as a result of punishment is secondary in determining and meting out punishment. For example, if someone has stolen $5,000, a retributivist could justify a $5,000 fine in addition to an amount calculated to offset any additional advantages that resulted from that theft. Federal laws, for example, permit the federal government to seize property that has been purchased as a result of money acquired through illegal drug sales. In other words, for retributivism, people cannot gain from their wrongdoing. Laws that prohibit convicted criminals from making money from a book they write about their crimes are retributive in nature. Criminals are not to gain from their wrongdoing.[23] Retributivists, in short, are not *directly* interested in consequences such as deterrence. If a retributive punishment results in a lower crime rate, that is a fortuitous result, a bonus. But "benefits" or "beneficial consequences" of punishment in classical retributivism do not count in support of the justification of punishment.

Retributivism, then, holds that punishments are evaluated independent from any consequences, good or bad, that the punishment brings into existence. Criminal acts, in classical retributivism, must be punished to maintain a moral and social equilibrium in society. This general justification for punishment, then, seeks *primarily* to restore social order, not to *deter* future criminal acts. As noted previously, most punishments will have some deterrent effect. But even if punishment does not deter, society, from a retributivist viewpoint, still has an obligation to punish criminal wrongdoing. Lying before a grand jury, for example, from a retributivist perspective, constitutes an act of wrongdoing that should be prosecuted because a legal wrong has been committed. For society to show respect for its laws, it must punish people who break those laws. The punishment itself is based on what has been done, not on what will happen later as a result of punishment. Retributivists, then, in general, look to the past to determine what punishment, if any, is *deserved.*

Deterrence theory holds that punishment is justified only if it serves some greater social purpose, function, or goal. Punishments, on this view, to be morally justified, must achieve some desirable social end. Deterrence theory is a *consequential* philosophy in that punishments must deter criminal conduct or that punishment is illegitimate. Consequentialism, as the name implies, holds that actions are judged in terms of the consequences, good and bad, that the act brings into existence. From a consequential point of view, for example, an act of wrongdoing (e.g., prostitution) may not need to be prosecuted or punished if the consequences of the wrongdoing were either indefinable or socially beneficial. In short, deterrence theory, in contrast to retributive theory, looks to the future to determine what punishment, if any, is *necessary.*[24]

A brief but useful differentiation between retributive and deterrent justifications for punishment is offered by Immanuel Kant, one of the most formidable moral philosophers and retributivists in the history of philosophy. Kant describes the difference as follows:

Punishment in general is physical evil accruing from moral evil. It is either deterrent or else retributive. Punishments are deterrent if their sole purpose is to prevent an evil from arising; they are retributive when they are imposed because an evil has been done. Punishments are, therefore, a means of preventing an evil [deterrent] or of punishing it [retributive]. Those imposed by government are always deterrent. They are meant to deter the sinner himself or to deter others by making an example of him. But the punishments imposed by a being who is guided by moral standards are retributive.[25]

With these very general lines of distinction drawn, what, more specifically, defines retributive and deterrent justifications for punishment?

Retributivism is not, as some have argued, necessarily associated with the notions of revenge and vengeance.[26] Susan Jacoby, for example, misrepresents retributivism as follows: "Advocates of draconian punishment for crime invariably prefer 'retribution'—a word that affords the comfort of euphemism although it is virtually synonymous with 'revenge.'"[27]

Revenge may be indeed the best way to get even, but retributivists are not justifying punishment because they think that there is a need to get even. Punishment is justified under a retributive view because a wrong has been done, and a moral society cannot stand idly by while wrongs are being committed. David Lyons makes the following relevant observation: "Retributive theories of punishment maintain that retributive attitudes can be translated responsibly into practice. They do not celebrate vengeance or call for blind, unreflective revenge. They call for justice—the justice of treating people as they *deserve* to be treated by virtue of their conduct and the attitudes that conduct represents."[28] Even Kant, the quintessential retributivist, eschews revenge, vengeance, and hate as legitimate elements in punishment. For Kant, the only person entitled to seek vengeance is the "Supreme Moral Lawgiver,"[29] namely, God. Kant makes his position rather clear in the following reflection: "Thus it is a moral duty not only to refrain from returning vengeful hatred for the hostility of others, but also to refrain from summoning the Judge of the World to vengeance. This is partly so because man is so saddled with guilt of his own that he is much in need of pardon, but it is especially so because *no* punishment, from whomever it might be, may be inflicted in *hate.*"[30]

For the retributivist, punishment is right in itself, regardless of what the consequences (the deterrent perspective) are, including the consequences of "getting even." Indeed, what may sound somewhat paradoxical, punishment of wrongdoing is justified even if it leads to an increase in crime. For example, there have been isolated cases of murder committed specifically because the death penalty existed. John Kaplan tells the story of a baby-sitter who killed the children left in her care because she wanted to commit suicide but, for religious reasons, was unable to. By killing the children, she reasoned, the state would take her life, something she was religiously prohibited from doing. Logic aside, this example may be better used to indicate that no punishment will ever be completely effective, whether effective be defined in terms of retributive or deterrent theory.[31] Although these cases are rare, they still occurred because the murderer sought or embraced the death penalty. Now politically and legally society may well want to reject the death penalty if its presence increases the possibility for murder. From the retributive perspective, however, the death penalty remains morally defensible despite any increase in murders.

The retributive theory stresses the relationship between punishment and desert. That is, no one should be punished who is not culpably guilty; people should be punished only if they are guilty *and* deserve it. Thus, a criminal may be guilty of wrongdoing, but a punishment may not be deserved. For example, people who simply do not, or cannot, understand what it is they have done should not be punished. For good or for ill, people are not punished if they are impaired mentally (e.g., do not or cannot understand what it is they have done). A nine-year-old, one can argue, should not be punished formally (i.e., an adult prison or the death penalty) for having committed murder on the basis that nine-year-old children do not comprehend the nature and meaning of the act they have committed. Of course, one can argue that nine-year-old children in certain situations should be punished. My point is less controversial, namely, there are conditions—mental, physical, or otherwise—that render a person blameless, although the act itself is criminal. From a retributive point of view, punishment cannot be inflicted on people who, for whatever reason, cannot understand their criminal wrongdoing. Society simply cannot punish people who do not deserve it. Or, to make the same point, a person who has been punished must be one who *deserved* to be punished; otherwise, that person has been done an egregious injustice.

Furthermore, the retributivist maintains that there is a duty to punish the guilty. A criminal should not go free. Why? First, an illegal act has been committed, and, to show society's respect for law, punishment is required. If people are not punished for their wrongdoing, law becomes a mockery, a joke. Second, criminals who are not punished for their wrongdoing are denied their autonomy and individual worth as human beings. Retributivism upholds the moral worth and dignity of all human beings.[32] Not to punish wrongdoers, to place them in a rehabilitation program or to claim that they were not responsible for their actions but were instead victims of their environment, is to deny them their autonomy, moral worth, and human dignity. One brief example can illuminate what at times sounds positively bizarre.

I do not think that anyone, in reality, would insist on punishment as a means to maintain their autonomy, moral worth, and human dignity. But, in theory, is it possible that someone would ever claim that they want or demand to be punished? In Henrik Stangerup's *The Man Who Wanted to Be Guilty*,[33] the main character, Torbin, commits a particularly brutal act: he murders his wife. Once taken into custody, Torbin is taken away to undergo "retraining." His son has been taken to a "social center" in part to forget his past but also to adjust to life without parents. Torbin has been told that there never was a wife and a son. All traces of his wife's and his son's existence have been removed from their former apartment. Her blood can no longer be found dried on the floors and walls. Pictures that would prove that there was once a family have been destroyed. It is time for Torbin to start a new life as if there had never been an old one. In Stangerup's fictional society, there is no such thing as guilt and punishment for wrongdoing. At one point in a session with his therapist Torbin tries desperately to tell her that he has committed murder and that he and he alone is responsible for it. The following conversation ensues:

"I'm guilty of a *murder*."
    Now she [the therapist] looked at him angrily.

"Why do you say such nonsense?"

"It's true nonetheless."

"There's no such thing as guilt anymore, you know that . . ."

Something censorious, pedantic, tight-lipped (almost like an old-fashioned piano teacher) had come over her:

"It's always the circumstances that dictate our actions."[34]

Torbid tries to take responsibility for his actions; he tries, and indeed wants, to take responsibility for his wife's murder. But there is no wife. There is no evidence that a child was ever conceived. Torbid is free to start life over, to forget about his being a victim of "the circumstances." Torbid struggles in vain to take responsibility for one of the most hideous acts a human being can commit. In such a world, a person might very well demand punishment to begin to atone for his wrongdoing, to begin to recover his soul. To be restored to mental health Torbid discovers, contrary to the state's therapeutic program, that he must atone for his wrongdoing.

From the retributivist perspective, if there is no punishment, not only is there no crime but also there is no moral worth and human dignity, either for the victim or for the criminal. Punishment, as odd as this may sound, upholds the self-respect of criminals and affirms to them that they are not being used to serve the interests of society. It is society's duty, responsibility, and obligation, to punish the criminal. Society should not take delight in punishing people. People who applaud executions, for example, are not good retributivists. They are vindictive, revengeful. The feelings of revenge or vengeance on the part of the victim's family can be understood but not acted upon. Victims are not exactly in a rational and objective state of mind, and rightly and understandably so. To be victimized and yet indifferent to the loss might well indicate an irrationality of another sort. Regardless, victims are not exactly objective bystanders. The questionable involvement of victims in deciding a criminal's degree of guilt will be examined in several cases in chapter 4 and pursued more fully in chapters 5 and 6. The point here is that people cannot serve as judges in their own cases.[35] In addition, no one should derive pleasure or satisfaction from punishing someone. Some people may well feel satisfaction from the punishment, but that does not justify the punishment. Teachers, for example, should not take delight about a student's failure. It is the duty of a teacher to fail someone who has not met the minimum passing requirements for the course. There should be, from the retributivist's point of view, little, if any, satisfaction felt from failing the student. Regarding student assessment, teachers should feel satisfaction if the course was well taught, tests were fair and meaningful, and students were graded fairly and objectively. Deriving satisfaction from a student's failure or from a criminal's punishment does not define, and grossly misrepresents, retributivism.

Aligned with the retributive notions of desert and duty is the notion of justice. Justice requires, minimally, that people be treated equally. For the retributivist, justice requires that the guilty be punished and, furthermore, that the punishment fit the crime. To reiterate, the guilty must be punished even if the punishment does not deter. In addition, punishments must, as realistically as possible, match the seriousness of the crime committed. For example, a retributivist, in general, holds that two similarly situated individuals committing essentially identical crimes, say, first-degree murder, should receive the same punishment, such as the death penalty. Two Supreme Court cases illuminate this claim. In *Furman v. Georgia*,[36] as previously noted, the Supreme Court held that the imposition of the death penalty on convicted murderers was unconstitutional in part because the states did not have any consistent way to distinguish between murderers who should die and murderers who should not. The punishment was meted out in an arbitrary and haphazard manner. From a retributive point of view, the death penalty would be unconstitutional because it had not been imposed in a manner consistent with the Fourteenth Amendment's "equal protection of the laws" clause. Criminals, in short, were being treated unequally and therefore unconstitutionally. In *Coker v. Georgia*,[37] the Supreme Court argued that the death penalty was disproportionate for the crime of rape. Such an argument is retributive in nature. If punishments are too severe or too lenient, from a retributive point of view they are not justifiable. The death penalty for rape, the Court held, is disproportionate to the crime committed and therefore unconstitutional.

Thus, retributivism holds that punishment restores the moral and legal order; punishment is necessary to annul the wrong done by the criminal. The criminal has upset the balance of the moral, social, and legal order, and that balance can be restored only by making the criminal suffer in a manner consistent with the wrong done. A corollary claim asserts that the wicked should be punished so that they do not prosper at the expense of the innocent. The criminal, if not punished, has gained an unfair social advantage. Punishment is necessary to restore the social order. This does not mean that the social order returns to its unblemished state. Murder victims cannot be brought back to life and rape victims cannot have the rape undone. But the advantage the murderer or rapist obtained can be nullified.[38] The idea that people should not gain through their wrongdoing is retributive in nature. There can never be perfect restoration and restitution, but society must do what it can to maintain as close a balance as possible in the moral order.

Deterrence theory challenges retributive justifications for punishment. In general, deterrence theory holds that if the moral order cannot be restored, and if punishments cannot match exactly the crime, would society be better served by a philosophy that looks more closely at how it can benefit from punishment? Deterrence theory holds that retributive theory fails as a justification for punishment in part because it does not guarantee that a punishment will deter future criminal acts, which, in deterrence theory, constitutes the primary, if not the sole, justification for punishment. From a deterrent perspective, if a punishment does not deter, then the punishment is unjustifiable. In deterrence theory, people are not as likely to become victims of crime if punishment actually deters criminal conduct. Deterrence theory holds that punishment must produce change in human behavior that will benefit the social order. In this context, criminologists speak of two kinds of deterrence, general and special.[39]

General deterrence occurs if a punishment prevents law-abiding citizens from entering a life of crime. In theory, when people see the negative consequences that follow from illegal conduct, they will not engage in that conduct. Special deterrence occurs if a punishment serves to deter the convicted felon from engaging in additional criminal activity after the punishment has been inflicted. In theory, when people experience pain that follows directly from their illegal conduct, they will be reluctant to engage in it again. They may want to steal another car, but having spent eighteen months in jail for car theft, they overcome that desire so as to avoid another unpleasant penal experience. The justification for punishment on this view rests on the success punishments have in preventing crime in the first place (general deterrence) and on the success a particular punishment has on a specific offender (special deterrence). If a punishment either deters law-abiding citizens from engaging in criminal activity or deters convicted criminals from engaging in criminal activity in the future, then, in terms of deterrence, the punishment has been justified. An essential difference, then, between retributive and deterrent philosophies is that retributive theory looks to the past to determine a just punishment while deterrence theory looks to the future—for example, to a decrease in criminal activity—to determine a just punishment. In theory, then, if a particular punishment has no effect on either law-abiding citizens or on convicted criminals, that punishment, for all practical purposes, is useless and must be abandoned.

Deterrence theory also holds that the prescribed punishment should be neither more nor less than is necessary to deter criminal conduct. For example, if it costs $5 for people to park their cars, and there is a $2 fine for illegal parking, the fine will not be sufficient to deter anyone. If the fine were $50, it might be more than what is necessary to prevent people from parking illegally. Indeed, the ill will such a fine would generate would probably offset any deterrent value a fine might otherwise have. A $10 fine, however, might be just right. If, however, a $50 fine worked as well as a $10 fine, the $50 fine would be considered inappropriate (unjustifiable) because the same socially desired behavior can be obtained at a greatly reduced cost. Accordingly, punishments, in terms of deterrence, will be limited to what is necessary to reduce criminal conduct. Four deterrent principles identified by Jeremy Bentham, one of the greatest advocates for punishment to be determined in terms of deterrence, serve to explain the focus of this theory.

First, punishments "must not be less in any case than what is sufficient to outweigh that of the profit of the offence."[40] Any benefit accruing from the criminal act must be balanced by a punishment of sufficient substance to make the activity itself undesirable. For example, a six-month sentence for murder would probably increase the murder rate dramatically. However, if a term of five years for first-degree murder would reduce the homicide rate, that punishment could be all that is necessary to inflict on a murderer. An automatic fifty-year sentence, however, could be more than is necessary to deter first-degree murder.

Second, "[t]he greater the mischief of the offence, the greater is the expense, which it may be worth while to be at, in the way of punishment."[41] Consistent with the first rule, more serious crimes merit more substantial punishments. Here deterrence theory and retributive theory agree. Indeed, with respect to many punishments, both theories will result in similar, if not identical, recommendations for punishment. There are, for example, both retributive and deterrent arguments in defense of capital punishment. Although there may be no difference between the recommended deterrent punishment and the required retributive punishment, there is a significant difference in principle. In essence, deterrence theory holds that society should do no more than is necessary to deter criminal wrongdoing whereas the retributive holds fast to the deserved punishment, regardless of any deterrent effect. In the case of first-degree murder, retributivists, for the most part, argue that the death penalty is justified because it fits the crime. Advocates of deterrence theory, on the other hand, will recommend the death penalty only if it can be shown to be a more effective deterrent than some lesser punishment.

Third, "[w]here two offences come in competition, the punishment for the greater offence must be sufficient to induce a man to prefer the less."[42] Again, punishment is designed to prevent "mischief," but it must also limit the harm that will result from the criminal act. Someone intent on kidnapping, for example, should be motivated by punishment to commit kidnapping and not kidnapping and murder. If kidnapping were punishable by death, what would prevent the kidnapper from killing the victim? The punishment for kidnapping must not be so great that it would make no difference to the kidnapper if the victim were also murdered.

Fourth, "whatever mischief is guarded against, to guard against it at as cheap a rate as possible."[43] This reflects the cost/benefit element of deterrence theory. For example, even if the death penalty were morally justifiable, it would be economically foolish to use it if the same desired effect could be achieved in a less costly manner. This is the same idea as expressed earlier in terms of a fine for illegal parking.

These, then, are the two main theories relating to justifications for punishment. The retributive/deterrent debate defines, for the most part, the constitutional debates encountered in Supreme Court death penalty cases. At this point, it would be helpful to examine retributive and deterrent theories within the framework of a constitutional case. The following Supreme Court case, decided on June 20, 2002, serves this purpose.

ATKINS V. VIRGINIA

Mentally ill people have been executed.[44] In 1989, in *Penry v. Lynaugh,*[45] the Supreme Court held that the execution of a moderately retarded adult with the mental comprehension of a six-year-old did not violate any specific constitutional prohibition.[46] In *Penry,* however, the Court addressed neither retributive nor deterrent justifications for punishment. In *Atkins v. Virginia* (No. 00–8452, slip op. [U.S. Supreme Court, June 20, 2002]), Justice Stevens, for the Court, addressed these theories directly.

Darryl Atkins had been "convicted of abduction, armed robbery, and capital murder, and sentenced to death."[47] Once convicted of the capital crime, the jury had to determine the appropriate punishment under Virginia law. Atkins's defense attorney hired a forensic psychologist to evaluate Atkins's mental state. That psychologist testified that Atkins was "'mildly mentally retarded.'"[48] The psychologist, "based on interviews with people who knew Atkins, a review of school and court records, and the administration of a standard intelligence test,"[49] testified that Atkins had an IQ of 59. Initially, the jury sentenced Atkins to death. Due to an error at the trial court level, the Virginia Supreme Court "ordered a second sentencing hearing."[50] Atkins was once again sentenced to death. The Virginia Supreme Court upheld the sentence and Atkins appealed.

Justice Stewart, for the Court, overturned Atkins's death sentence in part because neither *retribution* nor *deterrence* are served by executing a mentally retarded person. Quoting from a 1976 Supreme Court case,[51] Stewart writes that "'retribution and deterrence of capital crimes by prospective offenders'" constitutes "the social purposes served by the death penalty."[52] Stewart continues, "With respect to retribution—the interest in seeing that the offender gets his 'just deserts'—the severity of the appropriate punishment necessarily depends on the culpability of the offender."[53] For Stewart, and for the Court's majority, the death penalty of a "mentally retarded offender surely does not merit that form of retribution."[54]

On deterrence, Stewart writes the following:

With respect to deterrence—the interest in preventing capital crimes by prospective offenders—"it seems likely that 'capital punishment can serve as a deterrent only when the murder is the result of premeditation and deliberation.'" Exempting the mentally retarded from that punishment will not affect the "cold calculus that precedes the decision" of other potential murderers. . . . The theory of deterrence in capital sentencing is predicated upon the notion that the increased severity of the punishment will inhibit criminal actors from carrying out murderous conduct. Yet it is the same cognitive and behavioral impairments that make these defendants less morally culpable—for example, the diminished ability to understand and process information, to learn from experience, to engage in logical reasoning, or to control impulses—that also make it less likely that they can process the information of the possibility of execution as a penalty and, as a result, control their conduct based on that information. Nor will exempting the mentally retarded from execution lessen the deterrent effect of the death penalty with respect to offenders who are not mentally retarded. Such individuals are unprotected by the exemption and will continue to face the threat of execution. Thus, executing the mentally retarded will not measurably further the goal of deterrence.[55]

Unlike *Gideon*, *Atkins* was not a unanimous decision. Justice Scalia, joined by Chief Justice Rehnquist and Justice Thomas, dissents for several reasons, one of which focuses on retribution and deterrence. Scalia argues that there is no evidence to indicate that all mentally retarded people are incapable of understanding the nature of the crime and the punishment that awaits them if they murder. Retribution, Scalia argues, may well be served in those cases where the legal culpability of the mentally retarded is assured. He writes:

Assuming, however, that there is a direct connection between diminished intelligence and the inability to refrain from murder, what possible scientific analysis can possibly show that a mildly retarded individual who commits an exquisite torture-killing is "no more culpable" than the "average" murderer in a holdup-gone-wrong or a domestic dispute? Or a moderately retarded individual who commits a series of 20 exquisite torture-killings? Surely culpability, and deservedness of the most severe retribution, depends not merely (if at all) upon the mental capacity of the criminal (above the level where he is able to distinguish right from wrong) but also upon the depravity of the crime—which is precisely why this sort of question has traditionally been thought answerable not by a categorical rule of the sort the Court today imposes upon all trials, but rather by the sentencer's weighing of the circumstances (both degree of retardation and depravity of crime) in the particular place. The fact that juries continue to sentence mentally retarded offenders to death for extreme crimes shows that society's moral outrage sometimes demands execution of retarded offenders.[56]

As for deterrence, Scalia argues that what is relevant for retribution is equally relevant for deterrence. There is no evidence that the death penalty cannot have an effect on a mentally retarded person. Again, that is up to the state and a jury to decide, not, according to Scalia, the United States Supreme Court. Indeed, for Scalia, the death penalty will never achieve complete deterrence, nor is it necessary that it do so.

But surely the deterrent effect of a penalty is adequately vindicated if it successfully deters many, but not all, of the target class. Virginia's death penalty, for example, does not fail of its deterrent effect because *some* criminals are unaware that Virginia *has* the death penalty. In other words, the supposed fact that *some* retarded criminals cannot fully appreciate the death penalty has nothing to do with the deterrence rationale.[57]

The retributive/deterrence debate remains part of the constitutional landscape as the Court continues to rule on the constitutionality of the death penalty. That debate, along with the more specific constitutional issues the death penalty raises, will be developed in the following chapters.

The death penalty raises one of those intractable social problems that does not appear resolvable. Reconciliation or compromise from either side of the debate suggests either that a victim has not had his or her right to life vindicated or that a defendant has or has not had his or her right to life respected. Either a victim's death means nothing or a defendant's life means nothing. Either the murderer should die or the misbegotten individual should be helped. Either the state executes a murderer or the state commits murder. People, for the most part, either support the death penalty or oppose it. And there is little doubt on either side as to who is correct.

The purpose of the arguments advanced here is to explore the constitutional world of the death penalty from the assumption that both sides to the debate consist of rational, well-intentioned individuals. Of course there are embarrassments on both sides. No one should be proud of those who applaud an execution. Even if executions are morally and constitutionally justifiable, execution requires a somber moment. Society may very well have to execute the most vicious people within it. That should not, however, be a moment to rejoice.[58] By the same token, opponents of the death penalty have with great insensitivity told victims' families that nothing can be done to bring the loved one back to life. Nothing can be more blatantly obvious and simultaneously insensitive.[59] I believe that there is a more productive and meaningful path for society to follow as it seeks to secure itself against the most vicious acts committed against its members.

Right or wrong, policy or no policy, our social position on the death penalty contributes to our definition of ourselves. The philosophical and psychological questions—"Who are we?" and "What are we?"—can be answered in part by one's position on the death penalty. Thus, people need to think very carefully about what they want. They may, after all, get their wish. The purpose of the following analysis is to explore the constitutional framework within which the death penalty is meted out. In addition, that analysis will enable people to make a more humane and moral response to one of the most difficult issues that ever faces society, namely, what should society do with individuals who commit the most egregious injuries to its members?

Chapter 2 explains the Supreme Court's position on the death penalty, on a selective case-by-case basis, from 1878 to 1972. Not all cases examined focus specifically on the death penalty. Rather, the cases examined here serve to introduce the historical background necessary to understand where we are today and how we got there. Chapter 3 lays out the nine separate opinions in the landmark decision *Furman v. Georgia.*[60] In this watershed case, the Justices examine the punishment not only constitutionally but also in terms of retributive and deterrent theory. Chapter 4 describes many of the legal arguments and cases that have come before the Court since the *Furman* holding. Once again, arguments about retributive and deterrent theory will be heard along with the Justices' opinions about the constitutionality of the death penalty. The cases examined in chapters 2, 3, and 4 present both plurality and dissenting opinions without any attempt to evaluate the strengths and weaknesses of the respective positions. Chapter 5 examines some of the constitutional issues that remain unresolved. These issues highlight the ambiguities Supreme Court Justices confront as they deliberate in this delicate area of law. In Chapter 6 I reflect on those constitutional concerns about the death penalty that I believe point unmistakably toward the abolition of the death penalty. But the abolition of the death penalty requires a punishment, or punishments, that can take its place. Several alternatives to the death penalty are considered in chapter 6 as well.

CHAPTER 2

1878–1971: Initial Forays into Cruel and Unusual Punishments

If the state officials deliberately and intentionally had placed the relator in the electric chair five times and, each time, had applied electric current to his body in a manner not sufficient, until the final time, to kill him, such a form of torture would rival that of burning at the stake. Although the failure of the first attempt, in the present case, was unintended, the reapplication of the electric current will be intentional. How many deliberate and intentional reapplications of electric current does it take to produce a cruel, unusual and unconstitutional punishment?

Justice Harold Burton, dissenting, *Louisiana ex rel Francis v. Resweber*

It is unlikely that any State at this moment in history would attempt to make it a criminal offense for a person to be mentally ill, or a leper, or to be afflicted with a venereal disease. A State might determine that the general health and welfare require that the victims of these and other human afflictions be dealt with by compulsory treatment, involving quarantine, confinement, or sequestration. But, in light of contemporary human knowledge, a law which made a criminal offense of such a disease would doubtless be universally thought to be an infliction of cruel and unusual punishment in violation of the Eighth and Fourteenth Amendments.

Justice Potter Stewart, *Robinson v. California*

The following case history reflects the efforts of the Supreme Court to defer to states' rights in matters concerning the use of the death penalty. Two cases[1] included in this history do not involve the death penalty directly. However, those two cases are included because they will become part of judicial reasoning regarding the death penalty beginning in 1972. In addition, not all death penalty cases between 1878 and 1971 are examined. The following case history focuses on those cases that help define the Supreme Court's approach to the death penalty during these years.

WILKERSON V. UTAH

Wilkerson v. Utah (99 U.S. 130 [1878]) was the first death penalty case to reach the Supreme Court. In 1878 Utah's method of execution was by firing squad, a method that still remains one of the options in Utah today. Wilkerson claimed that death by firing squad constituted cruel and unusual punishment as prohibited by the Eighth Amendment. Wilkerson does not deny that death by firing squad had been legislatively proscribed from 1852 to 1876. Justice Clifford, for the Court, notes that during that time period, Utah had several execution methods available. The Utah statute stated that a death sentence shall be " 'by being shot, hung, or beheaded, as the court may direct.' "[2] But that statute was no longer in effect, as Utah had passed a revised penal code that did not specify the means of execution.[3] Clifford then explains the different methods of execution that have been available, and remain available, even if no specific method has been legislatively mandated. In addition, there is nothing cruel or unusual about Utah's choice in its method of execution. "Cruel and unusual punishments are forbidden by the Constitution, but the authorities referred to show that the punishment of shooting as a mode of executing the death penalty for the crime of murder in the first degree is not included in that category, within the meaning of the eighth amendment."[4] Thus, if no method of execution has been specified, states are free to use any option as long as it is neither cruel nor unusual. More specifically, the Eighth Amendment clause prohibiting cruel and unusual punishment refers to punishments that involve torture. "Difficulty would attend the effort to define with exactness the extent of the constitutional provision which provides that cruel and unusual punishments shall not be inflicted; but it is safe to affirm that punishments of torture[5] . . . are forbidden by that amendment to the Constitution."[6] Execution by firing squad does not qualify as unusual because others, including the military, have used it. Consequently, execution by firing squad does not fall into the domain of cruel and unusual punishments. That being the case, the Court does not even consider whether the Eighth Amendment applies to the states through the Fourteenth Amendment. That challenge arrives in 1890 in *In re Kemmler.*

IN RE KEMMLER

In re Kemmler (136 U.S. 436 [1890] [argued 5/20/1890; decided 5/23/1890]) is the first case to test the constitutionality of the death penalty by use of the electric chair. Kemmler claims his sentence of death by electric chair constitutes a cruel and unusual punishment in violation of both the Constitution of the United States and the New York State constitution. Chief Justice Fuller cites approvingly the lower court county judge's finding that the " 'Constitution of the United States and that of the State of New York, in language almost identical, provide against cruel and inhuman punishment, but it may be remarked, in passing, that with the former we have no present concern, as the prohibition therein contained has no reference to punishments inflicted in state courts for crimes against the state, but is addressed solely to the national government, and operates as a restriction on its power.' "[7]

In 1890, courts were not prepared to claim that the Fourteenth Amendment to the Constitution placed restrictions on the operations of state legislatures in criminal justice matters. But Chief Justice Fuller goes further. He notes that the New York Supreme Court found that the use of the electric chair did not violate the New York State Constitution.[8] Chief Justice Fuller cites the following observation made by Justice Dwight of the New York Supreme Court:

"We have read with much interest the evidence returned to the county judge, and we agree with him that the burden of the proof [that the electric chair constitutes cruel and unusual punishment] is not successfully borne by the relator. On the contrary, we think that the evidence is clearly in favor of the conclusion that it is within easy reach of electrical science at this day to so generate and apply to the person of the convict a current of electricity of such known and sufficient force as certainly to produce instantaneous, and therefore painless, death."[9]

The federal court of appeals affirmed the Supreme Court of New York. According to that court the electric chair not only does not violate the cruel and unusual punishment clause in the New York State constitution, it actually offers a more humane means of administering the death penalty. It is hanging that is inhumane and antiquated. The governor of New York is quoted as follows: " 'The present mode of executing criminals by hanging has come to us from the dark ages, and it may well be questioned whether the science of the present day cannot provide a means for taking the life of such as are condemned to die in a less barbarous manner.' "[10] The New York legislature itself approved the use of the electric chair as a more humane method of execution. That does not mean, however, that any death penalty method would pass constitutional muster. Chief Justice Fuller writes that "if the punishment prescribed for an offense against the laws of the state were manifestly cruel and unusual, as burning at the stake, crucifixion, breaking on the wheel, or the like, it would be the duty of the courts to adjudge such penalties to be within the constitutional prohibition."[11] He continues, "Punishments are cruel when they involve torture or a lingering death; but the punishment of death is not cruel within the meaning of that word as used in the constitution. It implies there something inhuman and barbarous—something more than the mere extinguishment of life."[12]

Furthermore, the use of the electric chair, the Court noted, may be unusual, but that does not make its use illegitimate or unconstitutional. As long as the punishment does not reach one of the previously stated examples of a cruel and unusual punishment (e.g., burning at the stake), then courts must accept the judgment of the legislative branches of government. The Court must assume that the New York legislature had studied the use of the electric chair and had found it a more humane means of implementing the death penalty.[13] Chief Justice Fuller writes, "The decision of the state courts sustaining the validity of the act under the state constitution is not re-examinable here, nor was that decision against any title, right, privilege, or immunity specially set up or claimed by the petitioner under the constitution of the United States."[14] Fuller concludes as follows:

In order to reverse the judgment of the highest court of the state of New York, we should be compelled to hold that it had committed an error so gross as to amount in law to a denial by the state of due process of law to one accused of crime, or of some right secured to him by the constitution of the United States. We have no hesitation in saying that this we cannot do upon the record before us. The application for a writ of error is denied.[15]

As a result of *Kemmler*, the electric chair becomes perceived not only as constitutional but also as a more humane method of execution. It is important to note as well what the Court is saying by its silence. The question here concerns the appropriate method of punishment for murder, not whether the death penalty itself is an appropriate constitutional punishment. It is important to be aware of two questions, then, in capital cases, namely: Is capital punishment constitutional? and Is the method of carrying out the punishment constitutional? More often than not, the Court is interested far more in the latter question than in the former, but it is the former question that has yet to be answered.

LOGAN V. UNITED STATES

Logan v. United States (144 U.S. 263 [1892] [argued 1/26–27/1892; decided 4/4/1892]) generally does not receive Eighth Amendment attention. The case does raise one question, however, that continues to challenge the constitutionality of the death penalty, namely, On what basis can a juror be challenged for cause? To challenge a juror for cause is to "request to a judge that a prospective juror not be allowed to serve on the jury for some specific cause or reason, e.g., he is not qualified under the provisions of a statute."[16] In this case, the defendants challenged the prosecutor's right to challenge for cause jurors who had been summarily excused from serving on the jury because they had conscientious scruples about imposing a death sentence on a person convicted of murder. Justice Gray, writing for the majority, found that prosecuting attorneys do have the right to challenge for cause those individuals whose beliefs could preclude them from performing their constitutional duty. He writes:

As the defendants were indicted and to be tried for a crime punishable with death, those jurors who stated on voir dire that they had "conscientious scruples in regard to the infliction of the death penalty for crime" were rightly permitted to be challenged by the Government for cause. A juror who has conscientious scruples on any subject which prevent him from standing indifferent between the Government and the accused and from trying the case according to the law and the evidence is not an impartial juror. This Court has accordingly held that a person who has a conscientious belief that polygamy is rightful may be challenged for cause on a trial for polygamy.[17]

There are three questions *Logan* raises that are important for future cases. First, to what extent can a potential juror express some personal or moral concern about the death penalty before a prosecutor can challenge for cause? For example, can a potential juror express doubt about the wisdom of the proscribed punishment without being challenged for cause? Certainly the prosecutor does not want anyone on the jury who cannot bring in a guilty verdict if that verdict could invoke the death penalty. The prosecutor's responsibility is to represent the people. In theory, the death penalty, as approved by state and federal governments, reflects the will of the people. Governors and presidents sign death penalty legislation into law claiming to represent the will of the people. The will of the people should not be thwarted by jurors who claim that their personal, moral, or religious feelings or beliefs would make it impossible for them to bring in a guilty verdict because the potential punishment is death. But should potential jurors be excluded from jury duty simply because they express doubt about or concern with the wisdom or prudence of state or federal government use of the death penalty? Second, is a defendant's Sixth Amendment right to "an impartial jury" violated when potential jurors are challenged for cause due to their opposition to the death penalty? Again, in theory, a jury should represent a community's various constituencies. Juries composed of people with the same mind-set rarely reflect the oftentimes vast differences of view present in any community. Would not a jury so composed fail to meet the Sixth Amendment requirement of "an impartial jury"? Third, are juries composed of people who in general support the death penalty more likely to bring in a verdict of guilt? Opponents of the death penalty, for example, have argued that juries composed of people who can do their duty and sentence a person to death are more likely to bring in a conviction. Such juries are referred to as "death-qualified juries." There is some evidence that death-qualified juries are more prone to convict. If that is the case, then defendants will find that the alleged scales of justice have made a shift toward conviction, a shift that again raises Sixth Amendment concerns about "an impartial jury."

These questions will be explored more fully in later cases.[18] That questions about jury composition are raised as early as 1892 strikes me as noteworthy. Over 100 years later questions about jury composition linger.

WEEMS V. UNITED STATES

The noncapital Eighth Amendment cruel and unusual punishment case titled *Weems v. United States* (217 U.S. 349 [1910] [argued 11/30 and 12/1/1909; decided 5/2/1910]) contains two of the more contentious and challenging approaches to constitutional interpretation, namely, interpretivism and noninterpretivism. For my purpose, these approaches are defined succinctly as follows. Interpretivists "believe that the only valid norms are those deriving from the intent of the Framers as expressed in the text of the Constitution itself or reasonably to be inferred from the text."[19] Noninterpretivists, on the other hand, "believe that judges may look to evolving social norms and 'fundamental values' of society as the basis for constitutional judgments."[20] For example, an interpretivist will adhere as strictly as possible to the language of the Constitution. Because the language of the Fifth Amendment supports the taking of life under certain circumstances, the death penalty remains a constitutional right for the states and the federal government. A noninterpretivist, however, will look to a society's evolving standards of norms in evaluating a constitutional clause. The Eighth Amendment, for example, makes cruel and unusual punishments unconstitutional. But what is included in that concept? Are we to be limited to the world of the eighteenth century in applying this clause? Or is it possible that society has matured sufficiently to recognize that some, if not all, methods of execution are constitutionally suspect?

In this context the quintessential question—What is the nature, meaning, and scope of the cruel and unusual punishment clause?—is asked. Is the cruel and unusual punishment clause to be understood within the context of the framers' intent in 1791 (interpretivism) or is it to be understood within the context of a growing, dynamic, and evolutionary society (noninterpretivism)? The majority opinion in *Weems* reflects a noninterpretivist approach to constitutional understanding and interpretation, that is, the majority do not see themselves bound either to original intent or to a limited understanding of what the framers would have had in mind were they still living.

Writing for the majority, Justice McKenna establishes the tone of the opinion in the philosophical foundation for his decision as follows:

Legislation, both statutory and constitutional, is enacted, it is true, from an experience of evils but its general language should not, therefore, be necessarily confined to the form that evil had theretofore taken. *Time works changes, brings into existence new conditions and purposes. Therefore a principle, to be vital, must be capable of wider application than the mischief which gave it birth.* This is peculiarly true of constitutions. They are not ephemeral enactments, designed to meet passing occasions. They are, to use the words of Chief Justice Marshall, "designed to approach immortality as nearly as human institutions can approach it." . . . In the application of a constitution, therefore, our contemplation cannot be only of what has been, but of what may be. . . . The meaning and vitality of the Constitution have developed against narrow and restrictive construction.[21]

In other words, constitutional phrases such as "cruel and unusual punishment" must be reconsidered in light of new social sensitivities. Otherwise, the law and the Constitution will become "impotent and lifeless formulas."[22]

It is within this philosophical backdrop that Justice McKenna surveys the history of the meaning of the "cruel and unusual punishment" clause of the Eighth Amendment. From that survey he concludes that there can be no static meaning attached to that phrase.[23] Justice McKenna argues here that courts, especially courts of final judgment, must continually reexamine constitutional phrases, which do not, and should not, admit precise and unambiguous meaning and application.

What had *Weems* done, then, to merit such attention? As noted, this is not a death penalty case. It arose in the Philippines, and American control of the Philippines at that time gave the Supreme Court the opportunity to speak to the cruel and unusual punishment clause of the Eighth Amendment. Since the Philippine Bill of Rights contained essentially the same language on this matter as the Eighth Amendment, the Court felt on secure ground. Weems was convicted, in essence, of falsifying public records. Specifically, he had falsified documents to make it appear that funds had been dispersed when they had not.[24] What was Weems's punishment? McKenna states that the minimum punishment for Weems was "confinement in a penal institution for twelve years and one day, a chain at the ankle and wrist of the offender, hard and painful labor, no assistance from friends or relative, no marital authority or parental rights or rights of property, no participation even in the family council. These parts endure for the term of imprisonment."[25]

Weems committed this fraudulent act, as noted, in the Philippine Islands and therefore was tried under the provisions of the Philippine Islands Criminal Code of Procedure. Weems appealed the lower court decisions all the way to the Supreme Court. Justice McKenna notes that this draconian punishment is almost inconceivable to American ears. "Such penalties for such offenses amaze those who have formed their conception of the relation of a state to even its offending citizens from the practice of the American commonwealths, and believe that it is a precept of justice that punishment for crime should be graduated and proportioned to offense."[26]

Justice McKenna then tries to determine what, exactly, a cruel and unusual punishment could be.[27] Throughout this historical survey, McKenna argues that the phrase does appear to be flexible in nature. However, at no point does he conclude that the phrase precludes the use of the death penalty. What this opinion changes, however, from the perspective of the cruel and unusual punishment clause, is that that phrase need no longer be given a strict and narrow eighteenth-century definition and meaning. It is on the basis of Justice McKenna's claim here that will set in motion many of the constitutional arguments for and against the death penalty that will be encountered in future cases. This idea, that the Constitution cannot be limited to the narrow framework within which it was created, carries enormous implications for future constitutional decision making. The majority opinion, however, is not unanimous, and the dissenting opinion offers a clear contrast to the liberal position taken by McKenna. Indeed, Justice White's dissenting opinion takes the majority position apart systematically. It is worth noting.

There are several parts to the dissenting opinion of Justice White, each of which is designed to respond to the specific points and arguments made by Justice McKenna. First, White notes that at trial there was never any challenge to the statute on which Weems was prosecuted in terms of cruel and unusual punishments. In addition, there is no indication that a cruel and unusual punishment claim was raised on appeal. White writes:

Neither at the trial in the court of first instance nor in the supreme court of the Philippine Islands was any question raised concerning the repugnancy of the statute defining the crime and fixing its punishment to the provision of the Philippine Bill of Rights, forbidding cruel and unusual punishment. Indeed, no question on that subject was even indirectly referred to in the assignments of error filed in the court below for the purpose of this writ of error.[28]

Thus, according to White, there is no basis on which the claim can now be raised.

Second, because the Philippine Bill of Rights contains a cruel and unusual punishment clause identical to that found in the Eighth Amendment, the majority opinion erroneously applied the American understanding and application of the clause without regard for the Philippine conception. For Justice White, the pivotal point here is that we cannot make cross-cultural comparisons even if the words are the same, for the same words have different meanings in different cultures (not to mention the possibility that the same words can have different meanings at different times and in different contexts in the same culture). Accordingly, what the Supreme Court happens to be deciding in this case is not what the Philippine Bill of Rights refers to in claims regarding cruel and unusual punishments but rather what limitations, if any, are placed on Congress as it uses its statutory authority to make laws and establish appropriate punishments. It is simply unfair to compare American and Philippine experiences.[29]

Third, the majority opinion that the legislative motives must include a rehabilitative element strikes Justice White as incoherent. It is up to the legislative branch of government, not the courts, to determine what punishments are designed to do.[30]

Fourth, Justice White questions the judicial and constitutional legitimacy of courts having the right to overturn legislative punishments judges find too severe. From an interpretivist's perspective, the Court has engaged in some legislative decision making in which it is not entitled to engage.[31]

Not one of these majoritarian claims receives Justice White's approval. He concludes this brief delineation with the warning that the court may be moving down a slippery slope toward a day when legislators no longer have any independent power, a claim that continues to follow Supreme Court decisions in death penalty cases, among others.

When to this result is added the consideration that the interpretation, by its necessary effect, does not simply cause the cruel and unusual punishment clause to carve out of the domain of legislative authority the power to resort to prohibited kinds of punishments, but subjects to judicial control the degree of severity with which authorized modes of punishment may be inflicted, it seems to me that the demonstration is conclusive that nothing will be left of the independent legislative power to punish and define crime, if the interpretation now made be pushed in future application to its logical conclusion.[32]

Justice White then proceeds to offer his own understanding of the history of the cruel and unusual punishment clause, going back to the founding of this nation and including representative examples from various state statutes to demonstrate that the cruel and unusual punishment clause applies only to punishments that involve substantive and meaningful pain.

From all the considerations, which have been stated, I can deduce no ground, whatever which, to my mind, sustains the interpretation now given to the cruel and unusual punishment clause. On the contrary, in my opinion, the review which has been made demonstrates that the word "cruel," as used in the Amendment, forbids only the lawmaking power, in prescribing punishment for crime, and the courts from imposing punishment, from inflicting unnecessary bodily suffering through a resort to inhuman methods for causing bodily torture, like or which are of the nature of the cruel and methods of bodily torture which had been made use of prior to the Bill of Rights of 1689,[33] and against the recurrence of which the word "cruel" was used in that instrument. To illustrate. Death was a well-known method of punishment, prescribed by law, and it was, of course, painful, and in that sense was cruel. But the infliction of this punishment was clearly not prohibited by the word "cruel," although that word manifestly was intended to forbid the resort to barbarous and unnecessary methods of bodily torture in executing even the penalty of death.[34]

An interpretivist could not be happier.

POWELL V. ALABAMA[35] AND NORRIS V. ALABAMA

One contemporary issue that raises both moral and constitutional questions about the death penalty focuses on the relationship, if any, between race, conviction, and punishment. If prejudice exists at any level of the justice system, people are denied the equal protection of the laws, as guaranteed by the Fourteenth Amendment, because their case outcome depends more on irrelevant factors such race, creed, color, sex, or religion than on the case's merits. Currently, significant differences of opinion exist about the relationship between individual and social prejudices and a defendant's guilt and punishment. In Scottsboro, Alabama, in 1932, few can doubt realistically that race was a major factor in the conviction of eight of nine young black men on the charge of having raped two white women (*Powell v. Alabama*, 287 U.S. 45 [1932] [argued 10/10/32; decided 11/7/32]). Each received a death sentence.[36] On appeal, the Alabama Supreme Court affirmed the lower court judgment—with the exception of Alabama's Chief Justice Anderson, who did think that the young men had been denied a fair trial—for seven of the eight men convicted. The Alabama Supreme Court set aside one conviction because of his young age. The Supreme Court's decision in *Powell* is summarized well in Chief Justice Hughes's opening statement in *Norris v. Alabama* (294 U.S. 587 [1935] [argued 2/15, 18/35; decided 4/1/35]).

Petitioner, Clarence Norris, is one of nine negro boys who were indicted in March, 1931, in Jackson County, Alabama, for the crime of rape. On being brought to trial in that county, eight were convicted. The Supreme Court of Alabama reversed the conviction of one of these, and affirmed that of seven, including Norris. This Court reversed the judgments of conviction upon the ground that the defendants had been denied due process of law in that the trial court had failed, in the light of the circumstances disclosed, and of the inability of the defendants at that time to obtain counsel, to make an effective appointment of counsel to aid them in preparing and presenting their defense.[37]

The specific question *Powell* raises, according to Justice Sutherland, is "whether the defendants were in substance denied the right of counsel, and, if so, whether such denial infringes the due process clause of the Fourteenth Amendment."[38] Sutherland explains that the Scottsboro defendants had been denied their Fourteenth Amendment due process rights in two steps.

Justice Sutherland agrees with Alabama's Chief Justice Anderson that the defendants never had an opportunity to obtain counsel or even to call their families. The men were not from Alabama and therefore would need time to make contacts necessary to obtain legal assistance. Alabama's chief justice is quoted to the effect that the defendants easily could have been given the necessary time. "[They] had little time or opportunity to get in touch with their families and friends who were scattered throughout two other states, and time has demonstrated that they could or would have been represented by able counsel had a better opportunity been given by a reasonable delay in the trial of the cases, judging from the number and activity of counsel that appeared immediately or shortly after their conviction."[39]

Attorneys were present at the arraignment and during the trial. But no specific attorney had been designated to handle the case. The failure to guarantee counsel from arraignment through trial, according to Justice Sutherland, constituted a denial of the right to counsel.

In any event, the circumstance lends emphasis to the conclusion that, during perhaps the most critical period of the proceedings against these defendants, that is to say, from the time of their arraignment until the beginning of their trial, when consultation, thoroughgoing investigation and preparation were vitally important, the defendants did not have the aid of counsel in any real sense, although they were as much entitled to such aid during that period as at the trial itself.[40]

Sutherland, after reviewing lower court records, states that the "defendants were not accorded the right to counsel in any substantial sense."[41] In his lead opinion, Sutherland makes a comment, as relevant today as the day he wrote it, about the need to dispose of cases efficiently without sacrificing fairness.

It is true that great and inexcusable delay in the enforcement of our criminal law is one of the grave evils of our time. Continuances are frequently granted for unnecessarily long periods of time, and delays incident to the disposition of motions for new trial and hearings upon appeal have come in many cases to be a distinct reproach to the administration of justice. The prompt disposition of criminal cases is to be commended and encouraged. But, in reaching that result, a defendant, charged with a serious crime, must not be stripped of his right to have sufficient time to advise with counsel and prepare his defense. To do that is not to proceed promptly in the calm spirit of regulated justice, but to go forward with the haste of the mob.[42]

There are delays in the administration of justice, but that is not a problem in and of itself. The problem should focus on securing the rights of both law-abiding members of society while protecting the rights of those who may or may not have been falsely accused and not on serving social self-interests, real or imagined. The rights of defendants, in reality, constitute the fundamental rights of all people, regardless of which side of the fence they happen to fall on.

The denial of the right to counsel infringes the Fourteenth Amendment's due process clause that reads, "nor shall any State deprive any person of life, liberty, or property, without due process of law."[43] The Sixth Amendment guarantees the assistance of counsel, but the Supreme Court continued to interpret that guarantee against federal and not state encroachment. The Court was not ready to apply, through "incorporation," Sixth Amendment guarantees to the individual states. Indeed, the Alabama Constitution itself guaranteed a right to counsel that the Alabama Supreme Court maintained had been met. Justice Sutherland explains:

The Constitution of Alabama provides that, in all criminal prosecutions the accused shall enjoy the right to have the assistance of counsel, and a state statute requires the court in a capital case where the defendant is unable to employ counsel to appoint counsel for him. The state supreme court held that these provisions had not been infringed, and with that holding we are powerless to interfere. The question, however, which it is our duty, and within our power, to decide is whether the denial of the assistance of counsel contravenes the due process clause of the Fourteenth Amendment to the federal Constitution.[44]

According to Justice Sutherland's claim, then, the U.S. Supreme Court does not have a right to review a defendant's claim, in a state case, that his or her Sixth Amendment rights were infringed, for the Sixth Amendment does not apply to the individual states. Nonetheless, the Fourteenth Amendment does apply to individual states as regards "due process of law." What, then, is included in this due process of law idea?

Due process of law, according to Justice Sutherland, includes the "'fundamental principles of liberty and justice which lie at the base of all our civil and political institutions.'"[45] Sutherland quotes the following from another case:

[I]t is possible that some of the personal rights safeguarded by the first eight Amendments against National action may also be safeguarded against state action, because a denial of them would be a denial of due process of law. If this is so, it is not because those rights are enumerated in the first eight Amendments, but because they are of such a nature that they are included in the conception of due process of law.[46]

For Sutherland, the right to counsel most assuredly constitutes a fundamental right that neither the federal government nor state governments can deny. A trial cannot be fair if counsel does not represent defendants. And people, for the most part, cannot represent themselves.

Even the intelligent and educated layman has small and sometimes no skill in the science of law. If charged with crime, he is incapable, generally, of determining for himself whether the indictment is good or bad. He is unfamiliar with the rules of evidence. Left without the aid of counsel, he may be put on trial without a proper charge, and convicted upon incompetent evidence, or evidence irrelevant to the issue or otherwise inadmissible. He lacks both the skill and knowledge adequately to prepare his defense, even though he have a perfect one. He requires the guiding hand of counsel at every step in the proceedings against him. Without it, though he be not guilty, he faces the danger of conviction because he does not know how to establish his innocence. If that be true of men of intelligence, how much more true is it of the ignorant and illiterate, or those of feeble intellect? If in any case, civil or criminal, a state or federal court were arbitrarily to refuse to hear a party by counsel, employed by and appearing for him, it reasonably may not be doubted that such a refusal would be a denial of a hearing, and, therefore, of due process in the constitutional sense.[47]

Sutherland's powerful conclusion merits attention.

In the light of the facts outlined in the forepart of this opinion—the ignorance and illiteracy of the defendants, their youth, the circumstances of public hostility, the imprisonment and the close surveillance of the defendants by the military forces, the fact that their friends and families were all in other states and communication with them necessarily difficult, and, above all, that they stood in deadly peril of their lives—we think the failure of the trial court to give them reasonable time and opportunity to secure counsel was a clear denial of due process.

But passing that, and assuming their inability, even if opportunity had been given, to employ counsel, as the trial court evidently did assume, we are of opinion that, under the circumstances just stated, the necessity of counsel was so vital and imperative that the failure of the trial court to make an effective appointment of counsel was likewise a denial of due process within the meaning of the Fourteenth Amendment. Whether this would be so in other criminal prosecutions, or under other circumstances, we need not determine. All that it is necessary now to decide, as we do decide, is that, in a capital case, where the defendant is unable to employ counsel and is incapable adequately of making his own defense because of ignorance, feeble mindedness, illiteracy, or the like, it is the duty of the court, whether requested or not, to assign counsel for him as a necessary requisite of due process of law, and that duty is not discharged by an assignment at such a time or under such circumstances as to preclude the giving of effective aid in the preparation and trial of the case.[48]

There are two points to note here. First, the Sixth Amendment has not been incorporated to apply to the states. That will not occur until 1963, when the Supreme Court, as noted in chapter 1 in *Gideon v. Wainwright*,[49] will hold that all indigents facing felony charges must be guaranteed the right to counsel. Second, due process of law includes, at least in capital cases involving defendants unable to represent themselves, the right to legal representation.

As obvious as Justice Sutherland's point—that due process of law includes a right to counsel—might be, to some it is not at all obvious. In a dissenting opinion, Justice Butler argued that the Court had interfered unjustifiably in Alabama's right to manage its own criminal justice affairs. Justice Butler cites Justice Sutherland's lead opinion to the effect that " 'the failure of the trial court to make an effective appointment of counsel was likewise a denial of due process within the meaning of the Fourteenth Amendment.' "[50] He concludes as follows: "The record wholly fails to reveal that petitioners have been deprived of any right guaranteed by the Federal Constitution, and I am of opinion that the judgment should be affirmed."[51]

Norris raises another issue with respect to the Fourteenth Amendment, namely, does the systematic exclusion of people from a jury on the basis of race or color constitute a denial of "the equal protection of the laws"?[52] The Supreme Court answered affirmatively. Norris and the six remaining defendants were retried. Norris was the only defendant to be found guilty on retrial. He was sentenced to death. Norris appealed the conviction and sentence. The defense argued that the systematic denial of African Americans from jury duty constituted a denial of the equal protection of the laws. The trial judge denied that there was any systematic exclusion of potential jurors on account of race or color. After his conviction, Norris appealed to the Alabama Supreme Court. The judges there ruled that there had been no systematic exclusion of jurors on the basis of race or color. Norris's conviction and sentence were upheld. Thereupon he appealed to the United States Supreme Court.

The Supreme Court overturned the conviction on the basis that potential jurors had been excluded from jury duty on the basis of race or color. Justice Hughes explains the operative legal principle by quoting an earlier Supreme Court case: "Whenever, by any action of a State, whether through its legislature, through its courts, or through its executive or administrative officers, all persons of the African race are excluded solely because of their race or color, from serving as grand jurors in the criminal prosecution of a person of the African race, the equal protection of the laws is denied to him, contrary to the Fourteenth Amendment of the Constitution of the United States."[53]

Justice Hughes lays out the history of jury selection in the counties in Alabama relevant to Norris's case. In those counties there is no evidence, according to Justice Hughes, to indicate that African Americans had ever served on a jury. Regardless of the requirements for jury duty, it seemed, to Hughes, virtually impossible that no African American could be found to serve.[54] The state court, however, did not find any overt discrimination, and rejected the defense claim that qualified African Americans were intentionally omitted from jury duty on account of race.

The state court rested its decision upon the ground that, even if it were assumed that there was no name of a negro on the jury roll, it was not established that race or color caused the omission. The court pointed out that the statute fixed a high standard of qualifications for jurors, and that the jury commission was vested with a wide discretion. The court adverted to the fact that more white citizens possessing age qualifications had been omitted from the jury roll than the entire negro population of the county, and regarded the testimony as being to the effect that "the matter of race, color, politics, religion or fraternal affiliations" had not been discussed by the commission and had not entered into their consideration, and that no one had been excluded because of race or color.[55]

The Supreme Court did not accept that determination.

We are of the opinion that the evidence required a different result from that reached in the state court. We think that the evidence that, for a generation or longer, no negro had been called for service on any jury in Jackson County, that there were negroes qualified for jury service, that, according to the practice of the jury commission, their names would normally appear on the preliminary list of male citizens of the requisite age, but that no names of negroes were placed on the jury roll, and the testimony with respect to the lack of appropriate consideration of the qualifications of negroes established the discrimination which the Constitution forbids. The motion to quash the indictment upon that ground should have been granted.[56]

Justice Hughes concludes that no testimony or evidence exists necessary to show that the exclusion of African Americans from jury duty was based on anything other than racial discrimination and that accordingly Norris was denied the equal protection of the laws as guaranteed by the Fourteenth Amendment to the Constitution.[57]

LOUISIANA EX REL. FRANCIS V. RESWEBER

Willie Francis's execution raises questions about the unanimous decision reached in *Kemmler* that the electric chair does not constitute a cruel and unusual punishment. Writing for the majority of the Court, Justice Reed relates the facts of the case (*Louisiana ex rel. Francis v. Resweber*, 329 U.S. 459 [1947] [argued 11/18/46; decided 1/13/47]) as follows:

Upon a proper death warrant, Francis was prepared for execution and on May 3, 1946, pursuant to the warrant, was placed in the official electric chair of the State of Louisiana in the presence of the authorized witnesses. The executioner threw the switch, but, presumably because of some mechanical difficulty, death did not result. He was thereupon removed from the chair and returned to prison, where he now is. A new death warrant was issued by the Governor of Louisiana, fixing the execution for May 9, 1946.[58]

After his ordeal, Francis was to be "executed" once again. That decision, his attorneys believed, required an appeal.

Francis appealed the execution decision on two grounds. First, he claimed that a second execution attempt violates the double jeopardy principle of the Fifth Amendment clause "nor shall any person be subject for the same offence to be twice put in jeopardy of life or limb."[59] Second, a second execution attempt would constitute a "cruel and unusual punishment" prohibited by the Eighth Amendment. The Supreme Court agreed to review the second execution attempt under the assumption that the Fifth and Eighth Amendments to the Constitution applied to the states through the Fourteenth Amendment. The majority found no constitutional barriers to a second execution attempt.

In his lead opinion, Justice Reed finds each of Francis's claims unconvincing. There is no double jeopardy in a second execution. Reed compares the punishment to a prisoner who seeks review of his conviction. The Fifth Amendment, Reed argues, does not apply to a retrial. "But where the accused successfully seeks review of a conviction, there is no double jeopardy upon a new trial."[60] In addition, the Fifth Amendment protection from double jeopardy applies only to the federal government. As long as there was not direct, conscious effort on the state's part to subject a defendant to multiple trials or repeated attempts to punish, no constitutional provision violation occurred. "When an accident, with no suggestion of malevolence, prevents the consummation of a sentence, the state's subsequent course in the administration of its criminal law is not affected on that account by any requirement of due process under the Fourteenth Amendment."[61]

Justice Reed also argues that a second execution attempt does not meet the constitutional ban on cruel and unusual punishments. In a footnote Reed approvingly quotes the standard from *In re Kemmler*, namely, that "if the punishment prescribed for an offense against the laws of the state were manifestly cruel and unusual as burning at the stake, crucifixion, breaking on the wheel, or the like, it would be the duty of the courts to adjudge such penalties to be within the constitutional prohibition."[62] Reed's more general constitutional principle follows:

The cruelty against which the Constitution protects a convicted man is cruelty inherent in the method of punishment, not the necessary suffering involved in any method employed to extinguish life humanely. The fact that an unforeseeable accident prevented the prompt consummation of the sentence cannot, it seems to us, add an element of cruelty to a subsequent execution. There is no purpose to inflict unnecessary pain, nor any unnecessary pain involved in the proposed execution. The situation of the unfortunate victim of this accident is just as though he had suffered the identical amount of mental anguish and physical pain in any other occurrence, such as, for example, a fire in the cell block. We cannot agree that the hardship imposed upon the petitioner rises to that level of hardship denounced as denial of due process because of cruelty.[63]

Willie Francis just had a very bad day, an unlucky, unfortunate day. It could have been worse. For example, his cell block could have caught on fire, and he could have been burned to death. But because no evidence exists to demonstrate that those involved in the botched execution were in any way reckless or unprofessional, no constitutionally challengeable claim merits further review.

The Fourteenth Amendment claim that Francis has been denied the equal protection of the laws rings hollow as well. This constitutional claim assumes that the need to revisit the execution process constitutes inflicting "a more severe punishment than is imposed upon others guilty of a like offense."[64] Unfortunately, the fact that Willie will endure more physical and mental pain than other prisoners awaiting their execution does not constitute a denial of equal protection of the laws. "Equal protection does not protect a prisoner against even illegal acts of officers in charge of him, much less against accidents during his detention for execution."[65] The lack of coherence in this claim notwithstanding, Francis has been an innocent victim of nothing more than an unfortunate miscarriage, albeit an unintentional miscarriage, of an otherwise just punishment. No system, Justice Reed claims, can be made safe from freak accidents. "Laws cannot prevent accidents, nor can a law equally protect all against them. So long as the law applies to all alike, the requirements of equal protection are met. We have no right to assume that Louisiana singled out Francis for a treatment other than that which has been or would generally be applied."[66]

Finally, Francis's claim that the trial itself violated several constitutional rights is without merit. A review of the entire case, Justice Reed argues, presents no evidence that could sustain a constitutional challenge to any aspect of the case, including "the warrant for arrest, the indictment, the appointment of counsel and the minute entries of trial, selection of jury, verdict and sentence."[67]

Justice Reed concludes the majority position as follows: "Nothing is before us upon which a ruling can be predicated as to alleged denial of federal constitutional rights during petitioner's trial. On this record, we see nothing upon which we could conclude that the constitutional rights of petitioner were infringed."[68]

Justice Frankfurter's concurring opinion reveals the tensions that must exist when any judge is required to rule consistent with established law while believing that there is something unacceptable, perhaps immoral, with that law. In general, judges are not be free to make laws anymore than individuals are free to be judges in their own cases. Nothing could bring disrespect more quickly to law than a revelation that judges are free to vote their consciences or feelings. Frankfurter clearly opposes a second execution attempt.

I cannot bring myself to believe that for Louisiana to leave to executive clemency, rather than to require, mitigation of a sentence of death duly pronounced upon conviction for murder because a first attempt to carry it out was an innocent mis-adventure, offends a principle of justice "rooted in the traditions and conscience of our people." Short of the compulsion of such a principle, this Court must abstain from interference with State action no matter how strong one's personal feeling of revulsion against a State's insistence on its pound of flesh. One must be on guard against finding in personal disapproval a reflection of more or less prevailing con-demnation. Strongly drawn as I am to some of the sentiments expressed by my brother BURTON,[69] I cannot rid myself of the conviction that, were I to hold that Louisiana would transgress the Due Process Clause if the State were allowed, in the precise circumstances before us, to carry out the death sentence, I would be enforcing my private view, rather than that consensus of society's opinion which, for purposes of due process, is the standard enjoined by the Constitution.[70]

Two points stand out in these comments. First, Justice Frankfurter can-not believe that Louisiana does not offer any means, other than executive clemency, to set aside a death penalty in these types of situations. Surely a second execution attempt here "offends a principle of justice 'rooted in the traditions and conscience of our people.'"[71] Second, Frankfurter acknowl-edges the rights of the states to develop their own laws and procedures with respect to criminal law. He does not want to interfere with states' rights here—although he would like to—so as to maintain the traditional separation between federal and state jurisdictions. Third, while his moral and human sympathies rest with Justice Burton's dissent, Frankfurter can-not force his own "private view" on the "consensus of society's opin-ion."[72] The second point here requires closer scrutiny.

Justice Frankfurter begins and ends his opinion with a limited exegesis about the meaning and interpretation of the Fourteenth Amendment in terms of the "privileges or immunities" clause and the due process clause.[73] We have already touched on the claim that the Fourteenth Amendment incorporates or absorbs the Bill of Rights to extend constitu-tional safeguards against the federal government to state governments. Frankfurter hesitates to move in that direction. For Frankfurter, the privi-leges or immunities clause was not designed to force on the states, through incorporation, the limitations the first eight amendments placed on the federal government. "The notion that the Privileges or Immunities Clause of the Fourteenth Amendment absorbed, as it is called, the provisions of the Bill of Rights that limit the Federal Government has never been given countenance by this Court."[74]

Continuing, Justice Frankfurter argues that the due process of law clause does not apply to the states either, at least in their criminal law. "The Fourteenth Amendment placed no specific restraints upon the States in the formulation or the administration of their criminal law."[75] States must be free to establish their own notions and philosophies about the enforcement of law, as long as fundamental principles of justice are not violated. "In short, the Due Process Clause of the Fourteenth Amendment did not withdraw the freedom of a State to enforce its own notions of fairness in the administration of criminal justice unless, as it was put for the Court by Justice Cardozo, 'in so doing, it offends some principle of justice so rooted in the traditions and conscience of our people as to be ranked as fundamental.'"[76]

The Fourteenth Amendment, however, "did mean to withdraw from the States the right to act in ways that are offensive to a decent respect for the dignity of man, and heedless of his freedom."[77] *Francis* does not meet this broad standard. "Since I cannot say that it would be 'repugnant to the conscience of mankind' for Louisiana to exercise the power on which she here stands, I cannot say that the Constitution withholds it."[78]

These rarefied and abstract thoughts, however, do not appear to concern Justice Burton in his dissent. A second execution attempt in this case constitutes, for four members of the Court, a violation of the Eighth Amendment right that cruel and unusual punishments must not be inflicted.[79] How, then, does a second execution attempt become unconstitutional? Burton writes, "In determining whether the proposed procedure is unconstitutional, we must measure it against a lawful electrocution. The contrast is that between instantaneous death and *death by installments*— caused by electric shocks administered after one or more intervening periods of complete consciousness of the victim."[80] The fundamental and critically relevant difference between a constitutional and an unconstitutional execution is that a constitutional execution is virtually "instantaneous and substantially painless." Burton writes, "The all-important consideration is that the execution shall be so instantaneous and substantially painless that the punishment shall be reduced, as nearly as possible, to no more than that of death itself. Electrocution has been approved only in a form that eliminates suffering."[81] A second execution attempt is neither. That it is not instantaneous or painless is obvious. An instantaneous execution would have resulted in Francis's death. A painless execution would be one in which the defendant dies within minutes of electricity flowing through his body. "Painless," as peculiar and paradoxical as this sounds, is not "without" pain. Certainly some pain will result from 2,500 volts of electricity. The Supreme Court in *Kemmler* acknowledged the presence of pain, but the deciding factor in the electric chair was that it was, at the time, less painful than hanging, the previously approved method of execution. But it is not just the physical pain here that accrues from the electric chair. The entire death penalty process, which begins in this case with a transfer from one location to another and includes physical preparation (i.e., shaving one place on the head and one on the leg where the electrodes will be placed), involves psychological or emotional pain. Even if Willie committed the murder and deserved to die—and there are substantial reasons to believe that he did not commit murder—Burton argues that the failed attempt was so cruel and unusual that a second attempt must be unconstitutional.

On that record, denial of relief means that the proposed repeated, and at least second, application to the relator [Francis] of an electric current sufficient to cause death is not, under present circumstances, a cruel and unusual punishment violative of due process of law. It exceeds any punishment prescribed by law. There is no precedent for it. What then is it, if it be not cruel, unusual and unlawful? In spite of the constitutional issue thus raised, the Supreme Court of Louisiana treated it as an executive question not subject to judicial review. We believe that, if the facts are as alleged by the relator, the proposed action is unconstitutional. We believe also that the Supreme Court of Louisiana should provide for the determination of the facts, and then proceed in a manner not inconsistent with this opinion.[82]

Louisiana claimed that a second execution was constitutional because there had been no intent on the part of the executioner to make Willie suffer. Justice Burton does not buy that claim. "Lack of intent that the first application be less than fatal is not material. The intent of the executioner cannot lessen the torture or excuse the result. It was the statutory duty of the state officials to make sure that there was no failure."[83]

The botched execution of Willie Francis is not an isolated incident. Botched executions had occurred before Francis and have occurred after Francis.[84]

WILLIAMS V. PEOPLE OF STATE OF NEW YORK

The due process clause of the Fourteenth Amendment appears again. In *Williams v. People of State of New York* (337 U.S. 241 [1949] [argued 4/21/49; decided 6/27/49]), the trial judge set aside a jury recommendation of a life sentence for Williams and sentenced him instead to death. The trial judge made that judgment on the basis of information that was never introduced for jury or defense consideration.[85] Williams and his attorneys argue "that no person shall be tried and convicted of an offense unless he is given reasonable notice of the charges against him and is afforded an opportunity to examine adverse witnesses."[86] The Court, in sustaining the trial judge's judgment, maintains that there are both historical and practical reasons for allowing great latitude in sentencing judgments. For example, Justice

Black, for the Court, argued that "courts in this country and in England practiced a policy under which a sentencing judge could exercise a wide discretion in the sources and types of evidence used to assist him in determining the kind and extent of punishment to be imposed within limits fixed by law."[87] Justice Black notes several kinds of evidence that have been successful over the years, including out-of-court affidavits, prior knowledge about the defendant, and reports from probation officers, among others. The practical reasons focus on the prevention of jury confusion and the need for sentencing powers to consider all relevant, although at times extraneous, information. For example, the trial itself must be well defined. The jury's focus should be narrow and directed to the charges and the facts of the case. In addition, if a jury heard information unrelated to the charge under consideration, that jury might be more prone, in many cases, to convict. A sentencing judge, however, can consider more objectively information relating to the defendant. Black writes:

A sentencing judge, however, is not confined to the narrow issue of guilt. His task, within fixed statutory or constitutional limits, is to determine the type and extent of punishment after the issue of guilt has been determined. Highly relevant—if not essential—to his selection of an appropriate sentence is the possession of the fullest information possible concerning the defendant's life and characteristics. And modern concepts individualizing punishment have made it all the more necessary that a sentencing judge not be denied an opportunity to obtain pertinent information by a requirement of rigid adherence to restrictive rules of evidence properly applicable to the trial.[88]

Black concludes, "We cannot say that the due process clause renders a sentence void merely because a judge gets additional out-of-court information to assist him in the exercise of this awesome power of imposing the death sentence."[89] The defendant received, from Black's perspective, a fair hearing throughout the original trial and through the appeal process "to the highest court in the state."[90] Williams, Black concludes, was not denied due process and his conviction was confirmed.

Justice Murphy, however, did not agree. In dissent, Murphy argued that a jury trial rests on the idea that a jury represents the larger community of which it is a part. A judge should not be eager to override a jury's judgment. "A judge, even though vested with statutory authority to do so, should hesitate indeed to increase the severity of such a community expression."[91]

Murphy maintains that Williams was denied his due process of law rights because neither he nor the jury had access to the information on which the judge made his decision. Indeed, argues Murphy, some of the judge's "information" was based on hearsay. The trial judge's decision then did rest on information that due process of law requires be made to the defendant and to the jury. Murphy does not oppose the use of relevant information in sentencing decisions. He opposes the secrecy present in such a decision. Due process, for Murphy, requires that defendants and juries receive the same information and have the same opportunity to consider and rule on its relevance. Williams was denied, for Murphy, "the high commands of due process."[92] Murphy addresses the due process requirement specifically as follows:

Due process of law includes at least the idea that a person accused of crime shall be accorded a fair hearing through all the stages of the proceedings against him. I agree with the Court as to the value and humaneness of liberal use of probation reports as developed by modern penologists, but, in a capital case, against the unanimous recommendation of a jury, where the report would concededly not have been admissible at the trial, and was not subject to examination by the defendant, I am forced to conclude that the high commands of due process were not obeyed.[93]

Ultimately, it will be Murphy's dissenting opinion that will guide capital punishment sentencing practices.

TROP V. DULLES

In terms of influence, especially in terms of the cruel and unusual punishment clause, few cases have had the impact *Trop*[94] has had. Like *Weems*, *Trop* is not a death penalty case. Albert L. Trop had been court-martialed for desertion during World War II (he had escaped from a stockade in Casablanca and was gone about one day before he voluntarily surrendered to an Army officer) and had been sentenced for "three years at hard labor, forfeiture of all pay and allowances and a dishonorable discharge."[95] His application for a passport in 1952 had been denied on the basis that "he had lost his citizenship by reason of his conviction and dishonorable discharge for wartime desertion."[96] For all practical purposes, Trop was stateless. In 1955 he sought to have his citizenship restored on the basis that his punishment—expatriation—violated the Eighth Amendment's cruel and unusual punishment clause.

Chief Justice Earl Warren announced the 5–4 decision of the Court. For Chief Justice Warren, "citizenship is not subject to the general powers of the National Government and therefore cannot be divested in the exercise of those powers."[97] This is not to say, however, that one cannot relinquish one's citizenship or have it taken away.[98] Warren writes:

Citizenship is not a license that expires upon misbehavior. The duties of citizenship are numerous, and the discharge of many of these obligations is essential to the security and well being of the Nation. The citizen who fails to pay his taxes or to abide by the laws safeguarding the integrity of elections deals a dangerous blow to his country. But could a citizen be deprived of his nationality for evading these basic responsibilities of citizenship? In time of war, the citizen's duties include not only the military defense of the Nation, but also full participation in the manifold activities of the civilian ranks. Failure to perform any of these obligations may cause the Nation serious injury, and, in appropriate circumstances, the punishing power is available to deal with derelictions of duty. But citizenship is not lost every time a duty of citizenship is shirked. And the deprivation of citizenship is not a weapon that the Government may use to express its displeasure at a citizen's conduct, however reprehensible that conduct may be. As long as a person does not voluntarily renounce or abandon his citizenship, and this petitioner has done neither, I believe his fundamental right of citizenship is secure. On this ground alone, the judgment in this case should be reversed.[99]

Although this case raises several constitutional issues, I focus solely on the Eighth Amendment cruel and unusual punishment clause. The relevant question in this context is "whether denationalization is a cruel and unusual punishment within the meaning of the Eighth Amendment."[100] Or, as Chief Justice Warren writes, "The question subjects the individual to a fate forbidden by the principle of civilized treatment guaranteed by the Eighth Amendment."[101] Then comes what is one of the most frequently quoted passages in the ongoing debate about what constitutes a cruel and unusual punishment.

The exact scope of the constitutional phrase "cruel and unusual" has not been detailed by this Court. But the basic policy reflected in these words is firmly established in the Anglo-American tradition of criminal justice. The phrase in our Constitution was taken directly from the English Declaration of Rights of 1688 and the principle it represents can be traced back to the Magna Carta. The basic concept underlying the Eighth Amendment is nothing less than the dignity of man. While the State has the power to punish, the Amendment stands to assure that this power be exercised within the limits of civilized standards. Fines, imprisonment and even execution may be imposed depending upon the enormity of the crime, but any technique outside the bounds of these traditional penalties is constitutionally suspect. This Court has had little occasion to give precise content to the Eighth Amendment, and, in an enlightened democracy such as ours, this is not surprising. But when the Court was confronted with a punishment of 12 years in irons at hard and painful labor imposed for the crime of falsifying public records, it did not hesitate to declare that the penalty was cruel in its excessiveness and unusual in its character.[102] *The Court recognized in that case that the words of the Amendment are not precise, and that their scope is not static. The Amendment must draw its meaning from the evolving standards of decency that mark the progress of a maturing society.*[103]

In an interesting footnote,[104] Chief Justice Warren notes that the words cruel and unusual have never really been defined and that it is not clear if they have any separate and distinguishable meaning. In general, the cruel and unusual punishment clause has been informally defined as prohibit-

ing "inhuman treatment," a phrase equally subject to "the evolving standards of decency" criterion. Warren, for example, argues that denationalization violates the cruel and unusual clause of the Eighth Amendment.

We believe, as did Chief Judge Clark in the court below, that use of denationalization as a punishment is barred by the Eighth Amendment. There may be involved
no physical mistreatment, no primitive torture. There is, instead, the total destruc-
tion of the individual's status in organized society. It is a form of punishment more
primitive than torture, for it destroys for the individual the political existence that
was centuries in the development. The punishment strips the citizen of his status
in the national and international political community. His very existence is at the
sufferance of the country in which he happens to find himself. While any one
country may accord him some rights and, presumably, as long as he remained in
this country, he would enjoy the limited rights of an alien, no country need do so,
because he is stateless. Furthermore, his enjoyment of even the limited rights of an
alien might be subject to termination at any time by reason of deportation. In short,
the expatriate has lost the right to have rights.[105]

Then, in a passage reminiscent of Justice McKenna's opinion in *Weems*,
Chief Justice Warren writes:

We are oath-bound to defend the Constitution. This obligation requires that congressional enactments be judged by the standards of the Constitution. The Judiciary has the duty of implementing the constitutional safeguards that protect
individual rights. When the Government acts to take away the fundamental right
of citizenship, the safeguards of the Constitution should be examined with special
diligence.
    The provisions of the Constitution are not time-worn adages or hollow shibbo-
leths. They are vital, living principles that authorize and limit governmental powers in our Nation. They are the rules of government. When the constitutionality of
an Act of Congress is challenged in this Court, we must apply those rules. If we do
not, the words of the Constitution become little more than good advice.[106]

Ultimately, the "evolving standards of decency" concept may be the
benchmark against which all punishments are compared and evaluated.
    In a concurring opinion, Justice Black adds that even if a person can be
constitutionally stripped of citizenship, that expatriation cannot be done
by the military, as was the case here. Black writes, "Nothing in the Constitution or its history lends the slightest support for such military control
over the right to be an American citizen."[107]
    Justice Brennan offers as well a most interesting concurring opinion that
forecasts the constitutional position he will take in *Furman*.[108] Brennan was
vehemently opposed to the death penalty on moral and constitutional
grounds.[109] In a prescient passage relating to expatriation as punishment,
he writes:

The novelty of expatriation as punishment does not alone demonstrate its inefficiency. In recent years, we have seen such devices as indeterminate sentences and parole added to the traditional term of imprisonment. Such penal methods seek to achieve the end, at once more humane and effective, that society should make every effort to rehabilitate the offender and restore him as a useful member of that society as society's own best protection. Of course, rehabilitation is but one of the several purposes of the penal law. Among other purposes are deterrents of the wrongful act by the threat of punishment and insulation of society from dangerous individuals by imprisonment or execution. What, then, is the relationship of the punishment of expatriation to these ends of the penal law? It is perfectly obvious that it constitutes the very antithesis of rehabilitation, for instead of guiding the offender back into the useful paths of society, it excommunicates him and makes him, literally, an outcast. I can think of no more certain way in which to make a man in whom, perhaps, rest the seeds of serious anti-social behavior more likely to pursue further a career of unlawful activity than to place on him the stigma of the derelict, uncertain of many of his basic rights. Similarly, it must be questioned whether expatriation can really achieve the other effects sought by society in punitive devices. Certainly it will not insulate society from the deserter, for, unless coupled with banishment, the sanction leaves the offender at large. And, as a deterrent device, this sanction would appear of little effect, for the offender, if not deterred by thought of the specific penalties of long imprisonment or even death, is not very likely to be swayed from his course by the prospect of expatriation. However insidious and demoralizing may be the actual experience of statelessness, its contemplation in advance seems unlikely to invoke serious misgiving, for none of us yet knows its ramifications.[110]

Of course, *Trop* was decided by a 5–4 vote. Justice Frankfurter penned the dissenting opinion. Essentially, Frankfurter claims that Congress, in carrying out its war powers, may be required, in the name of national defense, to use severe means to achieve laudable ends.[111] More specifically, he continues:

Possession by an American citizen of the rights and privileges that constitute citizenship imposes correlative obligations, of which the most indispensable may well be "to take his place in the ranks of the army of his country and risk the chance of being shot down in its defense." Harsh as this may sound, it is no more so than the actualities to which it responds. Can it be said that there is no rational nexus between refusal to perform this ultimate duty of American citizenship and legislative withdrawal of that citizenship? Congress may well have thought that making loss of citizenship a consequence of wartime desertion would affect the ability of the military authorities to control the forces with which they were expected to fight and win a major world conflict. It is not for us to deny that Congress might reasonably have believed the morale and fighting efficiency of our troops would be impaired if our soldiers knew that their fellows who had abandoned them in their time of greatest need were to remain in the communion of our citizens.[112]

Justice Frankfurter offers additional rationale to support Congress's use of what might otherwise seem like a draconian punishment.[113] For Frankfurter, there is nothing in the nature of denationalization per se that would subject it to constitutional review under the cruel and unusual clause of the Eighth Amendment. In a telling conclusion that parallels Justice White's dissent in *Weems*, Frankfurter writes:

This legislation is the result of an exercise by Congress of the legislative power vested in it by the Constitution, and of an exercise by the President of his constitutional power in approving a bill and thereby making it "a law." To sustain it is to respect the actions of the two branches of our Government directly responsive to the will of the people and empowered under the Constitution to determine the wisdom of legislation. The awesome power of this Court to invalidate such legislation, because in practice it is bounded only by our own prudence in discerning the limits of the Court's constitutional function, must be exercised with the utmost restraint. Mr. Justice Holmes, one of the profoundest thinkers who ever sat on this Court, expressed the conviction that "I do not think the United States would come to an end if we lost our power to declare an Act of Congress void. I do think the Union would be imperiled if we could not make that declaration as to the laws of the several States." Holmes, Speeches, 102. He did not, of course, deny that the power existed to strike down congressional legislation, nor did he shrink from its exercise. But the whole of his work during his thirty years of service on this Court should be a constant reminder that the power to invalidate legislation must not be exercised as if, either in constitutional theory or in the art of government, it stood as the sole bulwark against unwisdom or excesses of the moment.[114]

WITHERSPOON V. STATE OF ILLINOIS

One of the issues raised in Logan concerned jury selection and composition. *Witherspoon v. State of Illinois* (391 U.S. 510 [1968] [argued 4/24/68; decided 6/3/68]) revisits that issue. By a majority vote of 6–3 the Court overturned Witherspoon's death penalty conviction on Witherspoon's Sixth Amendment right to a trial "by an impartial jury of the state and district wherein the crime shall have been committed." The denial of that right occurred when the state of Illinois excluded potential veniremen[115] for cause simply because they expressed some conscientious scruples about the death penalty. The Supreme Court holds that individuals with some conscientious scruples about the death penalty remain able to reach a decision consistent with state law. Only those individuals who state categorically that they could not invoke the death penalty can be excluded automatically from a jury in a death penalty case for these individuals in all likelihood cannot do what the state expects them to do, namely, bring in a sentence of death if the death penalty is warranted by the facts of the case. That is, someone categorically opposed to the use of the death penalty could, single-handedly, preclude the state of Illinois and the people in that state from exercising their constitutional right to impose the death penalty. Without substantial constitutional reason, no one can undermine legitimately the will of the people and therewith the will of the state. By the same token, the state cannot tip the scales of justice to its position. That did occur, according to the Court in *Witherspoon*, when the state of Illinois excluded potential jurors simply because they expressed some reservations about the use of the death penalty. They did not indicate that they could not do their lawful duty, namely, bring in a sentence of death, if the evidence so warranted. Such action, according to the Court, clearly violates the Sixth Amendment requirement of an impartial jury. As Justice Douglas notes in his concurring opinion, "The constitutional question is whether the jury must be 'impartially drawn from a cross-section of the community,' or whether it can be drawn with systematic and intentional exclusion of some qualified groups."[116] An indication that the state tipped the scales of justice in its favor came when the presiding trial judge remarked, early in the *voir dire*, "'Let's get these conscientious objectors out of the way, without wasting any time on them.'"[117]

One of the most succinct statements explaining the Court's view can be found in Justice Stewart's opinion for the Court.

If the state had excluded only those prospective jurors who stated in advance of trial that they would not even consider returning a verdict of death, it could argue that the resulting jury was simply "neutral" with respect to penalty. But when it swept from the jury all who expressed conscientious or religious scruples against capital punishment and all who opposed it in principle, the State crossed the line of neutrality. In its quest for a jury capable of imposing the death penalty, the State produced a jury uncommonly willing to condemn a man to die.[118]

It is important to note that the Court did not claim that a jury composed only of death penalty proponents would be conviction-prone. Yet today, while the Court continues to hold to that position, the subject remains contentious. The question, succinctly stated, is: Is a jury composed only of people in support of the death penalty more likely or less likely to return a guilty verdict? If yes, then a Sixth Amendment challenge to the death penalty could be raised that might preclude the use of the penalty, for the jury would not be impartial as the Sixth Amendment requires. Justice Black disagrees. Regarding a conviction-prone jury, Justice Black writes that he "cannot accept the proposition that persons who do not have conscientious scruples against the death penalty are 'prosecution prone.'"[119] He agrees with the following statement of the Court of Appeals for the District of Columbia Circuit: "'No proof is available, so far as we know, and we can imagine none, to indicate that, generally speaking, persons not opposed to capital punishment are so bent in their hostility to criminals as to be incapable of rendering impartial verdicts on the law and the evidence in a capital case. Being not opposed to capital punishment is not synonymous with favoring it.' "[120] Black argues that the Court not only has made it impossible to obtain an impartial jury in death penalty cases but also has frustrated Illinois's efforts to enforce its laws. He maintains that "the implication [of the Court's decision] is inevitably . . . that people who do not have conscientious scruples against the death penalty are somehow callous to suffering, and are, as some of the commentators cited by the Court called them, 'prosecution prone.' This conclusion represents a psychological foray into the human mind that I have considerable doubt about my ability to make, and I must confess that the two or three so-called "studies" cited by the Court on this subject are not persuasive to me."[121]

Justice White, writing in dissent, finds no difficulty with the state of Illinois trying to ensure that the will of the people, governed by constitutional democracy, is carried out. For Justice White, the desire to exclude potential jurors who express doubt and scruples about the death penalty "seems an entirely reasonable and sensible legislative act."[122] For Justice White, the Court should "leave the decision about appropriate penalties to branches of government whose members, selected by popular vote, have an authority not extended to this Court."[123]

Still, the majority of the Court certainly thought something did not look right. Justice Stewart argued that a jury should reflect the prevailing community standards in considering the death penalty. But if jurors with reservations about the death penalty are automatically excluded from jury duty, the jury comprised of only those for whom the death penalty remains totally unproblematic will not represent a fair cross-section of the community so vital to our right to an impartial jury. In this context Stewart does cite statistics to reflect the need for a more balanced jury. In 1966 Stewart notes that "42% of the American people favored capital punishment for convicted murders, while 47% opposed it and 11% were undecided."[124] In this connection Stewart argues that it is essential to have a jury selected from this cross-section if community standards are to be present in a trial, especially a trial that could result in an execution. Stewart notes that a jury, which must choose between life and death, must be able to express truly that range of community sentiment. He writes, "Yet, in a nation less than half of whose people believe in the death penalty, a jury composed exclusively of such people cannot speak for the community. Culled of all who have doubts about the wisdom of capital punishment—of all who would be reluctant to pronounce the extreme penalty—such a jury can speak only for a distinct and dwindling minority."[125] Stewart concludes his analysis as follows:

It is, of course, settled that a State may not entrust the determination of whether a man is innocent or guilty to a tribunal "organized to convict." It requires but a short step from that principle to hold, as we do today, that a State may not entrust the determination of whether a man should live or die to a tribunal organized to return a verdict of death. Specifically, we hold that a sentence of death cannot be carried out if the jury that imposed or recommended it was chosen by excluding veniremen for cause simply because they voiced general objections to the death penalty or expressed conscientious or religious scruples against its infliction. No defendant can constitutionally be put to death at the hands of a tribunal so selected. Whatever else might be said of capital punishment, it is at least clear that its imposition by a hanging jury cannot be squared with the Constitution. The State of Illinois has stacked the deck against the petitioner. To execute this death sentence would deprive him of his life without due process of law.[126]

Justice Douglas concurs with the majority in overturning Witherspoon's death sentence, but he thinks that the conviction should be overturned as well on the ground that the jury, from the outset, did not contain jurors "drawn from a cross-section of the community."[127] He bases his position in part on the dissenting opinion of Justice Murphy in *Fay v. New York*.[128] He quotes Murphy as follows:

"There is no constitutional right to a jury drawn from a group of uneducated and unintelligent persons. Nor is there any right to a jury chosen solely from those at the lower end of the economic and social scale. But there is a constitutional right to a jury drawn from a group which represents a cross-section of the community. And a cross-section of the community includes persons with varying degrees of training and intelligence and with varying economic and social positions. Under our Constitution, the jury is not to be made the representative of the most intelligent, the most wealthy or the most successful, nor of the least intelligent, the least wealthy or the least successful. It is a democratic institution, representative of all qualified classes of people."[129]

Douglas continues, "The idea that a jury should be 'impartially drawn from a cross-section of the community' certainly should not mean a selection of only those with a predisposition to impose the severest sentence or with a predisposition to impose the least one that is possible."[130]

Justice Douglas's point is that defendants have a right to an impartial jury, not a partial one. In general, prospective jurors who are challenged for reasons that do not undermine constitutional rights[131] do not pose a threat to an impartial jury. Those challenges, however, must remain largely individualized. That was not the case here. "In the present case, however, where the jury is given discretion in fixing punishment, the wholesale exclusion of a class that makes up a substantial portion of the population produces an unrepresentative jury."[132] But Douglas argues further, as previously noted, that the verdict, along with the sentence, is tainted.

The Court fails to find on this record "an unrepresentative jury on the issue of guilt." But we do not require a showing of specific prejudice when a defendant has been deprived of his right to a jury representing a cross-section of the community. We can as easily assume that the absence of those opposed to capital punishment would rob the jury of certain peculiar qualities of human nature as would the exclusion of women from juries. I would not require a specific showing of a likelihood of prejudice, for I feel that we must proceed on the assumption that in many, if not most, cases of class exclusion on the basis of beliefs or attitudes some prejudice does result and many times will not be subject to precise measurement. Indeed, that prejudice "is so subtly, so intangible, that it escapes the ordinary methods of proof."[133]

As of late 2002, the issues surrounding jury composition remain far from settled.

MCGAUTHA V. CALIFORNIA

McGautha v. California (402 U.S. 183 [1971] [argued 11/9/70; decided 5/3/71]) is more important for the dissents of Justices Douglas and Brennan than for the majority opinion penned by Justice Harlan, for just one year after *McGautha* the Court decided *Furman v. Georgia*,[134] arguably the most important capital punishment decision in constitutional law. *McGautha* included as well a petition from an Ohio defendant by the name of Crampton. A review of *McGautha* enables us to understand the constitutional and moral issues surrounding the death penalty debate, many of which remain unresolved. The case makes clear as well the different directions Supreme Court Justices have taken and will take.

McGautha raises two fundamental questions[135] regarding the constitutionality of the death penalty: (1) Can a jury impose a sentence of death independent from standards designed to guide it in the deliberative process? and (2) Can a state impose a death penalty in a case in which there has been a single trial where the jury decided guilt and punishment simultaneously? The first question relates to a constitutional need (a need based on the Due Process Clause of the Fourteenth Amendment) to guide jury decision making in capital cases. The second question raises a concern regarding a defendant's constitutional right to offer testimony regarding a potential sentence (for Crampton, a sentence of death or life imprisonment) without simultaneously leaving the defendant open to prosecutorial cross-examination regarding guilt. More specifically, if a defendant cannot offer testimony regarding a potential sentence without opening questions regarding guilt, does that not seriously jeopardize a defendant's Fifth Amendment right against self-incrimination? These two questions are far more substantive than they first appear.

McGautha was tried, along with his codefendant Wilkinson, according to California law on charges of murder. Consistent "with California pro-

cedure in capital cases, the trial was in two stages, a guilt stage and a punishment stage."[136] McGautha and Wilkinson were found "guilty of two
counts of armed robbery and one count of first-degree murder as
charged."[137] Both defendants testified at the sentencing stage of the trial
before the same jury that had convicted them.[138] The instructions given to
the members of the jury regarding their duty are noteworthy. Justice Harlan quotes the instructions as follows:

"In this part of the trial the law does not forbid you from being influenced by pity
for the defendants and you *may be governed by mere sentiment and sympathy for the
defendants* in arriving at a proper penalty in this case; *however, the law does forbid you
from being governed by mere conjecture, prejudice, public opinion or public feeling.*

"The defendants in this case have been found guilty of the offense of murder in
the first degree, and it is now your duty to determine which of the penalties provided by law should be imposed on each defendant for that offense. Now, in arriving at this determination you should consider all of the evidence received here in
court presented by the People and defendants throughout the trial before this jury.
You may also consider all of the evidence of the circumstances surrounding the
crime, of each defendant's background and history, *and of the facts in aggravation or
mitigation of the penalty which have been received here in court.* However, it is not
essential to your decision that you find mitigating circumstances on the one hand
or evidence in aggravation of the offense on the other hand.

" . . . Notwithstanding facts, if any, proved in mitigation or aggravation, in
determining which punishment shall be inflicted, you are entirely free to act
according to your own judgment, conscience, and absolute discretion. That verdict
must express the individual opinion of each juror.

"Now, beyond prescribing the two alternative penalties, the law itself provides
no standard for the guidance of the jury in the selection of the penalty, but, rather,
commits the whole matter of determining which of the two penalties shall be fixed
to the judgment, conscience, and absolute discretion of the jury. In determination
of that matter, if the jury does agree, it must be unanimous as to which of the two
penalties is imposed."[139]

McGautha was given the death penalty and the California Supreme Court
affirmed; Wilkinson was given a life sentence.

Crampton was charged with the murder of his wife, Wilma Jean.
According to Ohio law at the time, Crampton's "guilt and punishment
were determined in a single unitary proceeding."[140] Crampton did not
testify at his trial, in large part because it would open him up to cross-
examination by the prosecution regarding past crimes. Such cross-
examination could sway the jury toward conviction, thereby jeopardizing
Crampton's Fifth Amendment right not to "be compelled in any criminal
case to be a witness against himself."[141] Again, it is useful in this context to
note the instructions given to the Ohio jury to help it in its deliberations.
Justice Harlan quotes from the instructions as follows: " 'If you find the
defendant guilty of murder in the first degree, the punishment is death,

unless you recommend mercy, in which event the punishment is imprisonment in the penitentiary during life.' "[142] In addition, the jury was told the following: " 'You must not be influenced by any consideration of sympathy or prejudice. It is your duty to carefully weigh the evidence, to decide all disputed questions of fact, to apply the instructions of the court to your findings and to render your verdict accordingly. In fulfilling your duty, your efforts must be to arrive at a just verdict.' "[143] These brief comments reflect rather accurately the information about the sentencing philosophy of the state of Ohio, as well as that of the state court in which Crampton was being tried. To repeat, the Supreme Court is being asked, in part, if these instructions are sufficient to guide jury decision making in such as way so as to guarantee fundamental constitutional rights respecting a defendant's due process rights.

Before he responds with the majority opinion, Justice Harlan makes a comment relevant to the role the Supreme Court should play in evaluating capital sentences. He writes, "Our function is not to impose on the states, *ex cathedra*, what might seem to us a better system for dealing with capital cases. Rather, it is to decide whether the Federal Constitution proscribes the present procedures of these two states in such cases."[144] Justice Harlan's concern here is to ensure that the system of federalism upon which our country is based remains clear. In other words, the Supreme Court should not usurp state power in policy matters unless there is a clear conflict between state policies and constitutional rights. Thus, even if there are better ways to implement death penalty statutes, the Court's business is to determine if state policies violate constitutional guarantees.

The first issue addressed by Justice Harlan concerns the apparent lack of standards to guide juries in their decision-making responsibility. The defendants in these two cases claim that a lack of standards violates the Fourteenth Amendment guarantee of due process of law. Harlan writes:

To fit their arguments within a constitutional frame of reference petitioners contend that to leave the jury completely at large to impose or withhold the death penalty as it sees fit is fundamentally lawless and therefore violates the basic command of the Fourteenth Amendment that no State shall deprive a person of his life without due process of law. Despite the undeniable surface appeal of the proposition, we conclude that the courts below correctly rejected it.[145]

At this point Harlan offers an interesting history of efforts to draw lines between those murderers who should die and those who should not.[146] Among the points raised in this history, one in particular is important for us, namely, jury nullification.[147] Essentially, what might happen occasionally is that a jury would take the law into its own hands and do what was plainly contrary to established law. For example, while a defendant might be guilty of murder, certain conditions about the case would make the death penalty inappropriate, at least from the jury's perspective.[148] But rather than try to bring legislative changes (e.g., reducing the number of capital crimes or defining more clearly what constitutes first-degree murder) to eliminate or minimize jury nullification, legislatures "adopted the method of forthrightly granting juries the discretion which they had been exercising in fact."[149] Harlan notes as well that calls for more uniform sentencing standards have been made. He writes: "In recent years academic and professional sources have suggested that jury sentencing discretion should be controlled by standards of some sort."[150] Any such suggestions, however, although they may prove useful to legislatures as they consider their capital sentencing statutes, are not constitutionally mandated. Harlan continues: "In recent years, challenges to standardless jury sentencing have been presented to many state and federal appellate courts. No court has held the challenge good.... As petitioners recognize, it requires a strong showing to upset this settled practice of the Nation on constitutional grounds."[151] Actually, it will take just one year to "upset this settled practice."

The McGautha/Crampton challenge here is based on the claim that constitutional due process of law requirements are not met when there is no way to know when a person will receive the death penalty as opposed to a life sentence, perhaps even with the possibility of parole. At the very minimum, "due process of law" would seem to require some consistency in sentencing practice. Crampton, for example, stated before the sentencing court that he did not receive "a fair and impartial trial because the jury was prejudiced by [his] past record and the fact [that he] had been a drug addict."[152] If other defendants with arrest and conviction records comparable to Crampton's did not receive the death penalty, Crampton may have a point. Is it fair to treat similar cases dissimilarly? On what basis are we to distinguish between a death sentence and life imprisonment? Crampton's attorneys wanted the death penalty sentence overturned because standards do not exist to direct juries in the deliberative process. In short, they want Crampton's due process of law rights upheld. Justice Harlan, however, noted that Crampton's argument sounded convincing only in its generality. These general due process of law claims do not square with the history of legislative and judicial efforts to draw clear lines between alternative sentences. "To identify before the fact those characteristics of criminal homicides and their perpetrators which call for the death penalty, and to express these characteristics in language which can be fairly understood and applied by the sentencing authority, appear to be tasks which are beyond present human ability."[153] Thus, our inability to establish clear guidelines does not undermine constitutional due process requirements.[154]

To reinforce his position, Justice Harlan cites both the Royal Commission on Capital Punishment[155] and one version of a tentative draft of the

Model Penal Code to the effect that sentencing guidelines in capital cases are neither possible nor constitutionally necessary. Harlan offers the following quote from the ninth tentative draft of the Model Penal Code: "'[T]he factors which determine whether the sentence of death is the appropriate penalty in particular cases are too complex to be compressed within the limits of a simple formula.'"[156] Furthermore, "the sentencing authority should 'take into account the aggravating and mitigating circumstances enumerated . . . and any other facts that it deems relevant,' and that the court should so instruct when the issue was submitted to the jury."[157] Harlan notes that the best anyone can do in this context is to provide juries with minimal guidelines, albeit guidelines that any jury should feel free to ignore. He writes:

It is apparent that such criteria [aggravating and mitigating circumstances] do not purport to provide more than the most minimal control over the sentencing authority's exercise of discretion. They do not purport to give an exhaustive list of the relevant considerations or the way in which they may be affected by the presence or absence of other circumstances. They do not even undertake to exclude constitutionally impermissible considerations. *And, of course, they provide no protection against the jury determined to decide on whimsy or caprice. In short, they do no more than suggest some subjects for the jury to consider during its deliberations, and they bear witness to the intractable nature of the problem of "standards" which the history of capital punishment has from the beginning reflected.* Thus, they indeed caution against this Court's undertaking to establish such standards itself, or to pronounce at large that standards in this realm are constitutionally required.[158]

Justice Harlan's conclusion to this issue of jury discretion in capital cases merits citation for it captures what will become a major issue just one year later.

In light of history, experience, and the present limitations of human knowledge, we find it quite impossible to say that committing to the untrammeled discretion of the jury the power to pronounce life or death in capital cases is offensive to anything in the Constitution. The states are entitled to assume that jurors confronted with the truly awesome responsibility of decreeing death for a fellow human being will act with due regard for the consequences of their decision and will consider a variety of factors, many of which will have been suggested by the evidence or by the arguments of defense counsel. For a court to attempt to catalog the appropriate factors in this elusive area could inhibit rather than expand the scope of consideration, for no list of circumstances would ever be really complete. The infinite variety of cases and facets to each case would make general standards either meaningless "boiler-plate" or a statement of the obvious that no jury would need.[159]

The second constitutional issue raised here concerns Crampton's single trial which precluded him from offering evidence in mitigation without simultaneously enhancing the prosecution's case for conviction. The single-trial procedure in Ohio at this time subjected capital defendants to a kind of Catch-22. That is, if defendants did not offer testimony regarding the charges, they could not offer testimony in mitigation of punishment; if they offered testimony in mitigation of punishment, they could be questioned on the issue of guilt. Either way, Crampton's due process of law right to remain silent appears in jeopardy. The Fifth Amendment reads, to repeat, that no person "shall be compelled in any criminal case to be a witness against himself, nor be deprived of life, liberty, or property, without due process of law." This protection against compulsory self-incrimination was made applicable to the states in *Malloy v. Hogan*.[160] Citing *Malloy*, Crampton asserts "a constitutional right not to be compelled to be a witness against himself."[161] Justice Harlan explains Crampton's challenge as follows:

Yet, under the Ohio single-trial procedure, [Crampton] could remain silent on the issue of guilt only at the cost of surrendering any chance to plead his case on the issue of punishment. He contends that under the Due Process of Law Clause of the Fourteenth Amendment . . . he had a right to be heard on the issue of punishment and a right not to have his sentence fixed without the benefit of all the relevant evidence. Therefore, he argues, the Ohio procedure . . . creates an intolerable tension between constitutional rights. Since this tension can be largely avoided by a bifurcated trial, petitioner contends that there is no legitimate state interest in putting him to the election, and that the single-verdict trial should be held invalid in capital cases.[162]

Furthermore, Harlan argues, a defendant sometimes must evaluate a decision to testify: "Again, it is not thought inconsistent with the enlightened administration of criminal justice to require the defendant to weigh such pros and cons in deciding whether to testify."[163] In addition, throughout the sentencing process, in any sentencing decision, inconsistency in sentencing practice is not necessarily unconstitutional. "Even in noncapital sentencing the sciences of penology, sociology, and psychology have not advanced to the point that sentencing is wholly a matter of scientific calculation from objectively verifiable facts."[164] Harlan writes, "We conclude that the policies of the privilege against compelled self-incrimination are not offended when a defendant in a capital case yields to the pressure to testify on the issue of punishment at the risk of damaging his case on guilt."[165]

Moving, then, to determine the extent, if any, to which a constitutional right to be heard at sentencing is compromised by Ohio's policy, Justice Harlan writes:

This Court has not directly determined whether or to what extent the concept of due process of law requires that a criminal defendant wishing to present evidence or argument presumably relevant to the issues involved in sentencing should be permitted to do so. Assuming, without deciding, that the Constitution does require such an opportunity, there was no denial of such a right in Crampton's case. The Ohio Constitution guarantees defendants the right to have their counsel argue in summation for mercy as well as for acquittal.[166]

Harlan continues:

Even in a bifurcated trial, the defendant could be restricted to the giving of evidence, with argument to be made by counsel only. Petitioner's contention therefore comes down to the fact that the Ohio single verdict trial may deter the defendant from bringing to the jury's attention evidence peculiarly within his own knowledge, and it may mean that the death verdict will be returned by a jury which never heard the sound of his voice. We do not think that the possibility of the former is sufficiently great to sustain petitioner's claim that the single verdict trial may deprive the jury of a rational basis for fixing sentence. Assuming that in this case there was relevant information solely within petitioner's knowledge, we do not think the Constitution forbids a requirement that such evidence be available to the jury on all issues to which it is relevant or not at all. As to the largely symbolic value represented by the latter interest, Ohio has provided for retention of the ritual of allocution, albeit only in its common law form, precisely to avoid the possibility that a person might be tried, convicted, and sentenced to death in complete silence. We have held that failure to ensure such personal participation in the criminal process is not necessarily a constitutional flaw in the conviction. We do not think that Ohio was required to provide an opportunity for petitioner to speak to the jury free from any adverse consequences on the issue of guilt. We therefore reject this branch of petitioner's argument as well.[167]

Justice Harlan ends his opinion by reference once again to the fact that there may be better means by which states can try capital cases, but that does not mean that the Constitution requires the use of the best means available. The only constitutional requirement is that states ensure the fundamental constitutional rights of defendants. According to Harlan, Ohio has done just that. "The Constitution requires no more than that the trials be fairly conducted and that guaranteed rights of defendants be scrupulously respected."[168] Ohio's practice of a single trial to determine both guilt and punishment does not compromise those rights, according to the Court's majority. Regarding the claims of both McGautha and Crampton, Harlan concludes, "The procedures which petitioners challenge are those by which most capital trials in this country are conducted, and by which all were conducted until a few years ago. We have determined that these procedures are consistent with the rights to which the petitioners were constitutionally entitled, and that their trials were entirely fair."[169]

Justice Black's concurring opinion, albeit brief, is noteworthy for its language. Noting that, in his opinion, the defendants' trials were conducted fairly, Black writes, "The Constitution grants this Court no power to reverse convictions because of our personal beliefs that state criminal procedures are 'unfair,' 'arbitrary,' 'capricious,' 'unreasonable,' or 'shocking to our conscience.'"[170] For Black, there is nothing unconstitutional per se about the death penalty. If people oppose it, then the changes people demand must occur throughout the legislative process. In *Furman*, however, Black's language will be used in one form or another by five members of the Court to overturn Furman's death sentence. As I noted, however, the dissenting opinions in this case ultimately are more important than the plurality opinion.

Justice Douglas's dissent, joined by Justices Brennan and Marshall, states immediately that "the unitary trial which Ohio provides in first-degree murder cases does not satisfy the requirements of procedural Due Process under the Fourteenth Amendment."[171] Douglas reasons as follows.

According to Ohio law, the jury makes three determinations simultaneously, namely, sanity (if the issue has been raised), guilt, and punishment. But if a defendant chooses to testify, that defendant's right to be free from self-incrimination can be seriously jeopardized. Douglas explained the problem well:

If a defendant wishes to testify in support of the defense of insanity or in mitigation of what he is charged with doing, he can do so only if he surrenders his right to be free from self-incrimination. Once he takes the stand he can be cross-examined not only as respects the crime charged but also on other misdeeds. In Ohio impeachment covers a wide range of subjects: prior convictions for felonies and statutory misdemeanors, pending indictments, prior convictions in military service, and dishonorable discharges. Once he testifies he can be recalled for cross-examination in the State's case in rebuttal.[172]

Under Ohio law at the time, the only right the defendant had is the right of allocution (in essence, a right to speak before the court), but that right can be exercised only after the jury has reached a decision. The defendant, quite literally, is caught between a rock and a hard place. Douglas explained as follows:

If the right to be heard were to be meaningful, it would have to accrue before sentencing; yet, except for allocution, any attempt on the part of the accused during the trial to say why the judgment of death should not be pronounced against him entails a surrender of his right against self-incrimination. It therefore seems plain that the single-verdict procedure is a burden on the exercise of the right to be free of compulsion as respects self-incrimination. For he can testify on the issue of insanity or on other matters in extenuation of the crime charged only at the price of surrendering the protection of the Self-Incrimination Clause of the Fifth Amendment made applicable to the States by the Fourteenth.[173]

On the question of insanity and punishment the accused should be under no restraints when it comes to putting before the court and the jury all the relevant facts. Yet he cannot have that freedom where these issues are tied to the question of guilt. For on that issue he often dare not speak lest he in substance be tried not for this particular offense but for all the sins he ever committed.[174]

Throughout the remainder of his opinion, Justice Douglas focuses on the nature of procedural due process as a means to guarantee constitutional rights. For example, a two-stage or bifurcated trial is not constitutionally mandated, but due process of rights is. A two-stage trial may be the means by which due process rights are achieved. There may be means other than a two-stage trial by which due process of rights can be sustained.[175] In addition, Douglas explains that there are *expressed* procedural due process requirements and *implied* procedural due process requirements. Expressed procedural due process includes specific constitutional guarantees such as a speedy trial, a trial by a jury and a right to counsel, among others.[176] Implied procedural due process rights relate to the fundamental issue of fairness.[177] As such, we can say that such rights are elastic in nature. That is, they will expand as we mature in our understanding of what we need to guarantee that a defendant receives a fair trial. The right to be heard is an example of an implied right, and it is this right Crampton has been denied. Douglas needs to be heard on this issue.

Crampton had the constitutional right as a matter of procedural due process to be heard on the issue of punishment. . . .

But where the opportunity to be heard on the sentence is denied both counsel and the defendant, the denial reaches constitutional proportions.

Whether the voice speaking for the defendant be counsel's voice or the defendant's, the right to be heard is often vital at the sentencing stage before the law decides the punishment of the person found guilty. . . .

At least then, the right of allocution becomes a constitutional right—the right to speak to the issues touching on the sentencing before one's fate is sealed. Yet where the trial is a unitary one, the right of allocution even in a capital case is theoretical, not real, as the Ohio procedure demonstrates.[178]

In addition, Ohio's unitary trial places procedural due process rights in conflict with one another. That is, if a defendant chooses to speak, to exercise his right to be heard on the issue of punishment, he sacrifices his right to be free from self-incrimination. "Petitioner also had the protection of the Self-Incrimination Clause of the Fifth Amendment. To obtain the benefit of the former [the right to be heard on the issue of punishment] he would have to surrender the latter [the protection of the Self-Incrimination Clause]."[179] Douglas makes the same point somewhat more succinctly as follows: "For the unitary trial or single-verdict trial in practical effect allows the right to be heard on the issue of punishment only by surrendering the protection of the Self-Incrimination Clause of the Fifth Amendment."[180] Douglas would reverse both convictions.

Justice Brennan pursued a course similar to that of Justice Douglas, namely, procedural due process had not been followed in either case and both cases should be overturned.[181] Brennan's first criticism of the Court's opinion is that, contrary to Justice Harlan's claim, there are means by which a state can distinguish between lawful and unlawful execution. This first challenge to the majority opinion focuses on the nature of procedural due process as applied to these cases. Brennan writes, "Unlike the Court, I do not believe that the legislators of the 50 States are so devoid of wisdom and the power of rational thought that they are unable to face the problem of capital punishment directly, and to determine for themselves the criteria under which convicted capital felons should be chosen to live or die."[182]

The state legislators in California and Ohio, Justice Brennan argues, do not offer any standards under which juries can make reasoned judgments in capital cases. The standards themselves may not be complete, or they may be difficult to apply, but in these cases there simply are no standards to guide any jury in the sentencing process. Brennan explains as follows:

For the plain fact is that the legislatures of California and Ohio, whence come these cases, have sought no solution at all. We are not presented with a State's attempt to provide standards, attacked as impermissible or inadequate. We are not presented with a legislative attempt to draw wisdom from experience from a process looking toward growth in understanding through the accumulation of a variety of experiences. We are not presented with the slightest attempt to bring the power of reason to bear on the considerations relevant to capital sentencing. We are faced with nothing more than stark legislative abdication.[183]

In this context Justice Brennan argued that the Court has established some general principles designed to guide its review of state procedures as they bear on constitutional law. First, procedures must ensure reasonable consistency in decision making.[184] Second, procedures must offer all individuals affected by a state policy "a fair hearing of their state-law claims."[185] Third, state procedures must guarantee effective oversight of federally protected rights.[186] Fourth, to guarantee due process of law, state power must "be structured in such a way that, ultimately at least, fundamental choices among competing state policies are resolved by a responsible organ of state government."[187] The important point in this process for Brennan is the guarantee of individual rights. "The principal function of the Due Process Clause is to insure that state power is exercised only pursuant to procedures adequate to vindicate individual rights."[188] Brennan's extended analysis of these points leads to three specific and noteworthy conclusions:

First, due process of law requires the States to protect individuals against the arbitrary exercise of state power by assuring that the fundamental policy choices underlying any exercise of state power are explicitly articulated by some reasonable organ of government. *Second,* due process of law is denied by state procedural mechanisms that allow for the exercise of arbitrary power without providing any means whereby arbitrary action may be reviewed or corrected. *Third,* where federally protected rights are involved due process of law is denied by state procedures which render inefficacious the federal judicial machinery that has been established for the vindication of those rights.[189]

Justice Brennan's second line of attack focuses on the claim that guidelines necessary to distinguish between cases that warrant the death penalty from those that do not have not been defined with sufficient clarity to guide juries in their decision-making responsibility. Brennan argues that there is no reason why some guidelines—albeit, at times, imperfect guidelines—cannot be legislatively proscribed. Without some guidelines, juries, for all practical purposes, operate more according to the rule of the lawless than to the rule of law. Brennan writes, "The Court neglects to explain why the impossibility of perfect standards justifies making no attempt whatsoever to control lawless action."[190] The problem here remains a recurring one in the long-standing and fractious debate about the constitutionality of the death penalty, namely, can the imposition of a death sentence avoid the arbitrary and haphazard implementation of it? The importance of this question cannot be gainsaid or underestimated. The rule of law implies, at the very minimum, that people can, for the most part, understand what the law is and be able to conform their behavior to it accordingly. Under a rule of law, people can expect certain behavior to illicit certain kinds of responses. People need to know not only what the law is but also what will happen if the law is broken. We need some consistency to assure us that law is not some randomly applied set of rules. In this context, Brennan argues that there must be some social goals punishment serves, that is, goals that can direct legislative policy making. For example, a state that wants to secure stability and safety in society may decide to put to death twice-guilty murderers. Twice-guilty murderers, a state could argue, have made clear that they constitute an ongoing threat to our security. "The protection of society," then, becomes the general justification for putting twice-guilty murderers to death.[191] Brennan elaborates:

A State may seek to inflict retribution on a wrongdoer, inflicting punishment strictly in proportion to the offense committed. It may seek, by the infliction of punishment, to deter others from committing similar crimes. It may consider at least some wrongdoers likely to commit other crimes, and therefore seek to prevent these hypothetical future acts by removing such persons from society. It may seek to rehabilitate most offenders, reserving capital punishment only for those cases where it judges the likelihood of rehabilitation to be less than a certain amount. I may assume that many if not all States choosing to kill some convicted criminals intend thereby to further more than one of the ends listed above; and I need not doubt that some States may consider other policies as well relevant to the decision. But I can see no reason whatsoever that a State may be excused from declaring what policies it seeks to further by the infliction of capital punishment merely because it may be difficult to determine how those policies should be applied in any particular case. If anything, it would seem that the difficulty of decision in particular cases would support rather than weaken the point that uniform decisionmaking requires that state policy be explicitly articulated. Yet the Court seems somehow to assume that jurors will be most likely to fulfill their function and correctly apply a uniform state policy if they are never told what that policy is.[192]

States must justify the punishments they inflict on wrongdoers. Such general justifications enable citizens to conform their behavior to the law and guide juries as they decide to do what should be done to those who do not conform their behavior to the law. Such, at the very minimum, constitutes the rule of law. Otherwise, the difference between lawful and unlawful is nonexistent. "In sum," Justice Brennan writes, "I see no reason whatsoever to believe that the nature of capital sentencing is such that it cannot be surrounded with the protections ordinarily available to check arbitrary and lawless action."[193]

Neither California nor Ohio statutes provide the guidance and clarity of direction necessary to avoid arbitrary and haphazard jury decision making.[194] In essence, the Ohio and California statutes are the very antithesis of the rule of law, according to Brennan. Decisions that affect peoples' lives cannot be made on the basis of whim and caprice without comprising the integrity of constitutional democracy. And while government must adhere to the rule of law in establishing policies and procedures, nowhere is that requirement more critical than at the point where people become subject to the death penalty. Death, as is argued throughout moral and constitutional debates about capital punishment, is different, and for that reason is subject to even greater Supreme Court scrutiny, not to mention moral scrutiny. That is precisely the direction the Court took one year after *McGautha* and *Crampton*.

In summary, the first ninety-year Supreme Court decision making with respect to the Eighth Amendment focused more on legitimate constitutional procedures in applying the cruel and unusual punishment clause to the death penalty than on whether the death penalty itself constituted cruel and unusual punishment. *Furman* will change that one-dimensional approach to one in which both the procedures for and constitutionality of the death penalty will be examined critically and, at times, quite contentiously.

CHAPTER 3

1972: Death Takes a Hiatus

It is for Congress and not for us to decide whether it is wise public policy to inflict the death penalty at all.

Justice Hugo Black, *Robinson v. United States*

Obviously, concepts of justice change; no immutable moral order requires death for murderers and rapists. The claim that death is a just punishment necessarily refers to the existence of certain public beliefs. The claim must be that, for capital crimes, death alone comports with society's notion of proper punishment. As administered today, however, the punishment of death cannot be justified as a necessary means of exacting retribution from criminals. When the overwhelming number of criminals who commit capital crimes go to prison, it cannot be concluded that death serves the purpose of retribution more effectively than imprisonment. The asserted public belief that murderers and rapists deserve to die is flatly inconsistent with the execution of a random few. As the history of the punishment of death in this country shows, our society wishes to prevent crime; we have no desire to kill criminals simply to get even with them.

Justice Brennan, *Furman v. Georgia*

The Eighth Amendment, adopted at the same time as the Fifth, proscribes "cruel and unusual" punishments. In an effort to discern its meaning, much has been written about its history in the opinions of this Court and elsewhere. That history need not be restated here since, whatever punishments the Framers of the Constitution may have intended to prohibit under the "cruel and unusual" language, there

cannot be the slightest doubt that they intended no absolute bar on the
Government's authority to impose the death penalty.

Justice Powell, *Furman v. Georgia*

No one predicted or could have predicted the surprising turn the Supreme
Court took on the death penalty just one year after *McGautha*. In 1972 the
Court announced a decision that would constitute a watershed in moral
and constitutional thinking about capital punishment. That decision
remains as important today as it was the day it was handed down.

FURMAN V. GEORGIA

Furman v. Georgia (408 U.S. 238 [1972] [argued 1/17/72; decided
6/29/72]), along with its companion cases *Jackson v. Georgia* and *Branch v.
Texas*, remains the most important Supreme Court decision on the death
penalty for several reasons. First, and foremost, most of the arguments for
and against the death penalty, both moral and constitutional, are found
here. Second, at 232 pages, it is the longest Supreme Court decision on the
death penalty. Third, nine separate opinions comprise the 5–4 decision.
Fourth, it makes clear the range of opinions and the complexity of the
issues that permeate death penalty debates. Fifth, it rendered the death
penalty unconstitutional as it was then implemented and required both
state governments and the federal government to rethink and to rewrite
death penalty statutes. Sixth, after *Furman*, and because of *Furman*, constitutional challenges to the death penalty will engage the Supreme Court on
a yearly and seemingly endless basis. Indeed, any Supreme Court death
penalty decision after *Furman* can be referred to simply as post-Furman. It
would not be inappropriate to refer to Furman and post-Furman as
descriptive nouns. *Furman* is, in short, a decision we must understand if
we are to understand anything about the constitutional issues that confront the Court yearly.

The majority opinion, penned by Justice Douglas,[1] held the death
penalty unconstitutional on the grounds that it violates the cruel and
unusual punishment clause of the Eighth Amendment as applied to the
states through the Fourteenth Amendment. Douglas's position on the
constitutionality of the death penalty rests on its indeterminate and haphazard application. That is, if death penalties are selectively or discriminatorily applied, they are constitutionally suspect. Such indeterminate
application means necessarily, for Douglas, that the sentence is "unusual"
and consequently a violation of the Eighth Amendment. Douglas writes,
"It would seem to be incontestable that the death penalty inflicted on one
defendant is 'unusual' if it discriminates against him by reason of his race,
religion, wealth, social position, or class, or if it is imposed under a procedure that gives room for the play of such prejudices."[2] The death penalty

cannot be applied selectively, Douglas argues, without subjecting it to Supreme Court scrutiny. Douglas then quotes an essay by Justice Arthur Goldberg and Professor Alan Dershowitz[3] as follows: "'A penalty . . . should be considered 'unusually' imposed if it is administered arbitrarily or discriminatorily'" and "'[t]he extreme rarity with which applicable death penalty provisions are put to use raises a strong inference of arbitrariness.'"[4] Douglas cites as well one of the conclusions from "The President's Commission on Law Enforcement and Administration of Justice." "'Finally, there is evidence that the imposition of the death sentence and the exercise of dispensing power by the courts and the executive follow discriminatory patterns. The death sentence is disproportionately imposed, and carried out on the poor, the Negro, and the members of unpopular groups.'"[5] To support his position more fully, Douglas quotes Sing Sing Warden Lewis E. Lawes as follows:

"Not only does capital punishment fail in its justification, but no punishment could be invented with so many inherent defects. It is an unequal punishment in the way it is applied to the rich and to the poor. The defendant of wealth and position never goes to the electric chair or to the gallows. Juries do not intentionally favour the rich, the law is theoretically impartial, but the defendant with ample means is able to have his case presented with every favourable aspect, while the poor defendant often has a lawyer assigned by the court. Sometimes such assignment is considered part of political patronage; usually the lawyer assigned has had no experience whatever in a capital case."[6]

For Justice Douglas, the Eighth Amendment reflects the desire on the part of those who wrote the Bill of Rights to ensure equal protection of the laws.[7] Douglas's concern is that the selective application of the death penalty reflects a social division unjustifiable under a constitutional democracy that seeks to preserve a fundamental political and legal equality among all people. Any deviation from equal treatment under the law undermines the integrity and legitimacy of the Constitution. It is incumbent upon the Court to guarantee that laws are not selectively and arbitrarily applied, as they most certainly appear to be circa 1972. With respect to the death penalty, Douglas concludes:

The high service rendered by the "cruel and unusual" punishment clause of the Eighth Amendment is to require legislatures to write penal laws that are evenhanded, nonselective, and nonarbitrary, and to require judges to see to it that general laws are not applied sparsely, selectively, and spottily to unpopular groups.

Thus, these discretionary statutes are unconstitutional in their operation. They are pregnant with discrimination, and discrimination is an ingredient not compatible with the idea of equal protection of the laws that is implicit in the ban on "cruel and unusual" punishments.[8]

Justice Brennan's concurring opinion constitutes a directional change from his *McGautha* opinion. Henceforth, Brennan will argue that the death penalty is unconstitutional in violation of the Eighth Amendment's cruel and unusual punishment clause. He will never again deviate from the position delineated here in *Furman.*

In a historical survey regarding the cruel and unusual punishment clause, Justice Brennan notes that there was a concern among a few of the framers of the Constitution that future legislatures, without some constitutional limitation on their power to punish, might decide to opt for draconian punishments as a means to extract confessions or to appease the vindictiveness of an excited populace.[9] The authors of the Bill of Rights, Brennan argues, recognized that representatives, by virtue of their being representatives, do not necessarily don a mantle of virtue once elected. Thus, one specific conclusion that can be drawn from the very limited history of any debates over the cruel and unusual punishment clause is that the cruel and unusual punishment clause was included "precisely because the legislature would otherwise have had the unfettered power to prescribe punishments for crime."[10]

Justices are not, then, in their constitutional deliberations, limited to interpreting the Constitution consistent with the penalties readily acceptable to people in the eighteenth century. Brennan is asserting here a judicial power to place a "'restraint upon legislatures'" to permit the constitutional growth necessary to preserve the integrity of the rule of law while maintaining individual freedom.[11] It devolves to the Supreme Court, then, to determine when the cruel and unusual punishment clause has been violated by legislatures. That determination is made according to legal principles, principles that are not necessarily easy to identify, to understand, or to apply. Indeed, Brennan warns, consistent with *Weems,* that judges cannot casually substitute their opinions for legislative opinions. By the same token, judges cannot stand idly by while provisions of the Bill of Rights are threatened.[12] For Brennan, the Supreme Court's function requires it to interpret constitutional clauses as necessary in an expanding and more complex society.[13] Consequently, given his position on constitutional interpretation, Brennan believes the Supreme Court finds itself in the unique position to give new life to the meaning and scope of the constitutionality of the death penalty.

The guiding principle for deciding cruel and unusual punishment cases for Justice Brennan is that enunciated in *Trop,* namely, "the Clause 'must draw its meaning from the evolving standards of decency that mark the progress of a maturing society.'"[14] Thus, a "civilized" society will move forward in the area of punishment in the same way that a "civilized" society leaves its past behind in other areas. For example, if legislators and judges relied solely on the standards acceptable and available in 1787, they could retain the institution of slavery. Just as slavery could not stand the moral scrutiny of most people in society today, so capital punishment will not be able to withstand the moral scrutiny of a mature and civilizing society. What is at the heart of this claim? Brennan asserts here that the fundamental foundation for overturning a punishment accepted throughout centuries is the dignity of human beings. Human dignity precludes the use of the death penalty. Brennan writes, "At bottom, then, the Cruel and Unusual Punishments Clause prohibits the infliction of uncivilized and inhuman punishments. The State, even as it punishes, must treat its members with respect for their intrinsic worth as human beings. A punishment is 'cruel and unusual,' therefore, if it does not comport with human dignity."[15] But how are people to know when a punishment does not comport with "human dignity" that thereby compromises their constitutional guarantee against cruel and unusual punishments? Brennan offers the following four guidelines.

First, "a punishment must not be so severe as to be degrading to the dignity of human beings."[16] A severe punishment is one which involves either physical or mental suffering, or possibly both. Punishments degrade human dignity when "they treat members of the human race as nonhumans, as objects to be toyed with and discarded."[17] The constitutional guarantee against cruel and unusual punishments, then, proclaims "that even the vilest criminal remains a human being possessed of common human dignity."[18] Indeed, in some cases, any punishment can be degrading to human dignity. For example, punishing people for any mental or physical impairment over which they have no control would violate the cruel and unusual punishment clause.[19] The enormity of a punishment also degrades human dignity. "A prime example is expatriation . . . for it necessarily involves a denial by society of the individual's existence as a member of the human community."[20] These examples constitute just some of the ways in which a punishment can degrade human beings.

Second, a punishment does not comport with human dignity if it *arbitrarily* inflicts a severe punishment.[21] Punishments, especially severe punishments, cannot be arbitrarily inflicted on some and not on others who commit similar crimes. Severe punishments, such as death by firing squad, are constitutional, it would seem, if they are inflicted in most cases for which the punishment is available. "Arbitrary" punishments fail to meet the cruel and unusual punishment clause test.[22]

Third, "a severe punishment *must not be unacceptable* to contemporary society."[23] If a punishment is rejected by society, that serves as "a strong indication that a severe punishment does not comport with human dignity."[24] And how are people to determine when a punishment is unacceptable to society? "The acceptability of a severe punishment is measured, not by its availability, for it might become so offensive to society as never to be inflicted, but by its use."[25] Accordingly, even if a legislative act establishes a death penalty, that does not imply social acceptance.[26]

Fourth, and finally, "a severe punishment must not be excessive."[27] And just when does a punishment become excessive? "A punishment is excessive under this principle if it is unnecessary: The infliction of a severe punishment by the State cannot comport with human dignity when it is nothing more than the pointless infliction of suffering. If there is a significantly less severe punishment adequate to achieve the purposes for which the punishment is inflicted . . . the punishment inflicted is unnecessary and therefore excessive."[28]

To conclude Justice Brennan's review of decision-making principles as they relate to cruel and unusual punishments, it is important to recognize that these four principles do not operate in isolation; they are interrelated. It is not necessary for a punishment to violate each of these principles for it to be held unconstitutional. Rather, a punishment can be held unconstitutional when several of these principles taken together are violated. The violation, then, of two or more of these principles enables a court to "determine whether a challenged punishment comports with human dignity."[29] Brennan explains this cumulative test as follows:

The test, then, will ordinarily be a cumulative one: if a punishment is unusually severe, if there is a strong probability that it is inflicted arbitrarily, if it is substantially rejected by contemporary society, and if there is no reason to believe that it serves any penal purpose more effectively than some less severe punishment, then the continued infliction of that punishment violates the command of the Clause that the State may not inflict inhuman and uncivilized punishments upon those convicted of crimes.[30]

The third and final section of Brennan's opinion makes clear the basis on which he finds the death penalty unconstitutional. In the second section of his opinion, just reviewed, Brennan identified the principles that should guide the courts in finding punishments unconstitutional. There is no reason, he reiterates here, to believe that the framers of the Bill of Rights had endorsed the death penalty for all time.[31]

Applying the four principles delineated above, Justice Brennan argues as follows.

First, death constitutes an unusually and unnecessarily severe punishment, both physically and mentally. There is not only no way to guarantee a physically painless death, but also no way to prevent the psychological pains those on death row face daily.[32] Quoting the California Supreme Court, Justice Brennan writes that "'the process of carrying out a verdict of death is often so degrading and brutalizing to the human spirit as to constitute psychological torture.'"[33] Brennan notes as well Justice Frankfurter's observation that it is not unusual for some people sentenced to death to go insane while awaiting execution.[34] Consequently, "the deliberate extinguishment of human life by the State is uniquely degrading to human dignity. I would not hesitate to hold, on that ground alone, that death is today a 'cruel and unusual' punishment, were it not that death is a punishment of longstanding usage and acceptance in this country."[35]

Second, a state is precluded from inflicting arbitrarily an unusually severe punishment. On what basis can it be deduced that the death penalty is inflicted arbitrarily? Justice Brennan notes that the death penalty has become a rare occurrence over the forty-year period prior to *Furman* (1930–70). Each year, fewer and fewer criminals are put to death.[36] Brennan adds that, while thousands of murders and rapes[37] occur each year, there are only about fifty executions each year. For Brennan, that reality indicates "that the punishment is not being regularly and fairly applied . . . [and] that it is being inflicted arbitrarily."[38] In addition, since there are no guidelines to direct juries in their deliberations, the death penalty by definition guarantees its arbitrary implementation.[39] Although the "facts" are clear to Brennan here, he acknowledges that not everyone will accept them. He concludes his analysis of the second principle by saying that the probability of the arbitrary infliction of the death penalty suffices to raise doubts about its constitutionality. This principle, however, combined with the other three principles, will help sustain Brennan's final position on the constitutionality of the death penalty.[40]

Third, the rejection of a penalty by the people establishes the unconstitutionality of that punishment. "An examination of the history and present operation of the American practice of punishing criminals by death reveals that this punishment has been almost totally rejected by contemporary society."[41] On what basis can Justice Brennan make this claim? Several realities, he argues, establish this inference. To begin, Brennan notes that American history reveals that Americans have always rejected the more cruel methods of execution and have, whenever possible, opted for supposedly more humane methods of execution, such as electrocution and lethal gas. In addition, states no longer support public executions, a practice that debases and brutalizes all human beings.[42] Furthermore, the number of crimes for which the death penalty has been available have been reduced drastically to only the most heinous crimes, 99 percent of which are for murder and rape, 87 percent of which are for murder.[43] Also, mandatory death sentences have been abandoned both legislatively and through the practice of jury nullification. Jury nullification occurs, in part, when juries refuse to convict because they find mandatory death sentences offensive. Rather than try to refine guidelines for juries to follow in sentencing decisions, legislatures "adopted the method of forthrightly granting juries the discretion that they had been exercising in fact."[44] And at the time of *Furman*, fully nine states no longer permitted the death penalty, and five used it in only the rarest cases.[45] Based on these observations, Brennan concludes that the death penalty raises serious moral and religious questions among the people, which raise constitutional concerns about the punishment. Policies and practices, both federal and state, indicate a move away from the death penalty. That juries do not use the death penalty indicates to Brennan "that contemporary society views this punishment with substantial doubt."[46]

Fourth, "an unusually severe and degrading punishment may not be excessive in view of the purposes for which it is inflicted."[47] Justice Brennan does not want to become embroiled in the debate over the deterrent effect, if any, of the death penalty. The constitutionally relevant question is not whether the death penalty deters, but whether it deters more than a lesser punishment, for example, life imprisonment. If deterrence is a goal of a criminal justice system, then that justice system, to be taken seriously, must use the most effective and least intrusive punishment alternative. For Brennan, there is no evidence to indicate that the death penalty could be any more effective than a lesser punishment, such as life imprisonment without the possibility of parole.[48]

Justice Brennan next examines the retributive function of punishment. As noted in chapter 1, retribution is seen as a general justification for punishment in that punishment is given because the punishment is deserved. Retributivists, for the most part, want the punishment to fit the crime. In terms of capital punishment, the states that use the death penalty claim "that death is the only fit punishment for capital crimes and that this retributive purpose justifies its infliction."[49] For Brennan, however, there is no necessary correlation between the death penalty and the crimes for which it has been used. The death penalty, notes Brennan, was once the accepted punishment not only for murder and rape but also for forgery, among other illegal acts. Thus, society can change its conception of what punishment is necessary to achieve retributive goals. As society changes and matures, so its punishments will become more rational.[50] Brennan concludes as follows:

In sum, the punishment of death is inconsistent with all four principles: death is an unusually severe and degrading punishment; there is a strong probability that it is inflicted arbitrarily; its rejection by contemporary society is virtually total; and there is no reason to believe that it serves any penal purpose more effectively than the less severe punishment of imprisonment. The function of these principles is to enable a court to determine whether a punishment comports with human dignity. Death, quite simply, does not.[51]

Justice Stewart's opinion is refreshingly short at just four pages, but those four pages send a message as important as any delivered in this case.[52] While he maintains, contrary to Justice Brennan, that retribution does not offend any constitutional clauses or principles, he does hold that the death penalty's present implementation violates the Eighth Amendment's cruel and unusual punishment clause. Stewart explains:

These death sentences are cruel and unusual in the same way that being struck by lightning is cruel and unusual. For, of all the people convicted of rapes and murders in 1967 and 1968, many just as reprehensible as these, the petitioners are among a capriciously selected random handful upon whom the sentence of death has in fact been imposed. My concurring Brothers have demonstrated that, if any basis can be discerned for the selection of these few to be sentenced to die, it is the constitutionally impermissible basis of race. But racial discrimination has not been proved, and I put it to one side. *I simply conclude that the Eighth and Fourteenth Amendments cannot tolerate the infliction of a sentence of death under legal systems that permit this unique penalty to be so wantonly and so freakishly imposed.*[53]

The last phrase, "so wantonly and so freakishly imposed," may well turn out to be the means by which capital punishment is rendered unconstitutional.

Justice White, in a four-page opinion as well, agrees with Justice Stewart in that the death penalty is not unconstitutional per se. "In joining the Court's judgments, therefore, I do not at all intimate that the death penalty is unconstitutional *per se* or that there is no system of capital punishment that would comport with the Eighth Amendment. That question, ably argued by several of my Brethren, is not presented by these cases and need not be decided."[54]

Justice White raises several concerns about the constitutionality of the death penalty. First, common sense tells us that any punishment infrequently imposed fails to serve criminal justice goals. For White, criminal justice goals, consistent with general social goals, include retribution and deterrence. Among the defining characteristics of retribution is included the concept of proportionate punishments, that is, the punishment must fit the crime. From this perspective, murderers and rapists may well deserve the death penalty, that death may not be disproportionate for these crimes. But the infrequency with which capital punishment is used raises legitimate constitutional Eighth Amendment concerns regarding cruel and unusual punishment if for no other reason than that "there is no meaningful basis for distinguishing the few cases in which it [the death penalty] is imposed from the many cases in which it is not."[55] Retribution includes as well a concept of equality in that like cases are to be treated alike. All other things being equal, two people committing the same crime should receive essentially the same punishment. Retribution is not served by the infrequency with which it is carried out and is indeed undermined morally by the fact that it is a punishment unequally and hence unjustifiably imposed. Such inequality in criminal justice practices, for White, do not serve a retributive goal.[56]

Justice White accepts deterrence as well as a legitimate social goal and justification for punishment in general and for the death penalty in particular. "For present purposes, I accept the morality and utility of punishing

one person to influence another. I accept also the effectiveness of punishment generally, and need not reject the death penalty as a more effective
deterrent than a lesser punishment."[57] Unfortunately, deterrence, like retribution, is undermined by the infrequency with which the death penalty
is imposed. "Most important, a major goal of the criminal law—to deter
others by punishing the convicted criminal—would not be substantially
served where the penalty is so seldom invoked that it ceases to be the credible threat essential to influence the conduct of others."[58] White states his
position on the death penalty's constitutionality as follows:

At the moment that it ceases realistically to further these purposes, however, the
emerging question is whether its imposition in such circumstances would violate
the Eighth Amendment. It is my view that it would, for its imposition would then
be the pointless and needless extinction of life with only marginal contributions to
any discernible social or public purposes. A penalty with such negligible returns to
the State would be patently excessive and cruel and unusual punishment violative
of the Eighth Amendment.[59]

Justice Marshall's opinion is the longest in this case, coming in at virtually sixty pages, including appendixes.[60] For Marshall, the constitutionality of the death penalty comes down to one consideration, namely, Is the
death penalty consistent with a sense of self-respect? If it is not, then the
death penalty constitutes a cruel and unusual punishment in violation of
the Eighth Amendment. Marshall writes that the question before us "is
whether capital punishment is 'a punishment no longer consistent with
our own self-respect' and, therefore, violative of the Eighth Amendment."[61] Marshall answers that question when he states, quoting from
Trop, that the cruel and unusual punishment clause " 'must draw its meaning from the evolving standards of decency that mark the progress of a
maturing society.' "[62] For Marshall, "punishments" are not etched in stone.
The Court, for Marshall, is free to pursue a more enlightened interpretation and understanding of the cruel and unusual punishment clause. That
pursuit leads Marshall to assert that a punishment "may be cruel and
unusual because it is excessive and serves no valid legislative purpose" or
that it "may be invalid if popular sentiment abhors it."[63]

To determine if death is excessive or unnecessary, Justice Marshall examines the purposes of capital punishment to determine if the death penalty is
legislatively justifiable in terms of the cruel and unusual punishment clause
of the Eighth Amendment. He contends that if the purposes of capital punishment could be achieved with lesser punishments, then the death penalty
is unconstitutional because it would constitute unnecessary cruelty. For
example, if deterrence is a social goal of punishment and that goal could be
achieved with a two-week prison sentence, then there is no reason to
imprison someone for five weeks. Marshall argues that if social goals can be

achieved with less draconian punishments, then it is those punishments that are justifiable, not the excessive ones.[64]

What are the purposes of (or social goals served by) capital punishment? "There are six purposes conceivably served by capital punishment: retribution, deterrence, prevention of repetitive criminal acts, encouragement of guilty pleas and confessions, eugenics, and economy."[65] Marshall examines each of these purposes separately.

First, the concept of retribution, for Justice Marshall, confuses two questions: Why does society punish? What justifies societies in punishing others? The answer to the first question is that society punishes because a rule or law has been broken. "Thus, it can correctly be said that breaking the law is the *sine qua non* of punishment, or, in other words, that we only tolerate punishment as it is imposed on one who deviates from the norm established by the criminal law."[66] So society punishes someone because a law has been broken. But that does not entitle it to punish by any available means.[67] The second question requires that specific punishments be justified. The justification offered by retribution receives Marshall's close attention. For Marshall, retribution has never served as a legitimate justification for punishment. "Retaliation, vengeance, and retribution have been roundly condemned as intolerable aspirations for a government in a free society. Punishment as retribution has been condemned by scholars for centuries, and the Eighth Amendment itself was adopted to prevent punishment from becoming synonymous with vengeance."[68]

Thus, for Justice Marshall, retribution was never permissible under the Eighth Amendment. While societies punish because of retribution, specific punishments cannot be retributive in nature.[69] Marshall writes, "But, the fact that *some* punishment may be imposed does not mean that *any* punishment is permissible."[70] Indeed, Marshall argues that retribution could never have been the accepted justification for punishment, for that justification would enable states to invoke any penalty for any crime. "If retribution alone could serve as a justification for any particular penalty, then all penalties selected by the legislature would by definition be acceptable means for designating society's moral approbation of a particular act."[71] There is no doubt that many people, if not all people, have retributive moments, that is, moments in which they feel "that morality requires vengeance to evidence society's abhorrence of the act."[72] But, according to Marshall, the Eighth Amendment protects society from our vengeful moments. "But the Eighth Amendment is our insulation from our baser selves. The 'cruel and unusual' language limits the avenues through which vengeance can be channeled. Were this not so, the language would be empty, and a return to the rack and other tortures would be possible in a given case."[73]

Justice Marshall concludes his analysis of retribution as a justification for punishment as follows: "The history of the Eighth Amendment supports only the conclusion that retribution for its own sake is improper."[74] Of course, Marshall does not make clear the exact implications of this concluding statement. He could mean that punishment for the sake of punishment does not comport with Eighth Amendment history; on the other hand, he might mean that retribution should not stand as the sole justification for punishment in general and capital punishment in particular. It does not mean, however, that the death penalty is unwarranted or unconstitutional if other, more social, purposes merit its use. Thus, it is necessary to determine if other traditional justifications for punishment would sustain the constitutional use of the death penalty.

The second purpose for punishment is deterrence. Here society must ask if the death penalty serves as a better deterrent than life imprisonment. Because life imprisonment is often the preferred alternative to the death penalty, this is the alternative punishment Justice Marshall chooses to use in this context. "It must be kept in mind, then, that the question to be considered is not simply whether capital punishment is a deterrent, but whether it is a better deterrent than life imprisonment."[75] For Marshall, "[i]n light of the massive amount of evidence before us, I see no alternative but to conclude that capital punishment cannot be justified on the basis of its deterrent effect."[76]

The third purpose of the death penalty is to prevent recidivism. Clearly, any convicted criminal executed can no longer commit murder. But there is evidence that indicates that convicted murderers rarely commit murder again even if they are not sentenced to die.[77] Indeed, some become model citizens.[78] In addition, most criminals convicted of capital crimes are not sentenced to die, and there is no apparent rise in homicide.[79] It is clear, then, according to Justice Marshall, that the death penalty is excessive and unconstitutional from the recidivist perspective because the recidivism rate for murderers is at best negligible. Society does not need a punishment that severe to prevent additional murders.[80]

Justice Marshall examines the remaining purposes of the death penalty—encouraging guilty pleas and confessions, eugenics, and economy—together. First, the use of the death penalty to encourage guilty pleas and confessions is morally unconscionable and a violation of a defendant's Sixth Amendment right to a jury trial. In addition, there is no reason why a threat of life imprisonment cannot serve the same purpose. That is, life imprisonment remains a sufficiently severe punishment "which can be used as leverage for bargaining for pleas or confessions in exchange either for charges of lesser offenses or recommendations of leniency."[81]

Second, the use of capital punishment for eugenic purposes is both immoral and unconstitutional. For example, if society wants to eliminate those most likely to commit murder again, it does not have the means to distinguish between those who might and those who might not murder again. The inability to distinguish between curable and incurable constitutes a potential due process of law violation. Furthermore, to justify the death penalty for eugenic purposes, society would have to show that life imprisonment, treatment, and sterilization cannot achieve the same purpose. In addition, the United States "has never formally professed eugenic goals, and the history of the world does not look kindly on them."[82] For these reasons, capital punishment simply cannot be defended on eugenic grounds.

Third, the economic argument that the death penalty is cheaper than life imprisonment is less than clear, according to Justice Marshall. The costs for a capital trial are substantial. For example, jury selection in capital cases is far more time-consuming than in any other criminal trial. Capital trials, to meet constitutional requirements, present greater opportunities to appeal convictions. In order to ensure that innocent people are not executed, states bear the financial burden of processing numerous appeals. In short, the death penalty is no financial bargain.[83]

Justice Marshall concludes this analysis as follows: "There is but one conclusion that can be drawn from all of this—i.e., the death penalty is an excessive and unnecessary punishment that violates the Eighth Amendment."[84] Marshall, however, has not finished.

Justice Marshall next claims that the death penalty, even if some do not find it excessive and hence unconstitutional, "nonetheless violates the Eighth Amendment because it is morally unacceptable to the people of the United States at this time in their history."[85] Marshall begins this argument by noting that courts have determined that a punishment is morally acceptable "unless 'it shocks the conscience and sense of justice of the people.'"[86] The problem here is to determine if a punishment shocks and offends the people's sense of justice. The use of a public opinion poll would not help, Marshall argues, because the people surveyed may not comprehend fully the realities of the punishment to be considered. The determination of the moral acceptability of a punishment must be based "on whether people who were fully informed as to the purposes of the penalty and its liabilities would find the penalty shocking, unjust, and unacceptable."[87] Marshall continues, "In other words, the question with which we must deal is not whether a substantial proportion of American citizens would today, if polled, opine that capital punishment is barbarously cruel, but whether they would find it to be so in the light of all information presently available."[88]

But what kind of information about the death penalty does society lack? Justice Marshall offers the following observation.

It has often been noted that American citizens know almost nothing about capital punishment. Some of the conclusions arrived at in the preceding section and the supporting evidence would be critical to an informed judgment on the morality of the death penalty: e.g., that the death penalty is no more effective a deterrent than life imprisonment, that convicted murderers are rarely executed, but are usually sentenced to a term in prison; that convicted murderers usually are model prisoners, and that they almost always become law-abiding citizens upon their release from prison; that the costs of executing a capital offender exceed the costs of imprisoning him for life; that, while in prison, a convict under sentence of death performs none of the useful functions that life prisoners perform; that no attempt is made in the sentencing process to ferret out likely recidivists for execution; and that the death penalty may actually stimulate criminal activity.[89]

This kind of information, Marshall goes on to argue, might make it clear that the death penalty is unwise, but it would not necessarily convince someone that the punishment was immoral.

If people remain unconvinced about the meaning and effectiveness of the death penalty, they should consider the following: "capital punishment is imposed discriminatorily against certain identifiable classes of people; there is evidence that innocent people have been executed before their innocence can be proved; and the death penalty wreaks havoc with our entire criminal justice system."[90] For now, Justice Marshall concludes by claiming that capital punishment must be rejected. "Assuming knowledge of all the facts presently available regarding capital punishment, the average citizen would, in my opinion, find it shocking to his conscience and sense of justice. For this reason alone, capital punishment cannot stand."[91] Marshall concludes his analysis with the following moving summation.

In striking down capital punishment, this Court does not malign our system of government. On the contrary, it pays homage to it. Only in a free society could right triumph in difficult times, and could civilization record its magnificent advancement. In recognizing the humanity of our fellow beings, we pay ourselves the highest tribute. We achieve "a major milestone in the long road up from barbarism" and join the approximately 70 other jurisdictions in the world which celebrate their regard for civilization and humanity by shunning capital punishment.[92]

Such, then, are the opinions of those Justices who find, in *Furman*, constitutional problems with the death penalty. It must be remembered that only two Justices, Brennan and Marshall, found the death penalty inherently cruel and unusual and therefore a violation of the cruel and unusual punishment clause of the Eighth Amendment. Justices Douglas, Blackmun, and White found the process by means of which the death penalty was implemented constitutionally unacceptable, making clear that procedures guaranteeing due process of law would be necessary to bring the punishment in line with constitutional requirements. The remaining Justices found the death penalty constitutional in itself and, at least in *Fur-*

man, they do not have a problem with the due process issues previously raised.

Chief Justice Burger begins his opinion by stating that, were he a legislator, he would vote consistent with Brennan's and Marshall's position.[93] Judges, however, Burger argues, must interpret the Constitution independent from their ideological or philosophical positions. He offers seven considerations in support of the death penalty.

First, the Fifth Amendment, adopted on the same day as the Eighth Amendment, states that a person cannot be sentenced to death "unless on a presentment or indictment of a grand jury."[94] Furthermore, a person cannot be "twice put in jeopardy of life" for the same offense.[95] And no person can be "deprived of life, liberty, or property" without "due process of law."[96] For Chief Justice Burger, these elements of the Fifth Amendment to the Constitution offer clear and unmistakable evidence for the constitutionality of the death penalty. Why, for example, would the authors of the Bill of Rights deny in the Eighth Amendment what they had just affirmed in the Fifth Amendment? There simply is no evidence that the death penalty was to be included within the scope of the Eighth Amendment prohibition against cruel and unusual punishments.[97]

Second, until *Furman,* the Court has never questioned the constitutionality of the death penalty. "In the 181 years since the enactment of the Eighth Amendment, not a single decision of this Court has cast the slightest shadow of a doubt on the constitutionality of capital punishment. In rejecting Eighth Amendment attacks on particular modes of execution, the Court has more than once implicitly denied that capital punishment is impermissibly "cruel" in the constitutional sense."[98]

Third, Chief Justice Burger wants to know what, if anything, has happened since *McGautha* to raise new concerns relevant to the administration of the death penalty. Specifically, Burger notes that neither the physical nor the emotional (e.g., stress or "mental anguish") conditions have changed since 1791. Burger does recognize that the Court's application of the standard of cruelty can change as it did in *Weems* and *Trop.* There is nothing to suggest, however, that relevant changes have occurred in the administration of the death penalty that would suggest that the death penalty constitutes a cruel and unusual punishment. Burger writes, "To be sure, the ordeal of the condemned man may be thought cruel in the sense that all suffering is thought cruel. But if the Constitution proscribed every punishment producing severe emotional stress, then capital punishment would clearly have been impermissible in 1791."[99]

Fourth, Chief Justice Burger argues that changes in social mores are relevant in discussions on the just punishment, but the Court, he argues, is not the arena in which these mores are to be addressed. In a democracy, Burger argues, these changes are to be handled legislatively unless there is a clear and compelling reason for judicial override of a legislative judgment. Given that some thirty-eight states and the federal government have capital punishment statutes, there does not seem to be any change that would render death sentences cruel and unusual punishments. For Burger, the basic standards of decency in a democratic society are reflected in the election of those the majority of voters feel best represent their views.[100]

Fifth, Chief Justice Burger challenges Justices Brennan's and Marshall's claim that people find the death penalty morally repugnant. "There are no obvious indications that capital punishment offends the conscience of society to such a degree that our traditional deference to the legislative judgment must be abandoned."[101] The fact that capital punishment, at the time of *Furman*, was "authorized by statute in 40 States, the District of Columbia, and in the federal courts for the commission of certain crimes,"[102] indicates general social acceptance of the penalty, a support, for example, that burning at the stake would not have.[103] In general, there are no clear social indicators that support the Brennan and Marshall philosophy.[104]

Sixth, the few cases in which juries bring in a death penalty do not undermine support for the death penalty or indicate that the death penalty "is now regarded as intolerably cruel or uncivilized."[105] Indeed, the discretionary application of the death penalty indicates the seriousness with which juries take their responsibility. Chief Justice Burger cites both *Witherspoon* and *McGautha* to support the discretionary nature of the judgments on the death penalty that juries must inevitably exercise. That juries do not behave uniformly or predictably indicates not that jury judgments are arbitrary but that they take their responsibility seriously.[106] Burger finds that juries are moved by many decisional factors, including "[t]he motive or lack of motive of the perpetrator, the degree of injury or suffering of the victim or victims, and the degree of brutality in the commission of the crime."[107] Thus, the infrequent use of the death penalty is laudable. Certainly there are cases in which different juries would have brought in a different punishment than death in the same case. "However, this element of fortuity does not stand as an indictment either of the general functioning of juries in capital cases or of the integrity of jury decisions in individual cases."[108]

Seventh, Chief Justice Burger challenges Justice Marshall's claim that retribution is not a legitimate social goal of a criminal justice system. A case such as *Weems*, Burger argues, does not establish the principle that punishments must reflect some social utility, for example, deterrence. Rather, *Weems* holds sacred the principle that a punishment must not be disproportionate to the crime.[109] From Burger's perspective, the Court, in *Weems* "was making an essentially moral judgment, not a dispassionate assessment of the need for the penalty."[110] There is no evidence to indicate the illegitimacy, moral or legal, of retribution. "There is no authority suggesting that the Eighth Amendment was intended to purge the law of its retributive elements, and the Court has consistently assumed that retribution is a legitimate dimension of the punishment of crimes."[111] Burger continues, "It would be reading a great deal into the Eighth Amendment to hold that the punishments authorized by legislatures cannot constitutionally reflect a retributive purpose."[112] As far as deterrence is concerned, Burger claims that legislative decision making must evaluate the efficacy of punishments, not the courts. Furthermore, if states must prove the deterrent capability of the death penalty, why are they then not required to determine the deterrent effects of any punishment? What punishments produce desirable results, for Burger, "are beyond the pale of judicial inquiry under the Eighth Amendment."[113]

To conclude, Chief Justice Burger makes clear that the full impact of the Court's decision does not undermine the constitutionality of the death penalty since only Justices Brennan and Marshall have so argued. By the same token, the meaning of *Furman* in terms of state legislative decision making is less than clear. Burger notes that judges and juries will not be permitted to exercise the kind of discretion in capital cases they once exercised, but exactly how the system is to avoid the charge of "arbitrariness" and "capriciousness" remains ambiguous. There is no question but that legislatures, both state and federal, must design new statutes to meet the *Furman* challenge. And he does not object to Congress and state legislatures reconsidering the meaning of and justifications for the death penalty. He knows that there can be some important social benefits that result from people rethinking the nature and purpose of any governmental action. For example, people will need to reconsider the deterrent effects, if any, of the death penalty. States have an opportunity to consider alternatives to the death penalty that might serve equally as well the purpose(s) for which the death penalty was designed. Some states may reject the penalty, only to find in a few years that they must reintroduce it. Thus, the opportunity to revisit legislatively the death penalty issue is not undesirable. What is undesirable, for Burger, is for courts to be in the business of telling states what to do in this particularly vexatious area. The Court must defer, to some extent, to state and federal legislative decision making and the democratic processes they represent, unless, of course, some fairly substantial constitutional rights are jeopardized. Burger writes, "The complete and unconditional abolition of capital punishment in this country by judicial fiat would have undermined the careful progress of the legislative trend and foreclosed further inquiry on many as yet unanswered questions in this area. . . . The highest judicial duty is to recognize the limits on judicial power and to permit the democratic processes to deal with matters falling outside of those limits."[114] Burger's position, in essence, is that the Court has usurped state powers and undermined the democratic process in its evolutionary development.

Justice Blackmun writes eloquently in opposition to the death penalty, but from a legislative, not a judicial, perspective.

I yield to no one in the depth of my distaste, antipathy, and, indeed, abhorrence, for the death penalty, with all its aspects of physical distress and fear and of moral judgment exercised by finite minds. That distaste is buttressed by a belief that capital punishment serves no useful purpose that can be demonstrated. For me, it violates childhood's training and life's experiences, and is not compatible with the philosophical convictions I have been able to develop. It is antagonistic to any sense of "reverence for life." Were I a legislator, I would vote against the death penalty for the policy reasons argued by counsel for the respective petitioners and expressed and adopted in the several opinions filed by the Justices who vote to reverse these judgments.[115]

Despite his abolitionist philosophy, Blackmun has several problems with the majority opinion.

First, why the Court chose these particular cases to use to hold the death penalty unconstitutional is less than clear, since it had been just "one year since *McGautha* . . . 14 years since *Trop,* and 25 years since *Francis,*"[116] during which time no new and startling information has come available that would move the Court to strike down the death penalty as cruel and unusual punishment. Agreeing with *Weems* and *Trop* that constitutions are open for developmental changes, there still must be substantive evidence for the Court to move in such a dramatic manner. And there is no support to justify such a bold move. Essentially, "[t]he Court has just decided that it is time to strike down the death penalty."[117] There can be progress in society, but that progress must develop incrementally, not dramatically. It is that dramatic, sudden change that concerns Justice Blackmun. "My problem, however, as I have indicated, is the suddenness of the Court's perception of progress in the human attitude since decisions of only a short while ago."[118]

Second, and related to the first problem, although society is not confined to a rigid, narrow, and literal interpretation of a 200-year-old document, interpretational changes generally occur in a more coherent and orderly manner. Justice Blackmun would agree with the following point Justice Powell makes, "Nor are 'cruel and unusual punishments' and 'due process of law' static concepts whose meaning and scope were sealed at the time of their writing. They were designed to be dynamic and to gain meaning through application to specific circumstances, many of which were not contemplated by their authors."[119] But changes in interpretation and understanding remain connected to the past. The history of support for the death penalty in the United States precludes the possibility that people are ready to abolish it. Blackmun wants to think that society is moving in a more humanitarian direction in which it places greater emphasis on life than on death. Unfortunately, society does not seem to be headed in that direction. And even if it were, that change should come legislatively, not judicially.[120]

Third, the majority opinion ignores the degree to which Congress had most recently approved the death penalty. "It is impossible for me to believe that the many lawyer-members of the House and Senate—including, I might add, outstanding leaders and prominent candidates for higher office—were callously unaware and insensitive of constitutional overtones in legislation of this type."[121] Again, judges must be wary of substituting their wisdom for that of the general public. The Supreme Court, for example, must determine if a particular piece of legislation is or is not constitutional, but that does not permit those justices to substitute their legislative judgments for those who have been elected to exercise legitimate legislative judgment.[122]

Fourth, the majority opinion forgets that the crimes committed by these defendants were against innocent people. Justice Blackmun recognizes the reaction such a comment might generate, and he hopes that people will recognize what is being said here.

It is not without interest, also, to note that, although the several concurring opinions acknowledge the heinous and atrocious character of the offenses committed by the petitioners, none of those opinions makes reference to the misery the petitioners' crimes occasioned to the victims, to the families of the victims, and to the communities where the offenses took place. The arguments for the respective petitioners, particularly the oral arguments, were similarly and curiously devoid of reference to the victims. There is risk, of course, in a comment such as this, for it opens one to the charge of emphasizing the retributive. Nevertheless, these cases are here because offenses to innocent victims were perpetrated. This fact, and the terror that occasioned it, and the fear that stalks the streets of many of our cities today perhaps deserve not to be entirely overlooked. Let us hope that, with the Court's decision, the terror imposed will be forgotten by those upon whom it was visited, and that our society will reap the hoped-for benefits of magnanimity.[123]

In conclusion, Justice Blackmun writes with the following concern: "Although personally I may rejoice at the Court's result, I find it difficult to accept or to justify as a matter of history, of law, or of constitutional pronouncement. I fear the Court has overstepped. It has sought and has achieved an end."[124]

That same concern regarding the Court overstepping its legitimate limits is one Justice Powell spends fifty-two pages detailing. It is the longest dissenting opinion in this case, and his goal is to demonstrate that the majority opinion bears little resemblance to sound constitutional judgment. Noting that five members of the Court have held that the death penalty is unconstitutional as it was then administered, Powell writes that "none of these opinions provides a constitutionally adequate foundation for the Court's decision."[125] In language similar to Justice Blackmun's, Powell writes disapprovingly about the Court's decision:

In terms of the constitutional role of this Court, the impact of the majority's ruling is all the greater because the decision encroaches upon an area squarely within the historic prerogative of the legislative branch—both state and federal—to protect the citizenry through the designation of penalties for prohibitable conduct. It is the very sort of judgment that the legislative branch is competent to make, and for which the judiciary is ill equipped. Throughout our history, Justices of this Court have emphasized the gravity of decisions invalidating legislative judgments, admonishing the nine men who sit on this bench of the duty of self-restraint, especially when called upon to apply the expansive due process and cruel and unusual punishment rubrics. I can recall no case in which, in the name of deciding constitutional questions, this Court has subordinated national and local democratic processes to such an extent.[126]

Justice Powell's opinion begins by repeating what has been heard already from others, namely, the Constitution itself permits, but does not mandate, the death penalty. Specifically, the Fifth, Eighth, and Fourteenth Amendments authorize the death penalty as a legitimate legislative option in deciding on appropriate punishments: "[t]here cannot be the slightest doubt that they [the framers of the Bill of Rights] intended no absolute bar on the Government's authority to impose the death penalty."[127] This does not mean that the states or the federal government must have the death penalty, or, if they have it, that they must use it. Nor does it mean that the Court is powerless in this area to hold some punishments, including the death penalty, unconstitutional in violation of the Eighth Amendment prohibition against cruel and unusual punishments. For example, it is inconceivable that the Supreme Court would permit beheading or drawing and quartering.[128] Still, for Powell, no one can argue seriously that the death penalty constitutes, in the abstract, a cruel and unusual punishment.

Justice Powell next challenges petitioners' claim that the evolution of society has reached its logical end, namely, the death penalty is no longer socially necessary or wanted. At this point, Powell asserts the relevance of the doctrine of judicial restraint, claiming essentially that judges should hesitate to overrule legislative decision making without substantive cause. There are two clear reasons to move slowly in evaluating the constitutionality of legislative statutes. First, the terminology of the Amendments in question (Fifth, Eighth, Fourteenth) do or can admit of diverse interpretation, which enables judges to insert too easily subjective judgments for reasoned decision making. Second, the respective roles of legislative and judicial bodies are different. Legislative bodies designate punishments for crimes, not judicial bodies. When asked to overturn a legislatively prescribed punishment, courts must move with caution.

Powell writes, "When asked to encroach on the legislative prerogative we are well counseled to proceed with the utmost reticence. The review of legislative choices, in the performance of our duty to enforce the Constitution, has been characterized most appropriately by Justice Holmes as 'the gravest and most delicate duty that this Court is called on to perform.'"[129] Furthermore, the Court here is not ruling against one punishment option of one state. Rather, the Court is being asked to overturn one punishment option for thirty-nine states, the District of Columbia, and Congress. To overturn such legislatively and democratically established policies requires far greater judicial support than that on which the majority opinion rests its case.

For Justice Powell, there must exist virtually insurmountable evidence against the constitutionality of the death penalty before the Court can overturn state and federal law, court precedents, and the affirmative references to the death penalty in the Constitution. What evidence is there for the Court to overturn such a history? Petitioners, for example, contend that society has evolved (*Trop*) to the point where, for all practical purposes, the death penalty now constitutes a cruel and unusual punishment. On what basis is that claim made? There are, according to Powell, five objective criteria and two less substantive but nonetheless relevant considerations offered in support of petitioners' claims. The five objective criteria are stated as follows:

(i) a worldwide trend toward the disuse of the death penalty; (ii) the reflection in the scholarly literature of a progressive rejection of capital punishment founded essentially on moral opposition to such treatment; (iii) the decreasing numbers of executions over the last 40 years, and especially over the last decade; (iv) the small number of death sentences rendered in relation to the number of cases in which they might have been imposed; and (v) the indication of public abhorrence of the penalty reflected in the circumstance that executions are no longer public affairs.[130]

The two additional considerations are "first, that the penalty survives public condemnation only through the infrequency, arbitrariness, and discriminatory nature of its application, and, second, that there no longer exists any legitimate justification for the utilization of the ultimate penalty."[131]

Rather than challenge seriatim these five "objective" criteria, Justice Powell wants to note "several overriding considerations which petitioners choose to discount or ignore."[132] Powell claims that "the first indicator of the public's attitude must always be found in the legislative judgments of the people's chosen representatives."[133] And what does Powell find? He finds precisely what no one can deny, namely, some thirty-nine states, the District of Columbia, and the federal government have capital punishment statutes. In addition, throughout the 1960s different capital crimes were added to state and federal laws. Some states rewrote their capital punishment statutes narrowing the crimes for which death was seen as the appropriate punishment. Voters in several states approved in statewide referenda the death penalty. Some states recommended abolition of the penalty, whereas others recommended retention. Overall, the available evidence suggests that support for the death penalty seems substantive and widespread.[134]

Justice Powell then moves to consider what he feels the majority opinion illegitimately neglected. "The second and even more direct source of information reflecting the public's attitude toward capital punishment is the jury."[135] Powell argues that there is jury support for the death penalty while at the same time recognizing on the part of juries the need to make recommendations for death more carefully, selectively, and discriminatorily. Powell writes, "During the 1960's, juries returned in excess of a thousand death sentences, a rate of approximately two per week. Whether it is true that death sentences were returned in less than 10% of the cases, as petitioners estimate, or whether some higher percentage is more accurate, these totals simply do not support petitioners' assertion at oral argument that 'the death penalty is virtually unanimously repudiated and condemned by the conscience of contemporary society.'"[136] Powell then concludes that "contrary to petitioners' submission . . . the indicators most likely to reflect the public's view—legislative bodies, state referenda and the juries which have the actual responsibility—do not support the contention that evolving standards of decency require total abolition of capital punishment."[137]

There are two additional concerns Justice Powell raises. First, the death penalty, as do all punishments, "falls more heavily on the relatively impoverished and underprivileged elements of society."[138] If poverty and lack of social standing are relevant to abolishing the death penalty, are they not equally relevant with respect to any proscribed penalty or punishment?[139] Powell describes the overall problem of crime and punishment as follows:

The "have-nots" in every society always have been subject to greater pressure to commit crimes and to fewer constraints than their more affluent fellow citizens. This is, indeed, a tragic byproduct of social and economic deprivation, but it is not an argument of constitutional proportions under the Eighth or Fourteenth Amendment. The same discriminatory impact argument could be made with equal force and logic with respect to those sentenced to prison terms. The Due Process Clause admits of no distinction between the deprivation of "life" and the deprivation of "liberty." If discriminatory impact renders capital punishment cruel and unusual, it likewise renders invalid most of the prescribed penalties for crimes of violence. The root causes of the higher incidence of criminal penalties on "minorities and the poor" will not be cured by abolishing the system of penalties. Nor, indeed, could any society have a viable system of criminal justice if sanctions were abolished or ameliorated because most of those who commit crimes happen to be underprivileged. The basic problem results not from the penalties imposed for criminal conduct, but from social and economic factors that have plagued humanity since the beginning of recorded history, frustrating all efforts to create in any country at any time the perfect society in which there are no "poor," no "minorities" and no "underprivileged." The causes underlying this problem are unrelated to the constitutional issue before the Court.[140]

Second, Justice Powell finds the charge of discrimination unfounded. That juries make distinctions, thus sending some to death and others to life imprisonment, is no indication that the system can be characterized as somehow "discriminatory" in nature.[141] Nonetheless, the issue of discrimination based on race is a relevant and justifiable concern. If defendants can show that race is a factor, that more blacks, for example, than whites receive the death penalty for essentially the same types of crime, then there is a constitutional problem, namely, there would be a violation of the equal protection of the laws clause of the Fourteenth Amendment. But there is no reason to believe, at that time, according to Powell, that race played a factor in the cases presently before the Court. Powell concludes this point as follows:

A final comment on the racial discrimination problem seems appropriate. The possibility of racial bias in the trial and sentencing process has diminished in recent years. The segregation of our society in decades past, which contributed substantially to the severity of punishment for interracial crimes, is now no longer prevalent in this country. Likewise, the day is past when juries do not represent the minority group elements of the community. The assurance of fair trials for all citizens is greater today than at any previous time in our history. Because standards of criminal justice have "evolved" in a manner favorable to the accused, discriminatory imposition of capital punishment is far less likely today than in the past.[142]

Justice Powell next examines the claim that the death penalty constitutes "cruel and unusual punishment because it no longer serves any rational legislative interests."[143] Before he challenges this assertion, however, he makes two claims. "First, I find no support—in the language of the Constitution, in its history, or in the cases arising under it—for the view that this Court may invalidate a category of penalties because we deem less severe penalties adequate to serve the ends of penology."[144] Thus, as long as the punishment is not cruelly inhumane or cruelly excessive, there is neither history nor logic to the claim that the Court can overturn a proscribed legislative punishment because a lesser punishment serves the same purpose.[145] Second, it is not the states that need to justify their prescribed punishments. Rather, it is the Court's burden to demonstrate clearly and unmistakably the constitutional violations of those legislatively prescribed punishments. In other words, state legislative decisions "are entitled to a presumption of validity."[146]

Having made these points Justice Powell then returns to consider the challenges to retribution and deterrence made by Justices Brennan and Marshall. Powell finds no credible evidence that would indicate that retribution "is unworthy of a civilized people."[147] He notes further that even if reform and rehabilitation have been incorporated into our criminal justice goals, there is no reason to believe that they either replace or override retribution. Powell acknowledges that retribution alone might not offer a sufficient justification for particular punishments. Nonetheless, there is no reason that retribution cannot serve a useful social function. Here Powell quotes Justice Stewart's comment that retribution "'serves an important purpose in promoting the stability of a society governed by law.'"[148]

As for deterrence, Justice Powell acknowledges the indeterminate studies regarding the deterrent effect, if any, of the death penalty.[149] Essentially, neither side can make a case for or against deterrence regarding the death penalty. Thus, there is no evidence to indicate that legislatures that adopt the death penalty are without justification for so doing. At the very minimum, there is certainly no substantive challenge to deterrent claims by states that would serve as a rational basis on which to overturn that presumption of validity to which Powell earlier eluded.[150] Powell recognizes that there is certainly no means of guaranteeing a perfect match between crime and punishment. However, unless there is an overwhelming injustice relevant to Court review, then the Court should be silent and defer to the presumption of legislative legitimacy. Powell concludes his opinion by noting the inappropriate role the majority has assumed. He makes his frustrations clear as follows:

I now return to the overriding question in these cases: whether this Court, acting in conformity with the Constitution, can justify its judgment to abolish capital punishment as heretofore known in this country. It is important to keep in focus the enormity of the step undertaken by the Court today. Not only does it invalidate hundreds of state and federal laws, it deprives those jurisdictions of the power to legislate with respect to capital punishment in the future except in a manner consistent with the cloudily outlined views of those Justices who do not purport to undertake total abolition. Nothing short of an amendment to the United States Constitution can reverse the Court's judgments. Meanwhile, all flexibility is foreclosed. The normal democratic process, as well as the opportunities for the several States to respond to the will of their people expressed through ballot referenda (as in Massachusetts, Illinois, and Colorado), is now shut off.[151]

Powell certainly overstated the impact of the effect the majority opinion had, that it would take a constitutional amendment to reverse the Court's judgment. Still, his concern that an important part of the democratic process had been jeopardized is not without merit. It is doubtful that citizens will ever reach agreement on the appropriate role or roles the Supreme Court should serve as it functions in this tripartite separation of powers.

He does, however, offer a final quote for reflection a remark by Justice Frankfurter in *Trop:* "'[T]he whole of [Justice Holmes's] work during his thirty years of service on this Court should be a constant reminder that the power to invalidate legislation must not be exercised as if, either in constitutional theory or in the art of government, it stood as the sole bulwark against unwisdom or excesses of the moment.'"[152] Powell, then, clearly concurs with Chief Justice Burger's opinion that the Court has overreached its legitimate authority.

Justice Rehnquist focuses on the theme with which Justice Powell concluded, namely, the role of the judiciary in a constitutional democracy. For Rehnquist, the actions of the Court in this case are diametrically opposed to sound Court review of state and federal legislation. The Court, in declaring the death penalty unconstitutional, has undermined the legitimate exercise of judicial review, which, in turn, raises serious questions about the Court from the perspective of constitutional democracy. Rehnquist writes, "Whatever its precise rationale, today's holding necessarily brings into sharp relief the fundamental question of the role of judicial review in a democratic society. How can government by the elected representatives of the people coexist with the power of the federal judiciary, whose members are constitutionally insulated from responsiveness to the popular will, to declare invalid laws duly enacted by the popular branches of government?"[153]

Justice Rehnquist's concern is twofold, namely, that judicial activism will undermine the constitutionally established democratic processes and that Supreme Court Justices will be able to impose their versions of right and wrong without any accountability to the people or any input from the people. Sovereignty, for Rehnquist, resides in the hands of the people. Ultimate power, as the great seventeenth-century English philosopher John Locke would say, rests in the hands of the people.[154] In a constitutional democracy, a constitution reflects the will of the people as a general guide to limits of legislative judgments. It is indeed the role of the judiciary to ensure that state and federal legislatures do not override the will of the people and impose their own version of what is socially necessary. A constitution by definition is superior to individual legislating bodies, and courts can ensure that legislative acts do not infringe the rights granted in a constitution. Applied to the United States, the Constitution limits the power of legislative bodies to enact legislation that involves cruel and unusual punishment. Thus, the Court has every right to guarantee that states do not sustain draconian punishments. What passes for cruel and unusual punishment, however, is less than clear. Certainly medieval punishments such as the rack and the iron maiden would be rejected, along with drawing and quartering, and the use of the hot lead enema to extract confessions. But there is nothing in the Constitution that prohibits the death penalty on the basis that it is immoral or that it violates specific constitutional limitations placed on legislative bodies. Indeed, as previously and frequently noted, the Fifth Amendment states unequivocally that our society can take a life as long as due process of law is followed. By the same token, the Constitution does not require that states use a death penalty. States are free to pass legislation and impose punishments consistent with the Constitution, but they do not need to go as far as the Constitution allows. Thus, the Court can overturn a death penalty that requires burning at the stake, but the Court cannot overturn the death penalty simply because a majority of Justices find the penalty morally odious. ["The most expansive reading of the leading constitutional cases does not remotely suggest that this Court has been granted a roving commission, either by the Founding Fathers or by the framers of the Fourteenth Amendment, to strike down laws that are based upon notions of policy or morality suddenly found unacceptable by a majority of this Court."155 That move invalidates the will of the people in a democracy and leaves the Constitution powerless. The Constitution acts as a limit on authority. "The Founding Fathers thus wisely sought to have the best of both worlds, the undeniable benefits of both democratic self-government and individual rights protected against possible excesses of that form of government."156 For Rehnquist, it is essential for the Court's integrity to defer to the judgments of state and federal legislatures unless there is a clear and compelling reason to overturn their democratically established statutes. Although the Court has a legitimate power to exercise over legislative enactments, the Court cannot simply substitute its will for the will of the people. And the only restraint on the Court is self-restraint. Rehnquist quotes Justice Stone in this context: "'[W]hile unconstitutional exercise of power by the executive and legislative branches of the government is subject to judicial restraint, the only check upon our own exercise of power is our own sense of self-restraint.'"157

It must be recognized as well that judges are as prone to errors as are citizens. As courts consider the possibility for human error, they must decide from which side they are going to accept some human error. That is, should the Court err on the side of legislative enactments or on the side of individual claims of legislative injustices? Invariably, courts should err, for Justice Rehnquist, on the side that preserves the integrity of constitutional democracy. In the long run, that will be the least harmful judicial action.158 Rehnquist recognizes that the Court must review constitutional challenges to state and federal legislation. That responsibility cannot be eschewed. Still, Court review should "be approached with the deepest humility and genuine deference to legislative judgment."159 That deference, for Rehnquist, is not present in the Court's majority opinion in *Furman*. He claims, therefore, "that this decision holding unconstitutional capital punishment is not an act of judgment, but rather an act of will."160

Justice Rehnquist's disgust with the Court's action here is made unambiguously in his final paragraph:

The very nature of judicial review . . . makes the courts the least subject to Madisonian check in the event that they shall, for the best of motives, expand judicial authority beyond the limits contemplated by the Framers. It is for this reason that judicial self-restraint is surely an implied, if not an expressed, condition of the grant of authority of judicial review. The Court's holding in these cases has been reached, I believe, in complete disregard of that implied condition.[161]

Furman, while it has been overturned, remains a formidable challenge to anyone interested in the constitutionality of the death penalty. However, the predictions by Chief Justice Burger and Justices Blackmun, Powell, and Rehnquist to the effect that the states and the federal government would be unable to meet the minimum constitutional requirements necessary to sustain death penalty legislation proved to be in error. In addition, those who thought the death penalty had been eliminated as a punishment alternative had made a rash and erroneous judgment.[162] It would take just four years to overturn *Furman.*

CHAPTER 4

The Supreme Court since *Furman*

We are concerned here only with the imposition of capital punishment for the crime of murder, and when a life has been taken deliberately by the offender, we cannot say that the punishment is invariably disproportionate to the crime. It is an extreme sanction, suitable to the most extreme of crimes.

Justice Potter Stewart, *Gregg v. Georgia*

In sum, we cannot say that the judgment of the Georgia Legislature that capital punishment may be necessary in some cases is clearly wrong. Considerations of federalism, as well as respect for the ability of a legislature to evaluate, in terms of its particular State, the moral consensus concerning the death penalty and its social utility as a sanction, require us to conclude, in the absence of more convincing evidence, that the infliction of death as a punishment for murder is not without justification, and thus is not unconstitutionally severe.

Justice Potter Stewart, *Gregg v. Georgia*

It took just four years for the Supreme Court to return to its history of support for the constitutional legitimacy of the death penalty. As noted in *Furman*, the Supreme Court did not declare the death penalty constitutionally invalid or infirm per se. Three of the five Justices in the majority ruled that the procedures used to distinguish between those individuals who deserve and those who do not deserve the death penalty result in the haphazard, arbitrary, and capricious infliction of a punishment inconsistent with general constitutional protections that guarantee people the ideal of equal dignity under the law. Stated alternatively, as well as retributively, people who commit similar crimes deserve similar punishments. No social or political system ever achieves the ideals these principles embody. All social systems are vulnerable to charges of arbitrary, capricious, and haphazard implementation and enforcement of its rules. When those charges can be substantiated, however, change should occur. When the implementation and enforcement involve ending a human life, however, slow change can mean, and has meant, that people die. *Furman* made clear that any new death penalty legislation must contain sentencing procedures that would avoid, as much as humanly possible, the arbitrary infliction of a life-ending verdict. That opportunity presented itself in 1976 in another Georgia case. Since then, no Supreme Court majority has ever held that the death penalty constitutes cruel and unusual punishment in violation of the Eighth and Fourteenth Amendments.

GREGG V. GEORGIA

In *Gregg v. Georgia,* 482 U.S. 153 (1976) (argued 3/31/76; decided 6/2/76), Gregg had been sentenced to death following a conviction for armed robbery and murder under Georgia's new capital punishment statute that was designed to overcome the constitutional objections to the death penalty raised in *Furman*. In essence, the Court, by a 7–2 vote (as opposed to a 5–4 vote in *Furman*), held that the death penalty is not unconstitutional per se and that the new Georgia death penalty statute overcomes the arbitrary and capricious use of the death penalty that was of such concern in *Furman*. Justices Stewart, Powell, and Stevens wrote the lead opinion.[1] They begin their opinion with a description of the legal process that the new Georgia statute requires in capital cases. That process, designed specifically to overcome *Furman*-type objections, has four steps.

First, capital trials in Georgia are bifurcated, that is, they involve two separate and distinct trial stages, namely, a guilt stage and a sentencing stage.[2] Second, upon a finding of guilt, the sentence must be determined by a consideration of aggravating and mitigating circumstances. The sentence can be determined either by a judge (in a bench trial) or a jury (in a jury trial).[3] Third, a sentence of death can be imposed only if the jury (or the judge in a bench trial) finds, beyond a reasonable doubt, at least one aggravating circumstance.[4] Fourth, a sentence of death must be reviewed by Georgia's Supreme Court to determine if the sentence in this particular case is appropriate. At this stage Georgia's Supreme Court must "consider 'the punishment as well as any errors enumerated by way of appeal.'"[5] In addition, the following conditions must be determined: "'(1) Whether the sentence of death was imposed under the influence of passion, prejudice, or any other arbitrary factor, and (2) Whether, in cases other than treason or aircraft hijacking, the evidence supports the jury's or judge's finding of a statutory aggravating circumstance, and (3) Whether the sentence of death is excessive or disproportionate to the penalty imposed in similar cases, considering both the crime and the defendant.'"[6] The Georgia statute also requires its Supreme Court, in cases where the death penalty is affirmed, to compare that decision with decisions reached in similar types of cases. Comparative review reflects one additional means Georgia has taken to avoid the arbitrary and capricious application of the death penalty.[7] Comparative review can be considered retributive in nature and consistent with equal justice under law. In essence, people who commit similar crimes should receive similar punishments, especially when life is at stake. The *Furman* decision made that concern—that similar cases be decided similarly—a high priority. Georgia uses comparative review to make death sentences consistent, predictable, and fair.

Given this background on Georgia's new capital punishment statute, the Court proceeds to respond to Gregg's appeal in two parts. First, is the death penalty itself an inherently cruel and unusual punishment and therefore in violation of the Eighth and Fourteenth Amendments? Second, if the death penalty is not an inherently cruel and unusual punishment, has Georgia correctly applied its statute in *Gregg*?

Consistent with the death penalty history as reviewed in *Furman*, the Court holds here "that the punishment of death does not invariably violate the Constitution."[8] That conclusion, according to Justice Stewart, follows from four Eighth Amendment considerations.

First, the Eighth Amendment prohibiting cruel and unusual punishments was designed to prevent government from inflicting "'tortures' and other 'barbarous' methods of punishment."[9] Second, from 1878–1971 most Eighth Amendment cases raised questions about the constitutionality of the methods (for example, firing squad and electrocution) of execution, not the execution itself. Third, the "cruel and unusual punishment" clause, the majority acknowledges, does not remain static, buried in eighteenth-century conceptions of punishment. For example, as previously noted, the Court has applied the cruel and unusual punishment clause as follows: the Eighth Amendment prohibits government from punishing people for a condition, such as a drug addiction (*Robinson*), prohibits punishments disproportionate to the crimes committed (*Weems*), and prohibits punishments inconsistent with "the dignity of man" (*Trop*). Fourth, while not dispositive, public opinion, in a constitutional democracy, is relevant in determining the constitutionality of legislative enactments. This point requires clarification.

Although public opinion cannot be allowed to override the Constitution, that opinion, the Court holds here, must be considered a relevant factor in constitutional adjudication. Barring a clear constitutional violation, the Court must defer to legislative judgment as representative of the people legislators were elected to serve. "Therefore, in assessing a punishment selected by a democratically elected legislature against the constitutional measure, we presume its validity. We may not require the legislature to select the least severe penalty possible so long as the penalty selected is not cruelly inhumane or disproportionate to the crime involved. And a heavy burden rests on those who would attack the judgment of the representatives of the people."[10] In addition, public opinion appears to support overwhelmingly the death penalty. That claim can be defended on two grounds. First, between *Furman* in 1972 and *Gregg* in 1976, the legislatures of thirty-five states and the United States Congress enacted legislation authorizing the use of the death penalty for certain crimes. The new legislation adopts specific procedures to meet the concerns raised in *Furman*. That legislation supports the view that the people continue to support the death penalty.[11] Second, juries, "a significant and reliable objective index of contemporary values, because it is so directly involved,"[12] continue to bring in death sentences. The Court quotes approvingly the following statement in *Witherspoon*: "'one of the most important functions any jury can perform in making . . . a selection [between life imprisonment and death for a defendant convicted in a capital case] is to maintain a link between contemporary community values and the penal system.'"[13]

Still, Justice Stewart recognizes that the public cannot serve as the final arbiter of what constitutes cruel and unusual punishment. "[T]he Eighth Amendment demands more than that a challenged punishment be acceptable to contemporary society."[14] The punishment itself, to repeat *Trop*, must comport "with the basic concept of human dignity." In addition, "the sanction imposed cannot be so totally without penal justification that it results in the gratuitous infliction of suffering."[15] What, then, constitutes "penal justification" as far as the death penalty is concerned?

According to Justice Stewart, the death penalty serves two purposes, "*retribution* and *deterrence* of capital crimes by prospective offenders."[16] Capital punishment can be understood as "an expression of society's moral outrage at particularly offensive conduct."[17] Stewart clarifies this idea more fully. "This [retributive] function may be unappealing to many, but it is essential in an ordered society that asks its citizens to rely on legal processes, rather than self-help, to vindicate their wrongs."[18] This idea is expressed as well in the following words: "Indeed, the decision that capital punishment may be the appropriate sanction in extreme cases is an expression of the community's belief that certain crimes are themselves so grievous an affront to humanity that the only adequate response may be the penalty of death."[19] There is, then, a clear sense that the death penalty serves a retributive function, a function that, for many on the Court, remains a legitimate justification for the death penalty. But does the death penalty serve a deterrent function as well?

For Justice Stewart, the deterrent function of the death penalty is less than clear. Some people are deterred by threats of punishment from a life of crime, but whether deterrence could be achieved by a less formidable means can never be known conclusively. For Stewart, absent evidence that the death penalty does not deter, deterrence remains a constitutionally sound punishment principle. Accordingly, given the legitimate penal justifications of retribution and deterrence, "the infliction of death as a punishment for murder is not without justification, and thus is not unconstitutionally severe."[20]

Finally, Justice Stewart considers whether the death penalty is disproportionate to the crime, in this case, murder. For such a crime, the death penalty cannot be considered disproportionate. "But we are concerned here only with the imposition of capital punishment for the crime of murder, and, when a life has been taken deliberately by the offender, we cannot say that the punishment is invariably disproportionate to the crime. It is an extreme sanction, suitable to the most extreme of crimes."[21]

The death penalty itself, then, from Justice Stewart's perspective, cannot be considered a cruel and unusual punishment in violation of the Eighth and Fourteenth Amendments. The first question answered, Stewart moves to determine if the death penalty has been applied correctly in *Gregg*.

The decision in *Furman* rested fundamentally on the capricious and arbitrary infliction of one of the most severe punishments a society could impose on one of its members. For the death penalty to be constitutional, death penalty legislation must minimize the possibility of capricious and arbitrary action.[22] The Court identifies two specific means by which arbitrary and capricious action can be acceptably minimized, if not eliminated.

First, capital trials should be bifurcated, that is, there should be two stages. "When a human life is at stake, and when the jury must have information prejudicial to the question of guilt but relevant to the question of penalty in order to impose a rational sentence, a bifurcated system is more likely to ensure elimination of the constitutional deficiencies identified in Furman."[23]

Second, because juries are not experienced in making sentencing decisions, they must be "given guidance regarding the factors about the crime and the defendant that the State, representing organized society, deems particularly relevant to the sentencing decision."[24] That guidance could come from a list of aggravating and mitigating circumstances that focus the jury's attention in a particular case.[25] Thus, a jury would not be left to its own devices and imagination to judge between the death penalty and life imprisonment. A jury would have a set of guidelines to direct its deliberations so as to overcome the constitutional concerns of *Furman*. As Justice Stewart notes, "[T]hese concerns are best met by a system that provides for a bifurcated proceeding at which the sentencing authority is apprised of the information relevant to the imposition of sentence and provided with standards to guide its use of the information."[26] Does

Georgia's statute satisfy these conditions?[27] Given the previously delineated components of Georgia's death penalty statute, Georgia has established, to the Court's satisfaction, a means to guard against capricious and arbitrary decisions on the death penalty.

Justices Brennan and Marshall filed separate dissenting opinions. Brennan's brief dissent reaffirms his position in *Furman*. In short, he argues "that the State, even as it punishes, must treat its citizens in a manner consistent with their intrinsic worth as human beings—a punishment must not be so severe as to be degrading to human dignity."[28]

Justice Marshall holds to his opinion in *Furman* as well. Here he limits his opinion to two points.

Justice Marshall still claims that an informed citizenry would reject the death penalty. Indeed, he has some minimal empirical support for his claim. "A recent study, conducted after the enactment of the post-*Furman* statutes, has confirmed that the American people know little about the death penalty, and that the opinions of an informed public would differ significantly from those of a public unaware of the consequences and effects of the death penalty."[29]

In addition, excessive punishments violate the Eighth Amendment's cruel and unusual punishment clause. But what, exactly, does it mean for a punishment to be excessive? To answer that question Justice Marshall considers the two justifications for punishment identified by Justice Stewart—retribution and deterrence.

The deterrent effect of the death penalty remains, for Justice Marshall, nonexistent. But even if the death penalty would deter, the punishment would be excessive if a less severe punishment would achieve the same goal. Although he does not indicate what punishments would achieve the same social goal, life imprisonment without the possibility of parole would be among the options. Indeed, in a footnote regarding the claim that the death penalty deters a murderer from murdering again, Marshall writes, "The only additional purpose mentioned in the opinions in these cases is specific deterrence—preventing the murderer from committing another crime. Surely life imprisonment and, if necessary, solitary confinement would fully accomplish this purpose."[30]

Retribution as a general justification for punishment does not find favor with Justice Marshall either. For example, Justice Stevens claimed that retributive feelings are instinctual and that if those instincts are not addressed, anarchy (e.g., vigilante justice and lynch law) could occur. Marshall finds that claim preposterous. "It simply defies belief to suggest that the death penalty is necessary to prevent the American people from taking the law into their own hands."[31] Furthermore, the retributive claim that the death penalty serves to reinforce moral values is equally disturbing. "It is inconceivable that any individual concerned about conforming his conduct to what society says is 'right' would fail to realize that murder is 'wrong' if the penalty were simply life imprisonment."[32]

Justice Marshall acknowledges that the retributive philosophy can avoid sounding utilitarian in nature by focusing solely on the claim that the death penalty is the appropriate punishment for some particularly heinous crimes, that is, that the punishment fits the crime. For Marshall, the idea that a punishment fits the crime does not reflect the Eighth Amendment concern that punishments reflect human dignity. "To be sustained under the Eighth Amendment, the death penalty must 'compor[t] with the basic concept of human dignity at the core of the Amendment.'"[33] Punishment for the sake of punishment, as retributivism is sometimes characterized, violates the very notions of dignity and worth. "Under these standards, the taking of life 'because the wrongdoer deserves it' surely must fall, for such a punishment has as its very basis the total denial of the wrongdoer's dignity and worth."[34] Marshall summarizes his position clearly and unambiguously: "The death penalty, unnecessary to promote the goal of deterrence or to further any legitimate notion of retribution, is an excessive penalty forbidden by the Eighth and Fourteenth Amendments. I respectfully dissent from the Court's judgment upholding the sentences of death imposed upon the petitioners in these cases."[35]

So ends the four-year hiatus of capital punishment. Henceforth, the Court will return to its historical role of determining not if the death penalty is constitutional but if the death penalty statutes guarantee that the constitutional rights of defendants will not be sacrificed, especially in terms of decisions that are capricious, arbitrary, and haphazard.

WOODSON V. NORTH CAROLINA

The issue in *Woodson v. North Carolina* (428 U.S. 280 [1976] [argued 3/31/76; decided 7/2/76]) concerns the imposition of the death penalty as a mandatory punishment for capital crimes.[36] The Court holds that mandatory death sentences are unconstitutional in that they violate the Eighth and Fourteenth Amendments. Specifically, the Court holds that mandatory death sentences do not curb the arbitrary and wanton jury discretion now prohibited by *Furman v. Georgia*. Furthermore, mandatory death sentences preclude any jury determination of the character and record of the defendant or the circumstances surrounding the crime. Such sentences therefore deny the respect for humanity assumed by the Eighth Amendment.

Woodson was a participant in a robbery in which a person was killed, but Woodson did not kill nor was there intent to kill. The North Carolina statute regarding murder at the time of the killing read:

Murder in the first and second degree defined; punishment—A murder which shall be perpetrated by means of poison, lying in wait, imprisonment, starving, torture, or by any other kind of willful, deliberate and premeditated killing, or shall be committed in the perpetration or attempt to perpetrate any arson, rape, robbery, kidnapping, burglary or other felony, shall be deemed to be murder in the first degree and shall be punished with death. All other kinds of murder shall be deemed murder in the second degree, and shall be punished by imprisonment for a term of not less than two years nor more than life imprisonment in the State's prison.[37]

Justices Stewart, Powell, and Stevens, writing the plurality opinion again,[38] state that the issue before the Court "involves the procedure employed by the State to select persons for the unique and irreversible penalty of death."[39]

There are essentially three points Justice Stewart makes against mandatory sentencing.[40] First, Stewart claims that the history of the United States from as early as 1794 has been against mandatory death sentences. He acknowledges the fact that "[a]t the time the Eighth Amendment was adopted in 1791, the States uniformly followed the common-law practice of making death the exclusive and mandatory sentence for certain specified offenses certain"[41] (e.g., "murder, treason, piracy, arson, rape, robbery, burglary, and sodomy"[42]). In 1794, states tried to address alleged public dissatisfaction with mandatory death sentences by limiting the types of crimes that would carry mandatory death sentences. Pennsylvania, for example, abolished capital punishment for all crimes except murder in the first degree.[43] Still, "[j]uries continued to find the death penalty inappropriate in a significant number of first-degree murder cases, and refused to return guilty verdicts for that crime."[44] In 1838, Tennessee, Stewart argues, introduced sentencing discretion in capital cases as a means to address jury unhappiness with mandatory death sentences. The history since 1838 continues to reflect a general dissatisfaction with mandatory death sentences. According to Stewart, mandatory death sentences have been abolished by virtually every state and by Congress for federal crimes. He concludes his brief historical review as follows: "The consistent course charted by state legislatures and by Congress since the middle of the past century demonstrates that the aversion of jurors to mandatory death statutes is shared by society at large."[45] In addition, Stewart notes that contemporary jury deliberations indicate an unwillingness to sentence defendants to death. Indeed, even with discretion, juries do not appear to impose the death penalty with any regularity. "The actions of sentencing juries suggest that under contemporary standards of decency death is viewed as an inappropriate punishment for a substantial portion of convicted first-degree murderers."[46] Despite this historical review, however, given the overwhelming response by thirty-five states to *Furman v. Georgia* (several of which had introduced mandatory death sentences), Stewart wants to know if state legislatures, along with the people they represent, either had changed their opinion about mandatory death sentences or whether they were just confused about how to write legislation to meet the constitutional issues raised in *Furman*.

Justice Stewart argues that states considering mandatory death sentences are trying to meet objections to the death penalty raised in *Furman*. Unfortunately, mandatory death sentences fail to meet contemporary constitutional requirements. He writes, "North Carolina's mandatory death penalty statute for first-degree murder departs markedly from contemporary standards respecting the imposition of the punishment of death and thus cannot be applied consistently with the Eighth and Fourteenth Amendments' requirement that the State's power to punish 'be exercised within the limits of civilized standards.'"[47]

Second, Justice Stewart questions mandatory death sentences as the means to avoid the arbitrary and haphazard imposition of capital sentences. Mandatory death sentences, according to North Carolina, eliminate the arbitrary and haphazard imposition of the death penalty because mandatory death sentences, obviously, do not permit jury discretion. But that assumption is in error, according to the Court. North Carolina's argument is, at best, disingenuous. For Stewart, "mandatory statutes enacted in response to *Furman* have simply papered over the problem of unguided and unchecked jury discretion." There is no evidence to indicate that jurors in 1976 were less reluctant to impose a mandatory death sentence than they were in 1949 when a North Carolina study commission proposed modifications in its "mandatory death sentence on any person convicted of rape or first-degree murder."[48] Indeed, between 1949 and 1970, North Carolina abandoned mandatory death sentences in rape and murder cases, opting instead for at least a limited domain of jury discretion consistent with that commission.

Consequently, rather than exercise discretion during the penalty phase of a capital trial, Justice Stewart argues, a jury will simply scrutinize more carefully, and therefore exercise possibly greater discretion, during the guilt phase of the trial. Juries will continue to act as they have in the past, that is, if they are not comfortable with a death penalty in a particular case, they may not convict. Thus, present mandatory death sentences remain as arbitrary and haphazard as they were before *Furman*, although now that arbitrariness occurs in the determination of guilt rather than in determination of sentence, where it properly rests. "North Carolina's mandatory death penalty statute provides no standards to guide the jury in its inevitable exercise of the power to determine which first-degree murderers shall live and which shall die."[49] The only thing that a mandatory death sentence might accomplish is to increase the number of people receiving the death penalty. But that is no guarantee that the process is more rational. Indeed, "a mandatory scheme may well exacerbate the problem identified in *Furman* by resting the penalty determination on the particular jury's willingness to act lawlessly."[50] Mandatory death sentences quite simply do not "fulfill *Furman*'s basic requirement by replacing arbitrary and wanton jury discretion with objective standards to guide, regularize, and make rationally reviewable the process for imposing a sentence of death."[51]

Third, the North Carolina statute fails to see each individual as unique. That is, *Furman* mandates that sentences reflect the character of the individual sentenced. A mandatory sentence treats all convicted defendants "as members of a faceless, undifferentiated mass to be subjected to the blind infliction of the penalty of death."[52] The death penalty, so the argument goes, is so qualitatively different from any other punishment, in part because it is so final, that society needs to assure, as best it can, the "reliability" of each particular death sentence.[53] Thus, the failure of North Carolina's mandatory death penalty statute to meet the above constitutional concerns renders that statute unconstitutional in violation of the Eighth and Fourteenth Amendments.

Justice Rehnquist dissents. In general, he reaffirms his opinion in *Furman* that there is nothing inherently cruel or unusual about the death penalty.[54] He then moves to the specific arguments advanced by Justice Stewart.

Justice Rehnquist initially disputes Justice Stewart's claim that the history of mandatory death penalties reflects growing opposition to mandatory death penalties. The rejection of mandatory death sentences, according to Rehnquist, came during the nineteenth century as juries rejected mandatory death sentences for offenses such as burglary and sodomy. There is no clear legislative evidence that people were, to any great extent, opposed to mandatory death sentences for murderers. Indeed, the move to a discretionary imposition of the death penalty does not necessarily reflect rejection of mandatory death sentences. Rehnquist notes here that those opposed to mandatory death sentences in the nineteenth century consisted primarily of the following two groups: (1) those opposed to the death penalty but who were willing to accept discretionary sentencing over mandatory sentencing as a halfway measure on the road to total abolition, and (2) those in support of mandatory death sentences but who found that juries were reluctant to impose a mandatory death penalty and were concerned that some murderers went free because there were no options (under a mandatory death penalty statute).[55] Rehnquist explains the motives of this second group as follows: "Change to a discretionary system was accepted by these persons not because they thought mandatory imposition of the death penalty was cruel and unusual, but because they thought that if jurors were permitted to return a sentence other than death upon the conviction of a capital crime, fewer guilty defendants would be acquitted."[56]

Of course, if juries failed at times to bring in guilty verdicts because of a mandatory sentence of death, would that not indicate jury opposition, which might reflect public opposition, to mandatory death sentences? Not necessarily. Because juries need to return a unanimous vote in mandatory death penalty cases, it would take only one juror to undermine the will of eleven. Of course, in theory, it could be the case that most jurors would oppose a mandatory death penalty. If we can assume, however, that legislators reflect majority will, which is a reasonable assumption in a constitutional democracy, then we can just as easily assume, if not more easily assume, that there was not widespread opposition to mandatory death penalties. For Justice Rehnquist, there is no evidence to support the majoritarian claim that "the evolving standards of decency" reached a point where most people would object to mandatory sentencing.[57]

Justice Stewart's charge against a mandatory death penalty, that "it has simply 'papered over' the problem of unchecked jury discretion,"[58] is without merit. Under mandatory sentencing, according to Stewart, juries can and do engage in jury nullification.[59] This raises one of the most debated issues relating to the constitutionality of the death penalty. In *Furman*, as previously noted, death penalties cannot be wantonly and freakishly imposed. Mandatory sentences, by eliminating jury discretion as it considers aggravating and mitigating circumstances, leaves juries open to nullify what might have been an otherwise guilty verdict, a nullification based perhaps on the whim of one juror who cannot accept the death penalty in this particular case. Justice Rehnquist's point, however, is that discretion will exist in any system, regardless of how well defined. Jury discretion exists, for example, in the consideration of aggravating and mitigating circumstances. Thus, removing discretion from one part of the trial does not mean that discretion will not occur elsewhere in the process. All systems will operate with some discretion and therefore will appear, at times, arbitrary and capricious.

The last concern raised in the plurality opinion relates to the need, when the death penalty is involved, to see each defendant as unique. Hence, there is a need to consider aggravating and mitigating factors in the sentencing process. For Justice Rehnquist, there is no constitutional requirement for the consideration of aggravating and mitigating circumstances. Governments may want to support such a process for guaranteeing a just decision, but that particular method is not a constitutional mandate. Furthermore, Rehnquist finds some inconsistency between the plurality's first and third arguments, namely, rejection of mandatory sentences and desire for individualized sentencing. For example, why is a statute mandating death for those already serving a life sentence not a legitimate option in particular kinds of cases? Not only is there no demonstrable prohibition against the death penalty, but also "particularized consideration" does not, in itself, speak against mandatory penalties.

In conclusion, Justice Rehnquist finds the plurality opinion specious at its best and willful legislation at its worst. The case, for Rehnquist, is "unsupported by any other decision of this Court."[60] The judgment for conviction should have been upheld.

PROFFITT V. FLORIDA AND JUREK V. TEXAS

The opinions in *Proffitt v. Florida* (428 U.S. 242 [1976] [argued 3/31/76; decided 7/2/76]) and *Jurek v. Texas* (428 U.S. 262 [1976] [argued 3/30/76; decided 7/2/76]) apply the Court opinion in *Gregg* to Florida and Texas death penalty statutes reenacted after *Furman*. There are slight differences between these state statutes, but they meet *Furman* requirements. For example, in Florida, the trial judge, not the jury, determines the sentence. Justice Stewart notes that the Court "has never suggested that jury sentencing is constitutionally required."[61] Indeed, "judicial sentencing should lead, if anything, to even greater consistency in the imposition at the trial court level of capital punishment, since a trial judge is more experienced in sentencing than a jury, and therefore is better able to impose sentences similar to those imposed in analogous cases."[62]

Like Georgia, the appellate review process enables the Supreme Court of Florida to overturn sentences it finds inconsistent with the aggravating and mitigating circumstances that resulted in a death sentence. The Florida Supreme Court has not shied away from that responsibility. "The Supreme Court of Florida, like that of Georgia, has not hesitated to vacate a death sentence when it has determined that the sentence should not have been imposed. Indeed, it has vacated 8 of the 21 death sentences that it has reviewed to date."[63]

Proffitt claims that the aggravating and mitigating circumstances defined by the Florida legislature "are so vague and so broad that virtually 'any capital defendant becomes a candidate for the death penalty.'"[64] Constitutional challenges to the aggravating and mitigating circumstances will continue to follow the Supreme Court in its death penalty deliberations. In *Proffitt*, the Court sustains the challenged statutory aggravating and mitigating circumstances against the charges of vagueness, incoherence, and imprecision. "The directions given to judge and jury by the Florida statute are sufficiently clear and precise to enable the various aggravating circumstances to be weighed against the mitigating ones. As a result, the trial court's sentencing discretion is guided and channeled by a system that focuses on the circumstances of each individual homicide and individual defendant in deciding whether the death penalty is to be imposed."[65]

Finally, Justice Stewart considers an additional charge that the Florida Supreme Court review process "is necessarily subjective and unpredictable."[66] That claim is quickly dismissed. "[A]ny suggestion that the Florida court engages in only cursory or rubber-stamp review of death penalty cases is totally controverted by the fact that it has vacated over one-third of the death sentences that have come before it."[67]

The Texas death penalty statute passes constitutional muster as well. There is one noteworthy difference between *Jurek* and *Gregg*, or, as far as that goes, between *Jurek* and *Proffitt*. In designing its post-*Furman* capital punishment statute, Texas limited its "capital homicides to intentional and knowing murders committed in five situations: murder of a peace officer or fireman; murder committed in the course of kidnaping [sic], burglary, robbery, forcible rape, or arson; murder committed for remuneration; murder committed while escaping or attempting to escape from a penal institution; and murder committed by a prison inmate when the victim is a prison employee."[68] Once a jury finds a defendant guilty, it must meet to determine if a death penalty is to be imposed. That determination is made on the basis of a jury's answer to the following questions:

(1) whether the conduct of the defendant that caused the death of the deceased was committed deliberately and with the reasonable expectation that the death of the deceased or another would result;
(2) whether there is a probability that the defendant would commit criminal acts of violence that would constitute a continuing threat to society; and
(3) if raised by the evidence, whether the conduct of the defendant in killing the deceased was unreasonable in response to the provocation, if any, by the deceased.[69]

If the jury can answer these questions affirmatively, the death penalty will be imposed. If any question is answered in the negative, then a life sentence will be imposed. The problem the Court notes here is that Texas does not establish a list of aggravating and mitigating circumstances that carefully guide a jury through deliberations that will meet *Furman* standards. Some form of aggravating and mitigating circumstances must exist, Justice Stewart argues, if death penalties are to be held constitutional. "Thus, the constitutionality of the Texas procedures turns on whether the enumerated questions allow consideration of particularized mitigating factors."[70] Although no formal set of mitigating circumstances have been established (whereas formal aggravating circumstances can be equated with a clear finding of guilt to one of the five capital homicide categories), Texas does "allow a defendant to bring to the jury's attention whatever mitigating circumstances he may be able to show."[71] The Texas statute, for Stewart, by allowing any mitigating circumstances a defendant can present, "has ensured that the sentencing jury will have adequate guidance to enable it to perform its sentencing function." Furthermore, "[b]y providing prompt judicial review of the jury's decision in a court with statewide jurisdiction, Texas has provided a means to promote the evenhanded, rational, and consistent imposition of death sentences under law. Because this system serves to assure that sentences of death will not be 'wantonly' or 'freakishly' imposed, it does not violate the Constitution."[72]

GARDNER V. FLORIDA

In *Gardner v. Florida* (430 U.S. 349 [1977] [argued 11/30/76; decided 3/22/77]), Gardner had been convicted of murdering his wife and sentenced to death. The jury, however, after considering aggravating and mitigating circumstances, concluded that the mitigating circumstances outweighed the aggravating circumstances and recommended a life sentence. The mitigating circumstances Gardner cited included his total state of inebriation at the time of the murder and that he remembered virtually nothing about the murder. Florida's mitigating circumstances included the following: "The capital felony was committed while the defendant was under the influence of extreme mental or emotional disturbance" and "[t]he capacity of the defendant to appreciate the criminality of his conduct or to conform his conduct to the requirements of law was substantially impaired."[73] The judge, however, overrode the jury's recommendation and sentenced Gardner to death. The decision to override the jury's recommendation was based in part on a "presentence investigation report."[74] More specifically, Justice Stevens noted "that his [the trial judge's] conclusion was based on the evidence presented at both stages of the bifurcated proceeding, the arguments of counsel, and his review of 'the factual information contained in said pre-sentence investigation.'"[75] Even though portions of the presentence report were shared with defense counsel, there was "a confidential portion which was not disclosed to defense counsel."[76]

Gardner claims that the failure to disclose the contents of the entire presentence report denied him his due process of law rights as he had no opportunity to challenge the report's confidential findings. The Supreme Court of Florida upheld the trial court's judgment without addressing Gardner's right to know what was contained in the confidential portion of that report. Florida asserts four arguments as to why the entire contents of the report cannot be disclosed. Justice Stevens rejects each argument.

First, Florida "argues that an assurance of confidentiality to potential sources of information is essential to enable investigators to obtain relevant but sensitive disclosures from persons unwilling to comment publicly about a defendant's background or character."[77] Without the assurance of confidentiality, Florida claims that all sentencing cases will be jeopardized. Justice Stevens, however, maintains that that confidential information carries the potential to include erroneous information or information that could be misinterpreted. "The risk that some of the information accepted in confidence may be erroneous, or may be misinterpreted, by the investigator or by the sentencing judge, is manifest."[78] Stevens claims that Florida's practice, especially in capital cases, is fraught with constitutional difficulty.

Second, Florida claims that the disclosure of all information could delay the sentencing process. Justice Stevens claims, however, that the alleged delay could be exaggerated. Even if the delay were not exaggerated, "the time invested in ascertaining the truth would surely be well spent if it makes the difference between life and death."[79]

Third, and somewhat mysteriously, Florida claims that disclosures of information can include psychiatric information that could affect rehabilitation efforts. Justice Stevens does not hesitate to note that the death penalty precludes rehabilitative efforts. "[T]he extinction of all possibility of rehabilitation is one of the aspects of the death sentence that makes it different in kind from any other sentence a State may legitimately impose."[80]

Fourth, "Florida argues that trial judges can be trusted to exercise their discretion in a responsible manner, even though they may base their decisions on secret information."[81] Justice Stevens notes here that *Furman* forecloses vesting such power in a judge's hands. Something more troubles Stevens about Florida's argument, namely, it "rests on the erroneous premise that the participation of counsel is superfluous to the process of evaluating the relevance and significance of aggravating and mitigating facts."[82] Denying defense attorneys the opportunity to challenge evidence known only to the sentencing judge denies defendants their due process right to respond to any allegations that could affect punishment. "We conclude that petitioner was denied due process of law when the death sentence was imposed, at least in part, on the basis of information which he had no opportunity to deny or explain."[83]

COKER V. GEORGIA

Georgia included rape among its capital offenses. The Supreme Court in *Coker v. Georgia* (433 U.S. 584 [1977] [argued 3/28/77; decided 6/29/77]) must determine if the death penalty can be sustained constitutionally for the crime of rape. Specifically, Justice White, for the Court, asks if the death penalty constitutes a disproportionate and excessive punishment in violation of the Eighth Amendment's cruel and unusual punishment clause. To make that determination, White explains the terms disproportionate and excessive as follows: "Under Gregg, a punishment is 'excessive' and unconstitutional if it (1) makes no measurable contribution to acceptable goals of punishment, and hence is nothing more than the purposeless and needless imposition of pain and suffering; or (2) is grossly out of proportion to the severity of the crime."[84] Although these twin requirements sound clear and coherent, White wants to know how they are to be applied objectively. He makes three observations relevant in implementing these requirements.

The majority of states in the twentieth century have never used the death penalty to punish rape crimes.[85] After *Furman,* only three states included rape as a capital crime when they rewrote their capital punishment statutes to meet *Furman* standards.[86] Since *Furman,* juries have been reluctant to impose the death penalty in those states that did retain the death penalty as an option for the crime of rape. While juries cannot serve as the sole means by which society, as well as the Supreme Court, evaluates the appropriateness of the death penalty for rape, it is nonetheless "a significant and reliable objective index of contemporary values."[87] Justice White notes that states have argued that the reluctance of juries to impose the death penalty might signify a belief on their part that only extreme cases of rape merit the extreme punishment. Still, "it is true that, in the vast majority of cases, at least 9 out of 10, juries have not imposed the death sentence."[88]

Justice White concludes this review by noting that, when all is said and done, Georgia remains the only state with a death penalty for the crime of rape of an adult woman.[89]

Based on these considerations, Justice White concludes that the death penalty is disproportionate and excessive. "[T]he legislative rejection of capital punishment for rape strongly confirms our own judgment, which is that death is indeed a disproportionate penalty for the crime of raping an adult woman."[90] The death penalty for rape cannot stand constitutionally.

Justice Powell agrees with the Court in Coker's case but does not agree with its judgment that the death penalty is always a disproportionate punishment. He clarifies his limited agreement as follows:

Although rape invariably is a reprehensible crime, there is no indication that petitioner's offense was committed with excessive brutality or that the victim sustained serious or lasting injury. The plurality, however, does not limit its holding to the case before us, or to similar cases. Rather, in an opinion that ranges well beyond what is necessary, it holds that capital punishment always—regardless of the circumstances—is a disproportionate penalty for the crime of rape.[91]

Justice Powell argues that there may well be aggravated cases of rape that cry out for the death penalty. The Court's decision precludes that possibility. "Today, in a case that does not require such an expansive pronouncement, the plurality draws a bright line between murder and all rapes—regardless of the degree of brutality of the rape or the effect upon the victim. I dissent because I am not persuaded that such a bright line is appropriate."[92] But, Powell cautions, "Some victims are so grievously injured physically or psychologically that life is beyond repair."[93] In such cases, Powell wants legislators and juries to determine the appropriateness of a death penalty response to heinous acts of rape.[94]

Chief Justice Burger, joined by Justice Rehnquist, dissents. Specifically, Burger agrees with Justice Powell that the Court has decided too much, that it should have limited its decision to the case itself rather than ruling unnecessarily that the death penalty for any rape constitutes a cruel and unusual punishment. The Court, for Burger, has reflected more on "societal mores and attitudes toward the generic crime of rape and the punishment for it" than on whether Georgia's death penalty statute was constitutionally acceptable in Coker's case. Burger maintains not only that the Georgia death penalty statute meets constitutional requirements but also that Georgia has been denied the opportunity to punish Coker meaningfully.[95] Burger makes four points in this context. First, Coker is serving such long sentences now that an additional sentence in the present case would be meaningless. Second, Coker's criminal record demonstrates that he remains indifferent to the safety and well-being of others, especially women. Third, he escaped from prison and has no reason not to try to escape in the future. Fourth, a successful escape again will result in additional rape attempts for there is no deterrent punishment available with which to sentence him. Burger would decide Coker as follows:

[D]oes the Eighth Amendment's ban against cruel and unusual punishment prohibit the State of Georgia from executing a person who has, within the space of three years, raped three separate women, killing one and attempting to kill another, who is serving prison terms exceeding his probable lifetime, and who has not hesitated to escape confinement at the first available opportunity? Whatever one's view may be as to the State's constitutional power to impose the death penalty upon a rapist who stands before a court convicted for the first time, this case reveals a chronic rapist whose continuing danger to the community is abundantly clear.[96]

Chief Justice Burger does not find any legitimate argument that would deny Georgia the right to determine the punishments it needs to effectively enforce its laws.[97] He concludes, "Whatever our individual views as to the wisdom of capital punishment, I cannot agree that it is constitutionally impermissible for a state legislature to make the 'solemn judgment' to impose such penalty for the crime of rape. Accordingly, I would leave to the States the task of legislating in this area of the law."[98]

LOCKETT V. OHIO

In *Lockett v. Ohio* (438 U.S. 586 [1978] [argued 1/17/78; decided 7/3/78]), Lockett had been convicted in the murder of a pawnbroker, although she only drove the getaway car. There was no evidence that she had intended the pawnbroker to die. She was not present in the shop when the pawnbroker was murdered. She challenged the constitutionality of Ohio's death penalty statute on four grounds, only one of which was successful.[99]

Her successful challenge focused on the severity of her punishment, death. Specifically, the Court considered "only her contention that her death sentence is invalid because the statute under which it was imposed did not permit the sentencing judge to consider, as mitigating factors, her character, prior record, age, lack of specific intent to cause death, and her relatively minor part in the crime."[100] Chief Justice Burger, for the Court, focuses on the constitutional guarantee of individualized sentencing, especially in capital cases. From *Furman, Gregg,* and *Woodson,* one clear and unmistakable point is that each defendant must receive all considerations relevant to their sentence determination. For Burger, "the Eighth and Fourteenth Amendments require that the sentencer, in all but the rarest kind of capital case, not be precluded from considering, as a mitigating factor, any aspect of a defendant's character or record and any of the circumstances of the offense that the defendant proffers as a basis for a sentence less than death."[101] Because there really is no comparable punishment to the death penalty, each individual must have the opportunity to present evidence in mitigation of that final punishment. "Given that the imposition of death by public authority is so profoundly different from all other penalties, we cannot avoid the conclusion that an individualized decision is essential in capital cases."[102] Burger holds, in general, that "a statute that prevents the sentencer in all capital cases from giving independent mitigating weight to aspects of the defendant's character and record and to circumstances of the offense proffered in mitigation creates the risk that the death penalty will be imposed in spite of factors which may call for a less severe penalty.[103] The Ohio death penalty statute, by allowing only three statutory mitigating circumstances, fails to meet the constitutional requirement that any mitigating circumstance must be allowed to defendants facing a death penalty.

In a separate concurring opinion, Justice Marshall gets to the point more directly and coherently. "The imposition of the death penalty for this crime totally violates the principle of proportionality embodied in the Eighth Amendment's prohibition; it makes no distinction between a willful and malicious murderer and an accomplice to an armed robbery in which a killing unintentionally occurs."[104] Speaking on the need for individuality in the sentencing process, Marshall writes, "Where life itself is what hangs in the balance, a fine precision in the process must be insisted upon. The Ohio statute, with its blunderbuss, virtually mandatory approach to imposition of the death penalty for certain crimes, wholly fails to recognize the unique individuality of every criminal defendant who comes before its courts."[105]

Justice Rehnquist dissents from the judgment to overturn Lockett's death sentence. He objects specifically to the open forum that will now exist that allows for the consideration of any kind of claim, however ludicrous, in mitigation. "We are now told, in effect, that, in order to impose a death sentence, the judge or jury must receive in evidence whatever the defense attorney wishes them to hear."[106]

Justice Rehnquist's objection is not just academic. The ramifications of allowing anything to be heard in mitigation could invite chaos. In an effort to individualize the sentencing process, the death penalty could, in effect, be implemented in a way that is more arbitrary and capricious than the system found unconstitutional in *Furman*. Rehnquist expresses this point as follows.

If a defendant, as a matter of constitutional law, is to be permitted to offer as evidence in the sentencing hearing any fact, however bizarre, which he wishes, even though the most sympathetically disposed trial judge could conceive of no basis upon which the jury might take it into account in imposing a sentence, the new constitutional doctrine will not eliminate arbitrariness or freakishness in the imposition of sentences, but will codify and institutionalize it. By encouraging defendants in capital cases, and presumably sentencing judges and juries, to take into consideration anything under the sun as a "mitigating circumstance," it will not guide sentencing discretion, but will totally unleash it.[107]

According to Rehnquist, Ohio is well within its constitutional rights to impose the death penalty on defendants who have participated in a criminal act that resulted in someone's death. Rehnquist does not know of any principle that prohibits states from holding individuals guilty of capital crimes even if they did not directly cause a person's death.[108] *Lockett* will be revisited at a later date. As it stood in 1978, a person who *just* aids and abets cannot be charged with a capital crime.

GODFREY V. GEORGIA

Godfrey had been tried, convicted, and sentenced to death for the murders of his wife and mother-in-law in *Godfrey v. Georgia* (446 U.S. 420 [1980] [argued 2/20/80; decided 5/19/80]). He challenged his death sentence on the ground that the aggravating circumstance that got him the death penalty was unconstitutionally vague. Georgia had included, among its aggravating circumstances, that "a person convicted of murder may be sentenced to death if it is found beyond doubt that the offense 'was outrageously or wantonly vile, horrible or inhuman in that it involved torture, depravity of mind, or an aggravated battery to the victim.'"[109] This particular aggravating circumstance was not seen as unconstitutional in *Gregg*, but since *Gregg* "many death sentences" have been "based in whole or in part" on this particular circumstance.[110]

In *Gregg,* the Court had accepted the constitutionality of this aggravating circumstance yet it had noted that "any murder involves depravity of mind or an aggravated battery."[111] The Court had no reason to assume that the Supreme Court of Georgia would allow such a wide latitude in the interpretation and application of this circumstance. Now, four years later, the Court reconsiders its decision on this aggravating circumstance.[112]

Godfrey was sentenced by the jury to death on the basis "'that the offense of murder was outrageously wanton or vile, horrible and inhuman.'"[113] The Georgia Supreme Court upheld that sentence. Justice Stewart, for the Court, finds the aggravating circumstance constitutionally unacceptable.

Beginning with *Furman,* Justice Stewart explains that the Court has maintained that the death penalty cannot "be imposed under sentencing procedures that create a substantial risk that the punishment will be inflicted in an arbitrary and capricious manner."[114] Among other things, this requirement means that people should be able to distinguish between those cases that call for a death penalty and those that do not. To meet this requirement, a state "has a constitutional responsibility to tailor and apply its law in a manner that avoids the arbitrary and capricious infliction of the death penalty."[115]

Justice Stewart examines the present case in terms of two previous death penalty convictions the Georgia Supreme Court had sustained. In one case, "the victim had been beaten, burned, raped, and otherwise severely abused before her death by strangulation." In the other case, "the convicted murderer had choked two 7-year-old boys to death after having forced each of them to submit to anal sodomy."[116] Stewart notes that, through these cases, the Georgia Supreme Court had three criteria to help explain and qualify the aggravating circumstance under review. These criteria are explained as follows:

The first was that the evidence that the offense was "outrageously or wantonly vile, horrible or inhuman" had to demonstrate "torture, depravity of mind, or an aggravated battery to the victim." The second was that the phrase, "depravity of mind," comprehended only the kind of mental state that led the murderer to torture or to commit an aggravated battery before killing his victim. The third . . . was that the word, "torture," must . . . require evidence of serious physical abuse of the victim before death.[117]

Justice Stewart argues that there is no indication that these criteria were used in *Godfrey.* For example, there is no evidence that Godfrey caused anyone "to suffer any physical injury preceding their deaths."[118] Godfrey's death sentence must be reversed, according to Stewart, because his "crimes cannot be said to have reflected a consciousness materially more 'depraved' than that of any person convicted of murder."[119] More specifically, "[t]here is no principled way to distinguish this case, in which the death penalty was imposed, from the many cases in which it was not."[120]

Chief Justice Burger and Justice White each wrote separate dissenting opinions. Burger's dissent captures the essence of both dissents.

Chief Justice Burger begins by noting that Godfrey himself had referred to his crime as "hideous," a description that reflected the jury's sentence recommendation, since the jurors "concluded that this 'hideous' crime was 'outrageously or wantonly vile, horrible and inhuman.'"[121] In addition, the decision suggests that the Court will be in the business "of determining on a case-by-case basis whether a defendant's conduct is egregious enough to warrant a death sentence." And a death sentence appears to be warranted only if there is "'evidence of serious physical abuse.'"[122] Burger believes that the Court's judgment is arbitrary and without constitutional foundation. He offers an example of a defendant who "killed a young woman for the thrill of it." Because it was *just* a killing, is a state precluded from imposing a death penalty? Burger does not believe so. He writes:

In short, I am convinced that the course the plurality embarks on today is sadly mistaken—indeed, confused. It is this Court's function to insure that the rights of a defendant are scrupulously respected; and in capital cases, we must see to it that the jury has rendered its decision with meticulous care. But it is emphatically not our province to second-guess the jury's judgment or to tell the states which of their "hideous," intentional murderers may be given the ultimate penalty. Because the plurality does both, I dissent.[123]

BECK V. ALABAMA

Justice Stevens, for the Court, explains the problem in *Beck v. Alabama* (447 U.S. 625 [1980] [argued 2/20/80; decided 6/20/80]) as follows: "May a sentence of death constitutionally be imposed after a jury verdict of guilt of a capital offense when the jury was not permitted to consider a verdict of guilt of a lesser included noncapital offense,[124] and when the evidence would have supported such a verdict?"[125]

The Alabama capital punishment statute in essence stated that juries have just two options in a capital case, namely, guilty of first-degree murder or not guilty. The first option required the jury to impose the death penalty on the defendant; the second option required the jury to let the defendant go free. Thus, faced with a defendant who was certainly guilty of something, the jury could only bring in a verdict that would require the death penalty or a verdict that would mean that a person who did in fact break some law would go free. The Court finds this statute an unconstitutional violation of a defendant's due process rights under the Fourteenth Amendment.

In essence, the Court argues that Alabama's statute creates an unacceptable risk of conviction, especially in a case like *Beck* where the defendant is
guilty of something. Justice Stevens notes that Alabama is unique in its
failure to provide juries the opportunity to convict a defendant of a lesser
included offense. The possibility that a defendant will be convicted of a
capital offense is substantively enhanced, Stevens believes, if a jury cannot
consider a lesser included offense. "For when the evidence unquestion-
ably establishes that the defendant is guilty of a serious, violent offense—
but leaves some doubt with respect to an element that would justify
conviction of a capital offense—the failure to give the jury the 'third
option' of convicting on a lesser included offense would seem inevitably
to enhance the risk of an unwarranted conviction."[126] Stevens notes as
well that the Court's position has been to require states to establish procedures that protect against the possibility of arbitrary or capricious decisions. For Stevens, the same oversight function applies in *Beck*. "Thus, if
the unavailability of a lesser included offense instruction enhances the risk
of an unwarranted conviction, Alabama is constitutionally prohibited
from withdrawing that option from the jury in a capital case."[127]

ADAMS V. TEXAS[128]

Adams v. Texas (448 U.S. 38 [1980] [argued 3/24/80; decided 6/25/80])
could be subtitled "*Witherspoon* Redux." The *Witherspoon* concern about
jury selection directs this Texas appeal. *Witherspoon* stands for the principle that prospective jurors cannot be excluded from jury duty in a capital
case because they have moral reservations about the death penalty. In
Adams, the relevance of that principle in the new bifurcated system is challenged. In reviewing cases that raised *Witherspoon*-type concerns, Justice
White, for the Court, summarizes the Court's history on this issue. "This
line of cases establishes the general proposition that a juror may not be
challenged for cause based on his views about capital punishment unless
those views would prevent or substantially impair the performance of his
duties as a juror in accordance with his instructions and his oath. The State
may insist, however, that jurors will consider and decide the facts impartially and conscientiously apply the law as charged by the court."[129]

The bifurcated trial, according to Justice White, carries the same principle with respect to jury selection as enunciated in *Witherspoon*. For example, under Texas's jury selection process, prospective jurors could be
excluded from jury duty who stated that they could be "affected" if they
had to bring in a death sentence. But that could mean only that they would
more carefully scrutinize the facts and the testimony presented at trial and
discussed in their deliberations. Prospective jurors could be excluded who
stated that they did not know, or were uncertain about, how they might be
affected if they had to bring in a sentence of death. Prospective jurors

could be excluded if they admitted that a capital case might require them to have a higher standard of what it means to be guilty "beyond a reasonable doubt." For White, the Texas statute leaves too many avenues open for excluding otherwise viable jurors. If each and every juror who expressed any reservation about the death penalty were excluded from jury duty, the defendant would be deprived "of the impartial jury to which he or she is entitled under the law."[130] In summary, White writes:

We repeat that the State may bar from jury service those whose beliefs about capital punishment would lead them to ignore the law or violate their oaths. But, in the present case, Texas . . . exclude[s] jurors whose only fault was to take their responsibilities with special seriousness or to acknowledge honestly that they might or might not be affected. It does not appear in the record before us that these individuals were so irrevocably opposed to capital punishment as to frustrate the State's legitimate efforts to administer its constitutionally valid death penalty scheme. Accordingly, the Constitution disentitles the State to execute a sentence of death imposed by a jury from which such prospective jurors have been excluded.[131]

BULLINGTON V. MISSOURI

If convicted of a capital offense in Missouri, the defendant, in this instance, *Bullington v. Missouri* (451 U.S. 430 [1981] [argued 1/14/81; decided 4/4/81]), at the sentencing stage of the trial, can receive either the death penalty or "life imprisonment without eligibility for probation or parole for 50 years."[132] Bullington was convicted in the drowning death of a young woman. To obtain a death penalty, Missouri had to prove beyond a reasonable doubt one or more of ten aggravating circumstances. In *Bullington,* the prosecutor identified two: "that '[t]he offense was committed by a person . . . who has a substantial history of serious assaultive criminal convictions,' and that '[t]he offense was outrageously or wantonly vile, horrible or inhuman in that it involved torture, or depravity of mind.'"[133] The jury found Bullington guilty of capital murder, but they sentenced him to "imprisonment for life without eligibility for probation or parole for 50 years."[134] Bullington appealed his conviction and asked for either acquittal or a new trial. He was granted a new trial.

At the new trial, the prosecution made it known that the death penalty would still be sought, relying in part on the same aggravating circumstances relied on in the first trial. Defense counsel objected on the grounds that that would violate Bullington's Fifth Amendment double jeopardy rights. The defense argued "that the Double Jeopardy Clause of the Fifth Amendment (as made applicable to the States through the Fourteenth Amendment) barred the imposition of the penalty of death when the first jury had declined to impose the death sentence."[135] Several attempts were made by both sides to reach a judgment about the constitutionality of the prosecution seeking a death penalty at a new trial that had been won on appeal. The Supreme Court of Missouri resolved the constitutional conflict as follows: "It held that neither the Double Jeopardy Clause nor the Eighth Amendment nor the Due Process Clause barred the imposition of the death penalty upon petitioner at his new trial, and that allowing the prosecution to seek capital punishment would not impermissibly chill a defendant's effort to seek redress for any constitutional violation committed at his initial trial."[136]

Justice Blackmun, for the Court, acknowledges that the double jeopardy clause prevents a person for being retried for a crime for which there was a previous acquittal. In addition, Blackmun notes "that the Double Jeopardy Clause imposes no absolute prohibition against the imposition of a harsher sentence at retrial after a defendant has succeeded in having his original conviction set aside."[137]

Justice Blackmun, however, does not accept the relevance of that position to *Bullington*. The present death penalty statute requiring a guilt stage and a sentencing stage works differently. Here, trying the defendant with the possibility of a death penalty would violate the double jeopardy clause. In *Bullington*, the jury had well-defined guidelines at sentencing determination. The jury's judgment in the first trial was not in question. Bullington's appeal is not of the sentence imposed but of the verdict reached. Blackmun writes, "A verdict of acquittal on the issue of guilt or innocence is, of course, absolutely final. The values that underlie this principle . . . are equally applicable when a jury has rejected the State's claim that the defendant deserves to die."[138] To subject Bullington to a second trial regarding punishment does indeed, for Blackmun, violate the double jeopardy clause. In addition, if that practice were allowed, it would have a chilling effect on prisoners. Why, for example, would someone appeal a conviction if winning a new trial could result in a punishment greater than the one received at the initial trial?

Justice Powell, joined by Chief Justice Burger and Justices White and Rehnquist, dissents. For Powell, the Court has deviated substantively and inexplicably from precedent. Prior to *Bullington*, Powell argues, no court had ever applied the double jeopardy clause to both parts of a capital trial. If a person wins a new trial, by what logic would that person be excluded from receiving a more severe sentence at a second trial? Powell argues that "[t]he reasons for considering an acquittal on guilt or innocence as absolutely final do not apply equally to a sentencing decision for less than the most severe sentence authorized by law. A retrial of a defendant once found to have been innocent 'enhanc[es] the possibility that, even though innocent, he may be found guilty.'" However, "when a defendant is found guilty, he must bear the ordeal of being sentenced just as he does the ordeal of serving sentence."[139]

For Justice Powell, there is no constitutional requirement that a defendant, upon winning a new trial, is precluded from receiving a more severe punishment if convicted at a second trial. At a new trial, the procedural guarantees for a fair trial are the same as at the first trial. In a capital case, this means those safeguards that have been established for a capital trial remain in effect in a new trial. In essence, for Powell, everything is the same as it was at the beginning.

ESTELLE V. SMITH

Chief Justice Burger, for the Court, succinctly states the issue in *Estelle v. Smith* (451 U.S. 454 [1981] [argued 10/8/80; decided 5/18/81]) as follows: "We granted certiorari to consider whether the prosecution's use of psychiatric testimony at the sentencing phase of respondent's capital murder trial to establish his future dangerousness violated his constitutional rights."[140]

Ernest Smith had been indicted for first-degree murder although he had not done the shooting that killed a clerk at a grocery store. Prior to his trial, Smith had been "informally ordered" to submit to a psychiatric examination "to determine [his] competency to stand trial."[141] Smith was found competent to stand trial, and he was convicted.

At the sentencing stage of Smith's trial, the psychiatrist was called to testify about Smith's future dangerousness. Over objections from defense counsel, the trial judge allowed the psychiatrist to testify. Based on just a ninety-minute "'mental status examination' of Smith," the psychiatrist testified before the jury as follows:

(a) that Smith "is a very severe sociopath"; (b) that "he will continue his previous behavior"; (c) that his sociopathic condition will "only get worse"; (d) that he has no "regard for another human being's property or for their life, regardless of who it may be"; (e) that "[t]here is no treatment, no medicine . . . that in any way at all modifies or changes this behavior"; (f) that he "is going to go ahead and commit other similar or same criminal acts if given the opportunity to do so"; and (g) that he "has no remorse or sorrow for what he has done."[142]

Based on that psychiatric testimony, the jury sentenced Smith to death. Chief Justice Burger, for the Court, argues that Texas violated Smith's Fifth and Fourteenth Amendment right not to speak at a pretrial psychiatric examination. Burger states that "the ultimate penalty of death was a potential consequence of what respondent told the examining psychiatrist."[143] In essence, Smith was not informed about his right against self-incrimination, as he had never been informed that his statements to the psychiatrist could be used against him. In addition, Smith's defense counsel had not been informed either that the psychiatrist would testify or to what the psychiatrist would testify. The psychiatrist's testimony went beyond an inquiry to determine Smith's competency to stand trial. As such, it compromised his right to remain silent on matters that could well condemn him to death. As Burger writes, "Just as the Fifth Amendment prevents a criminal defendant from being made 'the deluded instrument of his own conviction,' it protects him as well from being made the 'deluded instrument' of his own execution."[144]

Chief Justice Burger claims essentially that the two stages of a bifurcated trial remained governed by the same constitutional protections. "Given the gravity of the decision to be made at the penalty phase, the State is not relieved of the obligation to observe fundamental constitutional guarantees."[145] Consistent with the Fifth Amendment, Smith certainly cannot be made to testify against himself. In addition, "[t]he State's attempt to establish respondent's future dangerousness by relying on the unwarned statements he made to [the psychiatrist] similarly infringes Fifth Amendment values."[146] Burger notes further that "[t]he Fifth Amendment privilege is 'as broad as the mischief against which it seeks to guard,' and the privilege is fulfilled only when a criminal defendant is guaranteed the right 'to remain silent unless he chooses to speak in the unfettered exercise of his own will, and to suffer no penalty . . . for such silence.'"[147]

Smith's Sixth Amendment right to counsel was also effectively infringed. Smith had been indicted and had an attorney appointed to represent him. As Chief Justice Burger notes, the Sixth Amendment "provides that 'in all criminal prosecutions, the accused shall enjoy the right . . . to have the assistance of counsel for his defense.'"[148] Defense counsel was not present at the psychiatric examination. Defense counsel had never been notified that the psychiatrist's testimony would be used at a later stage. Accordingly, Smith was denied the opportunity to have counsel advise him regarding the psychiatric evaluation. Burger remarks, "Therefore, in addition to Fifth Amendment considerations, the death penalty was improperly imposed on respondent because the psychiatric examination . . . proceeded in violation of respondent's Sixth Amendment right to the assistance of counsel."[149] He concludes clearly and unmistakably, "Respondent's Fifth and Sixth Amendment rights were abridged by the State's introduction of [psychiatric] testimony at the penalty phase. . . . His death sentence must be vacated."[150]

EDDINGS V. OKLAHOMA

Sixteen-year-old Monty Eddings was convicted of and sentenced to die for killing an Oklahoma highway patrol officer in *Eddings v. Oklahoma* (455 U.S. 104 [1982] [argued 11/2/81; decided 1/19/82]). Even though Eddings was only sixteen at the time of the killing, Oklahoma tried him as an adult. The Oklahoma capital punishment statute provided the typical bifurcated trial, and the sentence was determined by aggravating and mitigating circumstances.

Oklahoma identified three aggravating circumstances: "[T]he murder was especially heinous, atrocious, or cruel, . . . the crime was committed for the purpose of avoiding or preventing a lawful arrest, and . . . there was a probability that the defendant would commit criminal acts of violence that would constitute a continuing threat to society."[151]

Eddings presented mitigating circumstances that focused on his "troubled youth," that included his parents' divorce when he was five, his life until age fourteen with a mother who set no rules and offered no supervision, and from there to his life with his physically abusive father.[152] In addition, testimony was presented that indicated that Eddings "was emotionally disturbed in general and at the time of the crime, and that his mental and emotional development were at least several years below his age."[153] There was testimony as well from a psychiatrist who stated that "Eddings had a sociopathic or antisocial personality and that approximately 30% of youths suffering from such a disorder grew out of it as they aged."[154] There was testimony from a sociologist who claimed "that Eddings was treatable" and from a psychiatrist who testified "that Eddings could be rehabilitated by intensive therapy over a 15- to 20-year period."[155]

The trial judge sentenced Eddings to death on the basis of the three aggravating circumstances. The only relevant mitigating circumstance the trial judge noted was Eddings's age. On appeal, "[t]he Court of Criminal Appeals affirmed the sentence of death."[156] On the basis that these courts had failed to take the mitigating circumstances into consideration, the Supreme Court overturned Eddings's death sentence.

Justice Powell, for the Court, based his decision on a rule that Chief Justice Burger enunciated in *Lockett*, namely, " '[W]e conclude that the Eighth and Fourteenth Amendments require that the sentencer . . . not be precluded from considering, as a mitigating factor, any aspect of a defendant's character or record and any of the circumstances of the offense that the defendant proffers as a basis for a sentence less than death.'"[157] Neither the trial judge nor the Court of Appeals considered the mitigating circumstances in Eddings life relevant to sentencing, with the exception that his age was noted. But other evidence was clearly ignored. Why, for example, is a traumatic divorce irrelevant in evaluating Eddings's behavior? Why ignore the fact that for several years Eddings was raised by a mother apparently oblivious to her son's needs? Why ignore the beatings of Eddings's father? The answers to these questions may or may not be relevant. But they must be considered. Powell writes that "[t]he sentencer, and the Court of Criminal Appeals on review, may determine the weight to be given relevant mitigating evidence. But they may not give it no weight by excluding such evidence from their consideration."[158]

Consequently, the Court overturned Eddings's death sentence and returned his case to Oklahoma to consider fully the relevance and strength of the mitigating circumstances.

Chief Justice Burger, joined by Justices White, Blackmun, and Rehnquist, dissents. Burger begins his dissent by noting that the Supreme Court agreed to hear this case to determine "whether the Eighth and Fourteenth Amendments prohibit the imposition of a death sentence on an offender because he was 16 years old in 1977 at the time he committed the offense."[159] Burger finds no justification for the Court's majority to go to the length it did to reach the decision it did. Indeed, Burger argues that the trial court judge's apparent dismissal of Eddings's mitigating circumstances does not necessarily imply that those circumstances were ignored. There is no way to know how those circumstances were weighed. It is entirely possible that the court considered Eddings's youth and family background and found that those circumstances did not offset the aggravating circumstances.[160]

Chief Justice Burger acknowledges that states must consider all mitigating circumstances. He stresses the point, however, that it is not the Supreme Court's responsibility to dictate the weight assigned to those circumstances. He maintains that *Lockett* holds only that all mitigating circumstances be considered. "We did not, however, undertake to dictate the weight that a sentencing court must ascribe to the various factors that might be categorized as 'mitigating', nor did we in any way suggest that this Court may substitute its sentencing judgment for that of state courts in capital cases."[161] Burger would have affirmed the judgments of both Oklahoma courts.

ENMUND V. FLORIDA

In *Enmund v. Florida* (458 U.S. 782 [1982] [argued 3/23/82; decided 7/2/82]), Enmund was tried, convicted, and sentenced to death in the killing of Thomas and Eunice Kersey. Enmund did not directly participate in the Kersey robbery or killings. He did, however, drive the getaway car.

Justice White, for the Court, overturns Enmund's death penalty sentence on the basis "that imposition of the death penalty in these circumstances is inconsistent with the Eighth and Fourteenth Amendments."[162] Comparing *Enmund* to *Coker* reveals a similar retributive principle, namely, punishments should not be excessive or disproportionate to the crime committed. White examines as well the practices in other states and finds that, for the most part, those states would not try Enmund for first-degree murder, much less expose him to the possibility of a death sentence.[163] White also examines the practices of juries in similar cases and again finds that most juries view the death penalty as excessive for people in similar situations as Enmund. "The evidence is overwhelming that American juries have repudiated imposition of the death penalty for crimes such as petitioner's."[164] For White, to punish someone "who aids and abets a felony in the course of which a murder is committed by others but who does not himself kill, attempt to kill, or intend that a killing take place or that lethal force will be employed,"[165] constitutes a cruel and unusual punishment in violation of the Eighth Amendment.

Justice White raises as well the relationship between Enmund's punishment and the twin justifications for punishment—retribution and deterrence. For White, "[u]nless the death penalty when applied to those in Enmund's position measurably contributes to one or both of these goals [retribution and deterrence], it 'is nothing more than the purposeless and needless imposition of pain and suffering,' and hence an unconstitutional punishment."[166] White develops these ideas more fully. As for deterrence, there is no convincing evidence, White argues, that suggests that the death penalty could serve as a deterrent to those who commit a felony in which killing was not an integral element of the crime. By and large, so few killings occur in the course of robberies that the death penalty would not be effective to deter would-be robbers. And retribution certainly is not served due to the difference in the degree of involvement, intent, and execution.[167] He concludes:

> For purposes of imposing the death penalty, Enmund's criminal culpability must be limited to his participation in the robbery, and his punishment must be tailored to his personal responsibility and moral guilt. Putting Enmund to death to avenge two killings that he did not commit and had no intention of committing or causing does not measurably contribute to the retributive end of ensuring that the criminal gets his just deserts. This is the judgment of most of the legislatures that have recently addressed the matter, and we have no reason to disagree with that judgment for purposes of construing and applying the Eighth Amendment.[168]

The death penalty for Enmund was overturned. The Court, however, was not unanimous.

Justice O'Connor, joined by Chief Justice Burger and Justices Powell and Rehnquist, dissents. O'Connor notes that the aggravating circumstances outweighed the mitigating circumstances. Indeed, there were no mitigating circumstances that applied to Enmund. In addition, Enmund was not a "'relatively minor'" player in the robbery. He participated in its planning and execution. That he was not directly involved in the killings is irrelevant for O'Connor. For example, "he 'planned the capital felony and actively participated in an attempt to avoid detection by disposing of the murder weapons.'"[169] O'Connor writes that "[u]nder Florida law at the time of the murders, 'if the accused was present aiding and abetting the commission or attempt of one of the violent felonies listed in the first-degree murder statute, he is equally guilty, with the actual perpetrator of the underlying felony, of first-degree murder.'"[170]

Fortunately for Enmund, only three Justices supported O'Connor's position.

ZANT V. STEPHENS

If a jury sentences a person to the death penalty on the basis of three aggravating circumstances and one of those circumstances turns out to be constitutionally illegitimate, does that finding nullify the sentence? In *Zant v. Stephens* (462 U.S. 862 [1983] [argued 2/24/82; decided 6/22/83]), the Supreme Court of Georgia, in reviewing Zant's trial, ruled that one of the three aggravating circumstances identified by the jury was invalid. Specifically, the first aggravating circumstance identified by the jury contained the constitutionally ambiguous phrase, "the offense of murder was committed by a person who has a substantial history of serious assaultive criminal convictions."[171] That finding did not nullify the sentence of death because "the two other aggravating circumstances adequately supported the sentence."[172]

The Supreme Court considered three separate questions relevant to Justice Stevens's conviction, only one of which needs to be noted here, namely, Does the finding of an invalid aggravating circumstance among one or more valid aggravating circumstances nullify the sentence of death? Stephens "contends that the death sentence was impaired because the judge instructed the jury with regard to an invalid statutory aggravating circumstance, [namely], a 'substantial history of serious assaultive criminal convictions.'" Stevens argues that an invalid aggravating circumstance does not undermine an otherwise constitutional finding.[173]

Justice Stevens maintains that the mandatory review of all death sentences in Georgia by the Georgia Supreme Court protects defendants from the arbitrary and capricious use of that penalty. Had the Georgia Supreme Court found that one constitutionally invalid statutory aggravating circumstance weighed substantively in the jury's decision, Stevens believes that the Georgia Supreme Court would have overturned that verdict. He writes, "We accept that court's view that the subsequent invalidation of one of several statutory aggravating circumstances does not automatically require reversal of the death penalty, having been assured that a death sentence will be set aside if the invalidation of an aggravating circumstance makes the penalty arbitrary or capricious."[174]

Justice Marshall, joined by Justice Brennan, dissents. Marshall argues that the invalid aggravating circumstance could have had an undue influence on the jury's decision. He maintains that "[t]here is no way of knowing whether the jury would have sentenced respondent to death if its attention had not been drawn to the unconstitutional statutory factor.[175]

Justice Marshall, in repeating his claims about the death penalty's unconstitutionality, focuses throughout his dissent on the potential influence that an unconstitutional aggravating circumstance could have had in jury deliberations. For example, he writes, "There is no basis for the Court's assumption that the jury did not attribute special significance to the statutory aggravating circumstances and did not weigh them, along with any other evidence in aggravation, against the evidence offered by respondent in mitigation."[176]

Justice Marshall refers here to the fundamental issues in *Furman* and *Gregg*, namely, juries need guidance in sentence determination to prevent defendants from being sentenced to death arbitrarily and capriciously. If unconstitutional statutory aggravating circumstances are before the jury, along with constitutional aggravating circumstances, is the jury really capable to distinguish between those defendants who deserve the death penalty and those who do not? For Marshall, the Court has ignored the substance of *Furman* and *Gregg*, thereby allowing juries to decide life and death matters without clearly defined guidelines.

BARCLAY V. FLORIDA

Barclay v. Florida (463 U.S. 939 [1983] [argued 3/30/83; decided 7/6/83]), like *Zant*, raised a constitutional question about the use of a non-statutory aggravating circumstance to sentence a person to death. Justice Rehnquist, for the Court, stated the issue in *Barclay*: "The central question in this case is whether Florida may constitutionally impose the death penalty on petitioner Elwood Barclay when one of the 'aggravating circumstances' relied upon by the trial judge to support the sentence was not among those established by the Florida death penalty statute."[177] Barclay claimed that the use of his prior criminal record was *not* a proper aggravating circumstance. Florida agreed that "[t]he State concedes that this is correct: Florida law plainly provides that a defendant's prior record is not a proper 'aggravating circumstance.'"[178]

Does the finding of one illegitimate aggravating circumstance, however, taint the entire judgment? Florida law required the finding of at least one aggravating circumstance before the death penalty could be imposed. In addition, aggravating and mitigating circumstances must be balanced and weighed, although no special standard exists to guide the weighing.[179] For the Florida Supreme Court, the finding of one invalid aggravating circumstance in most cases does not jeopardize the imposed sentence. The Florida Supreme Court weighs the constitutionally unsound aggravating circumstance against the remaining constitutionally sound aggravating circumstances. Based on the weighing of the aggravating circumstances, the use of one unconstitutionally sound aggravating circumstance constitutes "harmless error." In other words, the absence of that aggravating circumstance would not change the outcome of the sentence determination. Justice Rehnquist writes, "The crux of the issue, then, is whether the trial judge's consideration of this improper aggravating circumstance so infects the balancing process created by the Florida statute that it is constitutionally impermissible for the Florida Supreme Court to let the sentence stand."[180] Rehnquist does not find sufficient error to overturn Barclay's sentence. As long as no specific constitutional rights have been abridged—for example, a death sentence based solely on a nonstatutory aggravating circumstance— then the Court will not intervene in a state court decision. Rehnquist finds "no reason why the Florida Supreme Court cannot examine the balance struck by the trial judge and decide that the elimination of improperly considered aggravating circumstances could not possibly affect the balance."[181] Rehnquist then quotes from *Zant* to clarify: "'What is important . . . is an *individualized* determination on the basis of the character of the individual and the circumstances of the crime.'"[182]

Justice Marshall, joined by Justice Brennan, dissents. Marshall, in contrast to the Court's majority, does find constitutional error in the procedures that resulted in Barclay's death sentence. He writes, "The procedures by which Elwood Barclay was condemned to die cannot pass constitutional muster. First, the trial judge's reliance on aggravating circumstances not permitted under the Florida death penalty scheme is constitutional error that cannot be harmless. Second, the Florida Supreme Court's failure to conduct any meaningful review of the death sentence deprived petitioner of a safeguard that the Court has deemed indispensable to a constitutional capital sentencing scheme."[183] For Marshall, Florida has ignored its own statutory procedural requirements and thereby reintroduced whim and caprice into the sentencing system. The use of any nonstatutory aggravating circumstances, as Marshall recognized in *Zant*, introduces whim and caprice into the sentencing process.[184]

PULLEY V. HARRIS

Georgia and Florida use proportionality review as a means to guarantee that the death penalty is not imposed arbitrarily and capriciously. That is one method to insure against an arbitrary imposition of the death penalty as set forth in *Furman*. California, however, does not have proportionality review as part of its statutory review of death penalty sentences. In *Pulley v. Harris* (465 U.S. 37 [1984] [argued 11/7/83; decided 1/23/84]), Harris, convicted of murder and sentenced to die in California, claimed that without proportional review his sentence may be disproportionate to sentences imposed for similar kinds of murder cases. If that is the case, then the requirements of *Furman*—to impose the death penalty in a consistent, clear, and coherent way—have not been met. The Supreme Court does not agree that proportional review is an essential requirement in death penalty reviews. Justice White, for the Court, states the issue clearly and succinctly: "Harris claimed on appeal that the California capital punishment statute was invalid under the United States Constitution because it failed to require the California Supreme Court to compare Harris' sentence with the sentences imposed in similar capital cases and thereby to determine whether they were proportionate."[185]

Justice White acknowledges that the Court has on occasion "struck down punishments as inherently disproportionate, and therefore cruel and unusual, when imposed for a particular crime or category of crime."[186] There is a difference, however, between proportionality review to ensure that a given punishment is not out of line with a given crime and whether a given punishment is disproportionate to sentences for similar types of crime. For example, in *Coker* the Court found the death penalty to be disproportionate for the crime of rape. Even if every rapist, without exception, received the death penalty, the death penalty would still be cruel and unusual because the punishment does not fit the crime. This position reflects the retributive test of proportionality. What Harris seeks is not that the death penalty is disproportionate in the retributive sense but rather that without proportionality review, his sentence may be unconstitutionally disproportionate with sentences handed down to similar murders. White states that "this sort of proportionality review presumes that the death sentence is not disproportionate to the crime in the traditional [retributive] sense. It purports to inquire instead whether the penalty is nonetheless unacceptable in a particular case because disproportionate to the punishment imposed on others convicted of the same crime."[187]

Justice White argues that California's guidelines to juries provide sufficient protection from arbitrary and capricious judgments. In addition, White acknowledges that no system will be foolproof. "Any capital sentencing scheme may occasionally produce aberrational outcomes. Such inconsistencies are a far cry from the major systemic defects identified in *Furman*."[188] Proportionality review of death sentences, then, is not constitutionally mandatory, for several methods exist to guarantee that death sentences are not handed down capriciously.

Justice Brennan, joined by Justice Marshall, dissents. Brennan would constitutionally mandate proportionality review even if it only prevented a few questionable executions. He maintains that the results in states with proportionality review indicate that the practice "serves to eliminate some, if only a small part, of the irrationality that infects the current imposition of death sentences throughout the various States."[189]

WAINWRIGHT V. WITT

Witherspoon and *Adams* are revisited in *Wainwright v. Witt* (469 U.S. 412 [1985] [argued 10/2/84; decided 1/21/85]). The issue once again involves jury selection in a capital case. The question is, What beliefs must jurors hold relative to capital punishment to exclude them automatically from jury duty in capital cases?

Convicted of and sentenced to death for first-degree murder in Florida, Witt centered his hope for a new trial and a reduced sentence on the jury selection process. One of the potential jurors stated during voir dire that her opinion on the death penalty would "interfere with judging the guilt or innocence of the Defendant."[190] She was not allowed to serve on the jury as she might not be able to do what the law could require her to do, namely, bring in a death sentence. The issue of jury selection was raised originally in *Witherspoon*. Fundamentally, the Court in *Witherspoon* held that jurors could not be excluded simply because they may have some reservations about the death penalty. Justice Rehnquist, for the Court, quotes the standard in *Witherspoon* as follows: "[A] sentence of death cannot be carried out if the jury that imposed or recommended it was chosen by excluding veniremen for cause simply because they voiced general objections to the death penalty or expressed conscientious or religious scruples against its infliction."[191]

Justice Rehnquist finds the *Adams* standard, especially after *Furman* and *Gregg*, to be realistic. States cannot be frustrated in their efforts to enforce their statutes. Rehnquist explains that the state and the people need "jurors who will conscientiously apply the law and find the facts."[192] States need jurors who will not thwart the states' efforts to impose a constitutionally just punishment. In other words, Rehnquist restates the standard in *Adams* that jurors can be dismissed if their "views 'would prevent or substantially impair the performance of [their] duties as a juror in accordance with [their] instructions and [their] oath."[193]

Justice Brennan, joined by Justice Marshall, dissents. Brennan's concern remains directed to death-qualified juries. He argues that a decision, especially one that involves life or death, must be made by juries that compose a reasonable cross-section of society. Only then can there be the greatest likelihood that a defendant will receive a fair, unbiased hearing. Juries composed of people who have no qualms about the death penalty are, for Brennan, more likely to be biased against the defendant. After offering his own historical review of *Witherspoon*, Brennan argues that the exclusion of potential jurors opposed to the death penalty cannot help but result in a conviction-prone jury.[194]

For Justice Brennan, the Court's decision in *Witt* can only narrow the rights of defendants in capital cases. In essence, the Sixth Amendment's guarantee of a trial "by an impartial jury of the State and district wherein the crime shall have been committed" has been further eroded.

CALDWELL V. MISSISSIPPI

Caldwell v. Mississippi (472 U.S. 320 [1985] [argued 2/25/85; decided 6/11/85]) presents a procedural issue that focuses on a jury's ability to reach a decision free from undue influence on the prosecutor's side. Here the prosecutor informed the jury that its decision is not final, that all death sentences are automatically reviewed by the Mississippi Supreme Court. Would such an instruction from a prosecutor free a jury from serious reflection and decision making in a capital case? For example, some jurors might feel hesitant to bring in a death penalty sentence in close cases in which the evidence for guilt is sufficient but in which the aggravating and mitigating circumstances leave a jury uncertain about whether to impose the death penalty. Being reminded that in capital cases a sentence of death will be scrutinized on automatic appeal could allow a jury to reach a death penalty sentence knowing that it is not responsible for the death of a defendant. Justice Marshall, for the Court, maintains precisely that and vacates the death penalty sentence in this case. Marshall, for the Court, reverses the death penalty sentence here precisely because that instruction could have tainted the jury's considerations and decision.

Justice Marshall argues that no person should be subject to the death penalty by a jury that has been led to believe that it does not need to be all that concerned about recommending a death sentence. He states that "it is constitutionally impermissible to rest a death sentence on a determination made by a sentencer who has been led to believe that the responsibility for determining the appropriateness of the defendant's death rests elsewhere."[195] For Marshall, such an instruction makes it possible that a jury can feel less concerned about any error knowing that such an error can be corrected on appeal.[196]

Justice Rehnquist, joined by Chief Justice Burger and Justice White, dissents. He maintains that the Court has "overstated the seriousness of the prosecutor's remarks."[197] The focus of the Court's inquiry should have been directed to determine if prosecutorial remarks "rendered the proceedings as a whole fundamentally unfair."[198] For Rehnquist, even in light of the need in capital cases to proceed carefully, there is no basis on which the Court could reach objectively the decision it did.

SKIPPER V. SOUTH CAROLINA

Upon Skipper's conviction of capital murder in *Skipper v. South Carolina* (476 U.S. 1 [1986] [argued 2/24/86; decided 4/29/86]), South Carolina commenced the sentencing hearing. The state produced its list of aggravating circumstances and Skipper produced evidence in mitigation. Unfortunately, he was denied the opportunity to present all the evidence he wanted to submit. "Petitioner also sought to introduce testimony of two jailers and one 'regular visitor' to the jail to the effect that petitioner had 'made a good adjustment' during his time spent in jail."[199]

The jury sentenced Skipper to death. His appeal was based on what he considered an unconstitutional denial of all available mitigating circumstances. Justice White, for the Court, compares Skipper's case to *Lockett* and *Eddings*. White, quoting from *Eddings*, holds "that, in capital cases, 'the sentencer . . . not be precluded from considering, as a mitigating factor, any aspect of a defendant's character or record and any of the circumstances of the offense that the defendant proffers as a basis for a sentence less than death.'"[200]

Justice White argues that there can be no doubt but that Skipper was denied his constitutional rights to present any evidence, however remote, in mitigation. Even if the evidence does not relate directly to the crime, it could affect a jury's sentencing considerations. It could, for example, produce a sentence of life imprisonment with or without parole. Again, when life is at stake, it is incumbent to weigh all available evidence in mitigation. For example, the prosecutor, in his closing remarks to the jury, stated that Skipper "would pose disciplinary problems if sentenced to prison and would likely rape other prisoners."[201] Skipper, however, was precluded "from introducing otherwise admissible evidence for the explicit purpose of convincing the jury that he should be spared the death penalty because he would pose no undue danger to his jailers or fellow prisoners, and could lead a useful life behind bars if sentenced to life imprisonment."[202] Skipper's death sentence, as Eddings's, was overturned.

TURNER V. MURRAY

Turner v. Murray (476 U.S. 28 [1986] [argued 12/12/85; decided 4/30/86]) confronts the United States with a 350-year-old problem, namely, race. As noxious as the reality is that the race factor enters a courtroom, it is made all the more odious when a conviction results in a death sentence. One can reasonably ask even today, have things changed that much from 1986 when *Turner* was considered?

Turner was convicted of and sentenced to death for capital murder in the robbery/murder of a jewelry store owner. Turner was black and the victim was white.[203] Turner "requested and was granted a change of venue to Northampton County, Virginia some 80 miles from the location of the murder."[204] At voir dire, Turner's lawyer submitted several questions to the judge to ask prospective jurors, including the following: "The defendant, Willie Lloyd Turner, is a member of the Negro race. The victim, W. Jack Smith, Jr., was a white Caucasian.[205] Will these facts prejudice you against Willie Lloyd Turner or affect your ability to render a fair and impartial verdict based solely on the evidence?"[206]

The judge refused to ask that question, but he did ask the prospective jurors "whether any person was aware of any reason why he could not render a fair and impartial verdict, to which all answered 'no.'"[207] However, "the prospective jurors had no way of knowing that the murder victim was white."[208]

The jury, comprised "of eight whites and four blacks,"[209] convicted Turner and, after a sentencing hearing, recommended the death penalty. The judge accepted the recommendation and sentenced Turner to death. Turner appealed the conviction and sentence on the ground of the possibility of racial bias. After several appeals at all levels, the Supreme Court ruled that Turner's conviction must stand but that the death penalty must be vacated due to the possibility of racial bias, especially in Virginia, where the jury enjoys a greater discretion in sentence consideration than on other states. Justice White, for the Court, states that "Virginia's death-penalty statute gives the jury greater discretion than other systems which we have upheld against constitutional challenge."[210] Given as well that jurors make all kinds of subjective judgments in capital cases on the basis of individual uniqueness, the situation is ripe for hidden racial judgments. White concludes:

We hold that a capital defendant accused of an interracial crime is entitled to have prospective jurors informed of the race of the victim and questioned on the issue of racial bias. The rule we propose is minimally intrusive; as in other cases involving "special circumstances," the trial judge retains discretion as to the form and number of questions on the subject, including the decision whether to question the venire individually or collectively. Also, a defendant cannot complain of a judge's failure to question the venire on racial prejudice unless the defendant has specifically requested such an inquiry.[211]

Justice Brennan, concurring in part and dissenting in part, argues that this issue can be resolved easily by asking the question the defense attorney requested be asked, namely, "[t]he defendant, Willie Lloyd Turner, is a member of the Negro race. The victim, W. Jack Smith, Jr., was a white Caucasian. Will these facts prejudice you against Willie Lloyd Turner or affect your ability to render a fair and impartial verdict based solely on the evidence?"

There is another issue here, however, that the Court's majority has completely overlooked or ignored, namely, any "prejudice" would affect not only the sentencing judgment but also the guilt judgment. For Justice Brennan, the entire case should be overturned and reheard with a jury that has been screened for prejudice. For Brennan, the entire trial was contaminated.

A trial to determine guilt or innocence is, at bottom, nothing more than the sum total of a countless number of small discretionary decisions made by each individual who sits in the jury box. The difference between conviction and acquittal turns on whether key testimony is believed or rejected; on whether an alibi sounds plausible or dubious; on whether a character witness appears trustworthy or unsavory; and on whether the jury concludes that the defendant had a motive, the inclination, or the means available to commit the crime charged. A racially biased juror sits with blurred vision and impaired sensibilities, and is incapable of fairly making the myriad decisions that each juror is called upon to make in the course of a trial. To put it simply, he cannot judge, because he has prejudged. This is equally true at the trial on guilt as at the hearing on sentencing.[212]

FORD V. WAINWRIGHT

One of the pillars of civilized society holds that some people are not responsible for their acts due to insanity. People will disagree about how that term is defined, or even if there is such a thing, but most people recognize, without argument, that punishing people who have no idea what it is they did or who could not understand the wrongfulness of what they did should not be punished. Punishment, for such cases, can rarely be justified according to any of the traditional justifications of punishment. For example, is retributivism served by punishing mentally ill people for acts committed as a direct result of that illness? A retributivist, in general, requires that a people can be punished for criminal wrongdoing only if they had intended it, planned it, and executed it. In terms of deterrence theory, how will punishing people who do not understand what they are doing or have done serve as a deterrent? In essence, punishing people for acts that they could not understand were criminal carries no deterrent meaning and serves no deterrent purpose, general or specific.[213] So I assume, without argument, that there are people who cannot be punished legitimately under any justifiable punishment model. But what happens if a person is completely sane at the time of the trial, knows clearly and unmistakably why he or she acted in that particular manner, was found guilty and sentenced to death, and then goes insane while awaiting execution? Can society carry out the execution knowing that the person being executed no longer understands anything about what is about to happen, or why it is about to happen? *Ford v. Wainwright* (477 U.S. 399 [1986] [argued 4/22/86; decided 6/26/86]) raises just that problem.

Justice Marshall, for the Court, reviews Ford's history of incarceration as he sat on death row:

After reading in the newspaper that the Ku Klux Klan had held a rally in nearby Jacksonville, Florida, Ford developed an obsession focused upon the Klan. His letters to various people reveal endless brooding about his "Klan work," and an increasingly pervasive delusion that he had become the target of a complex conspiracy, involving the Klan and assorted others, designed to force him to commit suicide. He believed that the prison guards, part of the conspiracy, had been killing people and putting the bodies in the concrete enclosures used for beds. Later, he began to believe that his women relatives were being tortured and sexually abused somewhere in the prison. This notion developed into a delusion that the people who were tormenting him at the prison had taken members of Ford's family hostage. The hostage delusion took firm hold and expanded, until Ford was reporting that 135 of his friends and family were being held hostage in the prison, and that only he could help them. By "day 287" of the "hostage crisis," the list of hostages had expanded to include "senators, Senator Kennedy, and many other leaders."[214]

There is no question but that Ford was sane at the time of the crime, the trial and conviction, and the sentence in 1974. But by 1982, Ford had developed aberrational behavior, consistent with Justice Marshall's description. Ford was examined by a psychiatrist who "concluded in 1983 that Ford suffered from 'a severe, uncontrollable, mental disease which closely resembles 'Paranoid Schizophrenia With Suicide Potential'—a 'major mental disorder . . . severe enough to substantially affect Mr. Ford's present ability to assist in the defense of his life.'"[215]

Florida's governor appointed three psychiatrists to determine if Ford was sufficiently sane to be put to death. Although all three psychiatrists found Ford's behavior slightly abnormal, they all agreed that he could be put to death because he did understand why he was being executed. The governor then signed a death warrant for Ford's execution. After several appeals to stay Ford's execution, the Supreme Court "granted Ford's petition for certiorari in order to resolve the important issue whether the Eighth Amendment prohibits the execution of the insane and, if so, whether the District Court should have held a hearing on petitioner's claim."[216]

Justice Marshall develops at great length the limitations in Florida's procedures at that time to guard against the execution of a person who has gone insane while awaiting execution.[217] Just as there are procedures to protect the defendant at trial, there must be procedures that provide for an objective review of a prisoner's mental state while in prison. The procedures in Florida at the time did not offer Ford the constitutional guarantees Marshall believes are critical to a civilized society. Just as standards have been developed to distinguish among those persons who deserve the death penalty and those who do not, procedures must be developed to protect those who may no longer understand why they are to be executed. Even though standards and procedures may differ slightly from state to state, the overall process must afford defendants guarantees to protect against unconstitutional executions. Florida's procedures simply do not offer the protection the Eighth Amendment guarantees.[218]

Justice Rehnquist, joined by Chief Justice Burger, dissents. His conclusion provides a good review of his position on this case.

Creating a constitutional right to a judicial determination of sanity before that sentence may be carried out, whether through the Eighth Amendment or the Due

Process Clause, needlessly complicates and postpones still further any finality in this area of the law. The defendant has already had a full trial on the issue of guilt, and a trial on the issue of penalty; the requirement of still a third adjudication offers an invitation to those who have nothing to lose by accepting it to advance entirely spurious claims of insanity. A claim of insanity may be made at any time before sentence and, once rejected, may be raised again; a prisoner found sane two days before execution might claim to have lost his sanity the next day, thus necessitating another judicial determination of his sanity, and presumably another stay of his execution.[219]

TISON V. ARIZONA

In *Tison v. Arizona* (481 U.S. 137 [1987] [argued 11/3/86; decided 4/21/87]), Ricky and Raymond Tison had been charged with murder, convicted, and sentenced to death despite the fact that they had neither killed anyone nor had any intention to kill anyone. They had, however, helped their father escape from an Arizona prison, a father who was in prison in part for killing a guard in an earlier attempted prison escape.[220] They were tried under Arizona law that at the time left the sentencing decision to the judge "to determine whether the crime was sufficiently aggravated to warrant the death sentence."[221] The judge, finding three statutory aggravating circumstances, no statutory mitigating circumstances, and three nonstatutory mitigating circumstances, weighed the aggravating and mitigating circumstances and sentenced the Tison brothers to death.[222]

The defense argued, in part, that *Enmund* precluded sentencing people to death who had no intention to kill and had not participated in the actual murder(s). The involvement of Ricky and Raymond in this case, however, differs substantively from the driver of the getaway car in *Enmund*.[223] For example, Ricky and Raymond knew their father would not hesitate to kill in order to escape. In addition, they brought an arsenal of weapons with them to the prison to effect the escape. They participated in the entire planning process of the escape, and they knew lives would be in danger. That simply was not the case with the driver of the getaway car in *Enmund*.

Justice O'Connor notes that justifications for punishment are not served in *Enmund* whereas in *Tison* they are. For example, the Court in *Enmund* "found that neither the deterrent nor the retributive purposes of the death penalty were advanced by imposing the death penalty on Enmund."[224]

Traditionally, punishments have been morally and constitutionally challenged if they are too lenient or too severe. In general, people who do not kill or who do not intend to kill, do not merit the death penalty. Justice O'Connor holds, however, "that substantial participation in a violent felony under circumstances likely to result in the loss of innocent human life may justify the death penalty even absent an 'intent to kill.'"[225] In addition, she argues "that the reckless disregard for human life implicit in knowingly engaging in criminal activities known to carry a grave risk of death represents a highly culpable mental state, a mental state that may be taken into account in making a capital sentencing judgment when that conduct causes its natural, though also not inevitable, lethal result."[226] Under these criteria, the Tisons merited the death penalty.

Justice Brennan, joined by Justice Marshall and in part by Justices Blackmun and Stevens, dissents. Although Brennan opposes the death penalty on both moral and constitutional grounds, he finds the death penalty in this case particularly odious on retributive grounds, namely, "a felon [should not] be executed for a murder that he or she did not commit or specifically intend or attempt to commit."[227] In addition, Brennan finds sufficient ambiguities in the sentencing process that should overturn the Tisons' death penalty. For example, the trial court gave insufficient attention to the Tisons' mental states, to their complete lack of involvement in the murders, and to their "expressed feelings of surprise, helplessness, and regret."[228] Brennan argues additionally that the Court failed to consider as relevant a proportionality review, namely, does the Tisons' punishment really fit the crime?[229] For Brennan, the Tisons' death penalty clearly ignores the retributive principle that criminals get their just deserts. For him, "'a person who has not in fact killed, attempted to kill, or intended that a killing take place or that lethal force be used may not be sentenced to death.'"[230] For Brennan, no constitutional or moral principles can sustain the use of the death penalty in this case.

MCCLESKEY V. KEMP

If someone could establish beyond a reasonable doubt[231] that discrimination occurs in sentence determination, the death penalty would have to be suspended again as it was in *Furman*. As it turns out, there are a few statistical studies that indicate that the death penalty continues to be imposed more on black Americans than on white Americans. In *McCleskey v. Kemp* (481 U.S. 279 [1987] [argued 10/18/86; decided 4/22/87]), McCleskey takes those statistics as the basis of his appeal to reverse his death penalty sentence.[232] He argues that he has been denied the Fourteenth Amendment's equal protection of the laws clause on the basis of the discriminatory differences in sentencing blacks and whites to different punishments for similar crimes. Justice Powell offers several examples from the Baldus study, one of which will suffice to demonstrate the types of discriminatory patterns that can be found in the distribution of the death penalty. Powell writes that Baldus

found that the death penalty was assessed in 22% of the cases involving black defendants and white victims; 8% of the cases involving white defendants and white victims; 1% of the cases involving black defendants and black victims; and

3% of the cases involving white defendants and black victims. Similarly, Baldus found that prosecutors sought the death penalty in 70% of the cases involving black defendants and white victims; 32% of the cases involving white defendants and white victims; 15% of the cases involving black defendants and black victims; and 19% of the cases involving white defendants and black victims.[233]

The Court, however, rejects McCleskey's claim. Justice Powell, for example, argues that "a defendant who alleges an equal protection violation [has] the burden of proving 'the existence of purposeful discrimination.'" Powell also points out "that a criminal defendant must prove that the purposeful discrimination 'had a discriminatory effect' on him."[234] Powell claims that there is no evidence that would establish the validity of those claims. Powell argues, despite the Baldus study, that so many variables enter into a sentencing process that results in a death penalty that it might be impossible to ever account for apparent differences in sentencing decisions. He writes, "The unique nature of the decisions at issue in this case also counsels against adopting such an inference from the disparities indicated by the Baldus study. Accordingly, we hold that the Baldus study is clearly insufficient to support an inference that any of the decisionmakers in McCleskey's case acted with discriminatory purpose."[235]

Justice Brennan, joined by Justice Marshall and in part by Justice Blackmun, dissents. Brennan maintains that the Baldus studies do indeed indicate the presence of sentencing processes that may well result in an infringement of the equal protection of the laws clause. The facts, for Brennan, are disturbing. According to Brennan, if the Baldus studies reflect at least part of the truth in sentencing decisions, the possibility exists that a defense attorney would have to point out to black defendants that they would be more likely to get the death penalty since their victim was white. Paraphrasing Baldus, Brennan writes that the defense attorney would have to point out that "6 of every 11 defendants convicted of killing a white person would not have received the death penalty if their victims had been black."[236] Brennan adds that "the Baldus study . . . in light of both statistical principles and human experience, reveals that the risk that race influenced McCleskey's sentence is intolerable by any imaginable standard."[237] Accordingly, Brennan argues throughout his extended dissent that "evidence shows that there is a better than even chance in Georgia that race will influence the decision to impose the death penalty; a majority of defendants in white-victim crimes would not have been sentenced to die if their victims had been black."[238]

BOOTH V. MARYLAND

At issue in *Booth v. Maryland* (482 U.S. 496 [1987] [argued 3/24/87; decided 6/15/87]) is the inclusion of a victim impact statement (VIS) in a presentence report.[239] Prior to sentencing, "the State Division of Parole and Probation (DPP) compiled a presentence report that described Booth's background, education and employment history, and criminal record."[240] In addition, a presentence report contained a victim impact statement that described "the effect of the crime on the victim and his family."[241] Such reports contain any information relevant to sentencing, such as the economic impact on the family, the psychological trauma and loss the victim's family experience, and any physiological effects (such as a sudden inability to sleep).[242]

At least four considerations offer compelling reasons to disallow the use of victim impact statements. First, the focus of a criminal case should be on the defendant's guilt and degree of culpability or blameworthiness. For example, murderers "rarely select their victims based on whether the murder will have an effect on anyone other than the person murdered. Allowing the jury to rely on a VIS therefore could result in imposing the death sentence because of factors about which the defendant was unaware, and that were irrelevant to the decision to kill."[243]

Second, what happens when the victims have no family? Does that make the murder less offensive, less punishable?[244]

Third, would murdering a highly valuable member of the community be more reprehensible than murdering an incorrigible alcoholic?[245]

Fourth, can the information presented in a VIS be challenged? What if the victim's family exaggerated the importance of the family member? What if some of the family's statements were outright lies? As Justice Powell writes, "A threshold problem is that victim impact information is not easily susceptible to rebuttal."[246]

Justices White and Scalia offer separate dissenting opinions and are joined in those opinions by Chief Justice Rehnquist and Justice O'Connor. For these Justices, the consideration of the impact of a crime as heinous as murder introduces materially relevant evidence for jury consideration in sentencing. Just as there are distinctions of blameworthiness in criminal law (e.g., between first-degree murder and second-degree murder), so are there distinctions in punishment based on impact. The Justices here do not find any constitutional barrier to victim impact statements. Their dissent will soon become a majority opinion.[247]

LOWENFIELD V. PHELPS

In *Lowenfield v. Phelps* (484 U.S. 231 [1988] [argued 10/14/87; decided 1/13/88]), Lowenfield challenged his death sentence on two grounds. First, the trial court "coerced the jury to return a sentence of death."[248] Second, the aggravating circumstance used had already been used at the trial stage to obtain a guilty verdict and could not be used again at the sentencing stage without violating his due process rights.

The judge's instruction to the jury as it began its deliberations on the sentence "included the familiar admonition that the jurors should consider the views of others with the objective of reaching a verdict, but that they should not surrender their own honest beliefs in doing so."[249] After the jurors failed to reach agreement, the judge further instructed them that they should consult with one another, but that they should not change their opinion merely to bring the case to a close. In addition, the judge reiterated that a failure to reach a punishment would require the judge to sentence Lowenfield to "Life Imprisonment without benefit of Probation, Parole, or Suspension of Sentence."[250]

After that additional clarification, the jury returned in thirty minutes "with a verdict sentencing petitioner to death on all three counts of first-degree murder."[251] On its face, the verdict appears questionable. For several hours the jury was unable to reach any decision. Then, after further clarification from the judge, which included the point that if the jurors could not agree on a sentence the judge must sentence Lowenfield to life imprisonment. Lowenfield had been found guilty on three charges of first-degree murder. Did that additional instruction taint jury deliberations? Knowing that a murderer would be free to murder again, at least in prison, did the jurors decide that it was time for Lowenfield to die for his criminal wrongdoing? In short, did parts of the judge's instructions for jury deliberations contain, whether intentional or not, elements of coercion? After considering the various kinds of instruction that can be legitimately given, along with the recognition that defense counsel did not object to the instructions at the time those instructions were presented, Chief Justice Rehnquist holds that the instructions were not coercive elements. "We are mindful that the jury returned with its verdict soon after receiving the supplemental instruction, and that this suggests the possibility of coercion. We note, however, that defense counsel did not object to . . . the supplemental instruction. We do not suggest that petitioner thereby waived this issue, but we think such an omission indicates that the potential for coercion argued now was not apparent to one on the spot."[252]

The second appeal for dismissal rested on a claim that the use of a fact in the guilt stage of the trial could not be used as well at the sentencing phase of the trial. In other words, a defendant convicted of murder under a statute that is repeated as an aggravating circumstance at the sentencing stage appears to jeopardize the integrity of the judicial process. Chief Justice Rehnquist explains the alleged conflict as follows: "Petitioner was found guilty of three counts of first-degree murder: '[T]he offender has a specific intent to kill or to inflict great bodily harm upon more than one person.' The sole aggravating circumstance both found by the jury and upheld by the Louisiana Supreme Court was that 'the offender knowingly created a risk of death or great bodily harm to more than one person.' In these circumstances, these two provisions are interpreted in a 'parallel fashion' under Louisiana law. Petitioner's argument that the parallel nature of these provisions requires that his sentences be set aside rests on a mistaken premise as to the necessary role of aggravating circumstances."[253] This overlap, for Rehnquist, presents no constitutional difficulty. Aggravating circumstances merely narrow the use of the death penalty to particularly heinous murders. Rehnquist sees no reason why this narrowing function may not be performed by jury findings at either the sentencing phase of the trial or the guilt phase.[254] Rehnquist concludes, "There is no question but that the Louisiana scheme narrows the class of death-eligible murderers, and then, at the sentencing phase, allows for the consideration of mitigating circumstances and the exercise of discretion. The Constitution requires no more."[255]

Justice Marshall, joined by Justices Brennan and Stevens, dissents. Although Marshall acknowledges his general opposition to the death penalty, he bases his position here on the same facts as does the Court's majority. He claims, however, that these "facts" dictate a different outcome for two reasons.

First, the jury that sentenced Leslie Lowenfield was subjected during the penalty phase of the trial to a combination of practices that courts have viewed as coercive in far less sensitive situations. The use of these practices in this case presents an unacceptable risk that the jury returned a sentence of death for reasons having nothing to do with proper constitutional considerations. Second, even in the absence of coercion, the jury's sentence of death could not stand because it was based on a single statutory aggravating circumstance that duplicated an element of petitioner's underlying offense. This duplication prevented Louisiana's sentencing scheme from adequately guiding the discretion of the sentencing jury in this case, and relieved the jury of the requisite sense of responsibility for its sentencing decision. As we have recognized frequently in the past, such failings may have the effect of impermissibly biasing the sentencing process in favor of death in violation of the Eighth and the Fourteenth Amendments.[256]

Marshall finds that the process in Lowenfield's case easily could have denied him the unbiased hearing to which he is constitutionally entitled. Marshall concludes, "It is impossible to know what finally prompted the jury to return its sentence of death, but the coercive practices engaged in by the trial court, or the prosecutor's argument that a key aggravating circumstance already had been established at the guilt phase, may well have tipped the balance."[257] For Marshall, Lowenfield "was denied the individualized and reasoned consideration of his penalty that the Constitution promises him."[258]

SATTERWHITE V. TEXAS

Satterwhite v. Texas (486 U.S. 249 [1988] [argued 12/8/87; decided 5/31/88]) revisits *Estelle* regarding the introduction of psychiatric testimony into a trial, especially without having consulted with the defendant or the defendant's attorney. Justice O'Connor, for the Court, explains: "In *Estelle v. Smith* . . . we recognized that defendants formally charged with capital crimes have a Sixth Amendment right to consult with counsel before submitting to psychiatric examinations designed to determine their future dangerousness. The question in this case is whether it was harmless error to introduce psychiatric testimony obtained in violation of that safeguard in a capital sentencing proceeding."[259]

Before Satterwhite had counsel, Texas had Satterwhite examined by a psychologist, Betty Lou Schroeder, to determine if he was competent to stand trial, if he was sane when he committed the act, and if he posed future danger to the community. At the request of the district attorney, Satterwhite was examined a second time by Schroeder and by a psychiatrist, John T. Holbrook. Defense counsel was not notified of this exam. These exams occurred in March and April. Then, on May 3, 1979, another psychiatrist, James P. Grigson, examined Satterwhite "pursuant to a court order." In a May 18, 1979, letter to the trial court, Grigson wrote that "Satterwhite has 'a severe antisocial personality disorder and is extremely dangerous and will commit future acts of violence.'"[260]

Satterwhite was convicted of murder. At the sentencing hearing, and over the objections of defense counsel, "Dr. Grigson testified that, in his opinion, Satterwhite presented a continuing threat to society through acts of criminal violence."[261] Justice O'Connor explains the process of deliberation that will determine Satterwhite's sentence as follows: "At the conclusion of the evidence, the court instructed the jury to decide whether the State had proved, beyond a reasonable doubt, (1) that 'the conduct of the defendant that caused the death [was] committed deliberately and with the reasonable expectation that the death of [the victim] would result,' and (2) that there is 'a probability that the defendant would commit criminal acts of violence that would constitute a continuing threat to society.'"[262]

Justice O'Connor focuses her majority opinion on Grigson's testimony. If his testimony to Satterwhite's future dangerousness was considered by the jury in its deliberations, those deliberations would be suspect. O'Connor notes that the Texas Court of Criminal Appeals considered Grigson's testimony, at worst, as harmless error and that even without Grigson's testimony a reasonable jury would have concluded that Satterwhite posed continuing threats to society. The Texas Court of Criminal Appeals did not find Grigson's testimony problematic, especially in light of the evidence presented at the sentencing phase of the trial. For example, "Satterwhite had four prior convictions of crimes ranging from aggravated assault to armed robbery." There was testimony that Satterwhite shot one of his mother's husbands. Dr. Grigson's testimony, Texas argued, did not contribute to the jury's death penalty recommendation. O'Connor disagrees. She writes:

The finding of future dangerousness was critical to the death sentence. Dr. Grigson was the only psychiatrist to testify on this issue, and the prosecution placed significant weight on his powerful and unequivocal testimony. Having reviewed the evidence in this case, we find it impossible to say beyond a reasonable doubt that Dr. Grigson's expert testimony on the issue of Satterwhite's future dangerousness did not influence the sentencing jury. Accordingly, we reverse the judgment of the Texas Court of Criminal Appeals insofar as it affirms the death sentence, and we remand the case for further proceedings not inconsistent with this opinion.[263]

MAYNARD V. CARTWRIGHT

In *Maynard v. Cartwright* (486 U.S. 356 [1988] [argued 4/19/88; decided 6/6/88]), Cartwright had been convicted of murder and sentenced to death on the basis of two aggravating circumstances: "first, the defendant 'knowingly created a great risk of death to more than one person'; second, the murder was 'especially heinous, atrocious, or cruel.'"[264] After several appeals the Court of Appeals for the Tenth Circuit found that one of the two aggravating circumstances was invalid, namely, "the words 'heinous,' 'atrocious,' and 'cruel' did not, on their face, offer sufficient guidance to the jury to escape the strictures of our judgment in *Furman v. Georgia*."[265] In addition, the Oklahoma statute under which Cartwright was convicted and sentenced did not contain any provision that would allow for a reexamination of the death penalty when one of the aggravating circumstances was declared invalid. Accordingly, the Tenth Circuit reversed the death penalty conviction and returned the case to Oklahoma for further action.

Once again an aggravating circumstance comes under judicial scrutiny. The challenge here concerns the meaning of the phrase "heinous, atrocious, or cruel." What criteria, if any, will classify a murder as heinous, atrocious, or cruel? What makes these words unconstitutionally vague in a way that precludes their use in capital cases? Justice White, for the Court, explains the Court's understanding of the Oklahoma aggravating circumstance as follows:

As we understand the argument, it is that a statutory provision governing a criminal case is unconstitutionally vague only if there are no circumstances that could be said with reasonable certainty to fall within reach of the language at issue. Or, to put it another way, that if there are circumstances that any reasonable person would recognize as covered by the statute, it is not unconstitutionally vague even if the language would fail to give adequate notice that it covered other circumstances as well.[266]

Justice White argues that these terms remain sufficiently vague in a way that precludes jurors from distinguishing between defendants who deserve the death penalty and those who do not. The problem focuses again on *Furman* requirements that juries and judges have clear guidelines that enable them to make informed, reasonable, and defensible judgments. White writes, for example, that Oklahoma's aggravating circumstance of especially heinous, atrocious, or cruel "fails adequately to inform juries what they must find to impose the death penalty and as a result leaves them and appellate courts with the kind of open-ended discretion which was held invalid in *Furman*."[267] The death penalty, for White, cannot be imposed under aggravating circumstances that prove unconstitutionally vague.[268]

MILLS V. MARYLAND

While in prison, Mills murdered his cellmate, was found guilty in *Mills v. Maryland* (486 U.S. 367 [1988] [argued 3/30/88; decided 6/6/88]), and, as the jury found no mitigating circumstances, sentenced Mills to death. The Maryland capital punishment statute at the time Mills was convicted held that the death penalty would be imposed "if the jury unanimously found an aggravating circumstance, but could not agree unanimously as to the existence of any particular mitigating circumstance."[269]

Mills appealed his conviction in part on the fact that the jury could not consider any mitigating circumstances that were not agreed upon unanimously by the jury. In other words, if the jury found one aggravating circumstance but could not agree unanimously upon any mitigating circumstances, then the death penalty must be imposed. The result of such legislation must be, in certain situations, tantamount to the imposition of a mandatory death sentence which violates the Eighth and Fourteenth Amendments.

The Maryland Court of Appeals, however, did not accept Mills's interpretation of the Maryland capital punishment statute. The Maryland Court of Appeals agreed that, if jurors understood the statute as Mills claimed they did, then "jurors *would be* improperly prevented from giving due consideration to mitigating evidence."[270] The Appeals Court rejected Mills's interpretation. The Appeals Court held that the jury must be unanimous on any aggravating and mitigating circumstance before a judgment could be reached. Accordingly, if the jury cannot agree on any aggravating and mitigating circumstances, then "the statute required the imposition of life imprisonment."[271]

Justice Blackmun, for the Court, states that these two different interpretations of Maryland's capital punishment statute require Supreme Court review. He begins his analysis with two hypothetical situations, one put forth by Mills and one put forth by the dissent in the Maryland Court of Appeals. Blackmun quotes the following hypothetical situation from a brief for Mills: "If eleven jurors agree that there are six mitigating circumstances, the result is that no mitigating circumstance is found. Consequently, there is nothing to weigh against any aggravating circumstance found, and the judgment is death, even though eleven jurors think the death penalty wholly inappropriate."[272] Blackmun explains the hypothetical scenario from the dissent in the Appeals Court as follows: "All 12 jurors might agree that some mitigating circumstances were present, and even that those mitigating circumstances were significant enough to outweigh any aggravating circumstance found to exist. But unless all 12 could agree that the same mitigating circumstance was present, they would never be permitted to engage in the weighing process or any deliberation on the appropriateness of the death penalty."[273]

Justice Blackmun argues that it is not illogical to think the jury thought as Mills alleges. "While conceding that the Court of Appeals' construction of the jury instructions and verdict form is plausible, we cannot conclude, with any degree of certainty, that the jury did not adopt petitioner's interpretation of the jury instructions and verdict form."[274] After an extended analysis developing the potential problems in Maryland's capital punishment statute, Blackmun writes, "There is, of course, no extrinsic evidence of what the jury in this case actually thought. We have before us only the verdict form and the judge's instructions. Our reading of those parts of the record leads us to conclude that there is at least a substantial risk that the jury was misinformed."[275] Blackmun argues overall that the power to take life requires the closest scrutiny in death penalty decisions. Any ambiguities warrant judicial review, and any finding of any ambiguities warrants a reconsideration of the death penalty.

Chief Justice Rehnquist, joined by Justices O'Connor, Scalia, and Kennedy, dissents. Rehnquist does not find the ambiguity in Maryland's capital punishment statute as it relates to how juries are to reach decisions free from constitutional error. For Rehnquist, there is no evidence that indicates the jury was in any way confused about its task or how to proceed to carry out that task. Rehnquist emphasizes the trial court's instructions to the jury to explain why the alleged ambiguities did not exist in *Mills*.

Over and over again, the trial court exhorted the jury that *every* determination made on the sentencing form had to be a unanimous one. This repeated emphasis . . . simply had to alert the jury to the requirement of unanimity. To conclude otherwise, as the Court does, applies to the deliberations of jurors and the instructions of judges a requirement of freedom from any ambiguity more suitable to mathematics or the physical sciences than to the affairs of human beings.[276]

Chief Justice Rehnquist argues that the assumptions attributable to the jury by the Court cannot be sustained. For Rehnquist, "the instructions on the sentencing form and the charges given to the jury in this case are constitutionally unexceptionable, and petitioner's sentence should be upheld."[277]

THOMPSON V. OKLAHOMA

The United States has a history of executing children for their criminal wrongdoing.[278] Thompson was "15 years old at the time of his offense."[279] He was convicted and sentenced to death. The execution of a person whose crime was committed at fifteen years of age raises the following question: Is it a violation of the Eighth Amendment's cruel and unusual punishment clause to execute someone for a murder committed as a juvenile? Oklahoma tried Thompson as an adult in *Thompson v. Oklahoma* (487 U.S. 815 [1988] [argued 11/9/887; decided 6/29/88]). The jury that convicted and sentenced him based its death penalty determination on one aggravating circumstance, namely, "that the murder was *especially heinous, atrocious, or cruel.*"[280]

By way of analogy, Justice Stevens, for the Court, examines some of the laws that apply characteristically to juveniles in Oklahoma. For example, juveniles in Oklahoma cannot vote, sit on juries, get married without parental approval, or purchase alcohol or tobacco products. In addition, "most offenders under the age of 18 are not criminally responsible." However, there are statutes that allow for the death penalty for children sixteen and seventeen years of age to be tried as an adult. In addition, "there are no Oklahoma statutes, either civil or criminal, that treat a person under 16 years of age as anything but a 'child.'"[281] Stevens also points out that the death penalty for juveniles under sixteen years of age is inconsistent with state practices throughout the country.

Justice Stevens's position on the death penalty for juveniles focuses on two principal justifications for punishment—retribution and deterrence—as they apply to juveniles. Stevens points out that retribution, although a defensible penal philosophy, cannot be so easily employed in juvenile cases. "Given the lesser culpability of the juvenile offender, the teenager's capacity for growth, and society's fiduciary obligations to its children, [the death penalty] is simply inapplicable to the execution of a 15-year-old offender."[282]

Justice Stevens holds also that "deterrence" for those who commit crime under the age of sixteen is suspect for at least two reasons. First, juveniles under the age of sixteen, rarely, if ever, make a cost-benefit analysis of their actions. They simply do not have the cognitive understanding of someone sixteen years of age. Second, even if they knew and understood the consequences of their actions, they would likely not be deterred by the few examples of juveniles under the age of sixteen who have been executed. Stevens concludes, "In short, we are not persuaded that the imposition of the death penalty for offenses committed by persons under 16 years of age has made, or can be expected to make, any measurable contribution to the goals that capital punishment is intended to achieve. It is, therefore, 'nothing more than the purposeless and needless imposition of pain and suffering,' and thus an unconstitutional punishment."[283]

Justice Scalia, joined by Chief Justice Rehnquist and Justice White, dissents. Scalia explains the substantive involvement of Thompson in the crime so that there is no confusion about what Thompson did or the degree to which he participated. He begins with the trial. "The evidence at trial left no doubt that, on the night of January 22–23, 1983, Thompson brutally and with premeditation murdered his former brother-in-law, Charles Keene, the motive evidently being, at least in part, Keene's physical abuse of Thompson's sister. As Thompson left his mother's house that evening, in the company of three older friends, he explained to his girlfriend that 'we're going to kill Charles.'"[284]

For Justice Scalia, Thompson's involvement in the murder was not the involvement of a child. Thompson knew what he was doing, he planned it, and he executed it. Scalia finds no coherent reason why adult responsibility cannot be attributed to someone under the age of sixteen. Scalia would affirm the death penalty for Thompson.

GATHERS V. SOUTH CAROLINA

Victim impact statements are at issue once again in *Gathers v. South Carolina* (490 U.S. 805 [1989] [argued 3/28/89; decided 6/12/89]). Gathers, who had been convicted of first-degree murder and sentenced to death, appealed on the basis that the prosecutor's closing remarks prejudiced Gathers's case. Justice Brennan, for the Court, provides information about the victim, Richard Haynes. For example, Haynes "had been experiencing 'some mental problems,' and had been 'in and out of [a] mental hospital' three times." He considered himself a minister, which he was not, and referred to himself as Reverend Minister. He would talk to anyone about the Lord. He carried with him articles of identification and numerous religious items, "including two Bibles, rosary beads, plastic statues, olive oil, and religious tracts."[285] This information was introduced as evidence at the guilt stage of the trial without objection. No additional information was offered during the sentencing phase. However, the prosecuting attorney used parts of this evidence in his summation to the jury. It is the use of that material in summation that became problematic.

The prosecutor read from some of the tracts as emblematic of Haynes's life. In addition, the prosecutor spoke melodramatically about Haynes. For example, the prosecutor stated the following: "'Reverend Haynes believed in this community. He took part. And he believed that, in Charleston County, in the United States of America, that in this country, you could go to a public park and sit on a public bench and not be attacked by the likes of Demetrius Gathers.'"[286]

Based on its reading of *Booth*, the Supreme Court of South Carolina found the prosecutor's remarks unnecessarily inflammatory and irrelevant to the issue of guilt and punishment. The Supreme Court of South Carolina found that the remarks "'conveyed the suggestion appellant deserved a death sentence because the victim was a religious man and a registered voter.'"[287] Justice Brennan agrees with the Supreme Court of South Carolina. A defendant must be judged on the intent and nature of the crime. Gathers's intent, from what can be discerned, involved nothing more than to take a human life. He had no idea who he was killing. Had he read the religious tracts and seen the religious possessions and murdered Haynes because of his beliefs, then that material might well be germane to the punishment. But there is no indication that Gathers knew anything more than that here was a person to be killed. As Brennan maintains, people are to be judged on the basis of their motive and purpose for the crime, not on what the defendant could not have known. Brennan notes, for example, that Gathers's search among the victim's possessions for items to steal is relevant to the trial. But there is no evidence, beyond that obvious search of Haynes's possessions, that anything else was relevant to the murder. Unless a clear connection can be made between Haynes's personal life and Gathers's intention to murder Haynes because of his beliefs, the prosecutorial remarks were prejudicial to the defendant. Because the prosecutor's remarks went beyond what was directly relevant to Gathers's punishment, the death penalty cannot be sustained.[288]

Justice O'Connor, joined by Chief Justice Rehnquist and Justice Scalia, dissents. O'Connor maintains that VISs in no way jeopardize a defendant's constitutional rights. For O'Connor, information about the victim is not irrelevant to the sentence. As the dissent argued in *Booth*, if the defendant is entitled to state mitigating circumstances, the prosecutor should be entitled to present the victim's circumstances. Only in that way can justice be served. Because Gathers was permitted to present any mitigating evidence into consideration, O'Connor is baffled by the refusal to allow into evidence information about the victim and the victim's family. Logically, if a sentence must be limited to consider only what is relevant to the crime, then technically evidence in mitigation must be irrelevant. Why are mitigating circumstances relevant and a victim's personal circumstances irrelevant? O'Connor writes, "In my view, nothing in the Eighth Amendment precludes the prosecutor from conveying to the jury a sense of the unique human being whose life the defendant has taken."[289] O'Connor argues as well that that the consideration of the victim's life serves the legitimate retributive, correctional philosophy of punishment:

[O]ne of the factors that has long entered into society's conception of proper punishment is the harm caused by the defendant's actions. Thus, we have long recognized that retribution itself is a valid penological goal of the death penalty. Indeed, we have expressly noted that, while "retribution is an element of all punishments society imposes," it "clearly plays a more prominent role in a capital case." "The heart of the retribution rationale is that a criminal sentence must be directly related to the personal culpability of the criminal offender." Moreover, one essential factor in determining the defendant's culpability is the extent of the harm caused.[290]

Justice O'Connor maintains that as there is no discernible difference between the purpose of mitigating circumstances and the purpose of VISs, the life of the victim is relevant to sentence consideration. She writes, "Just as Gathers' own background was important to the jury's assessment of him as a "uniquely individual human bein[g]," so information about his equally unique victim was relevant to the jury's assessment of the harm he had caused and the appropriate penalty. Nothing in the Eighth Amendment precludes the community from considering its loss in assessing punishment nor requires that the victim remain a faceless stranger at the penalty phase of a capital trial.[291] O'Connor would sustain Gather's death penalty sentence.

PENRY V. LYNAUGH, PENRY V. JOHNSON, AND ATKINS V. VIRGINIA

The *Atkins v. Virginia* (No. 00-8452 [argued 2/20/02; decided 6/20/02]) case was examined in chapter 1 as an example of Supreme Court reasoning in terms of the dual justifications for the death penalty, namely, retribution and deterrence. Although Penry's appeals of his death sentence based on mental retardation are instructive in terms of how the Court changed its position, it is important to note that both of Penry's convictions were overturned by the Supreme Court, and both were overturned for the same reason: the juries were not clear as to what or how mitigating circumstances could be considered. *Penry v. Lynaugh* (492 U.S. 302 [argued 1/11/89; decided 6/26/89]) (*Penry I*) serves as a good case study for addressing constitutional challenges to the death penalty in terms of mitigating circumstances and mental retardation.

Penry I raised two questions: (1) Should Penry's jury have been allowed to "consider and give effect to his mitigating evidence in imposing its sentence" and (2) Does the Eighth Amendment prohibit "Penry's execution because he is mentally retarded"?[292]

Penry was tested by Dr. Jerome Brown, a clinical psychologist, who determined that Penry was "mentally retarded." His I.Q. was estimated to be between 50 and 63. In addition, "Dr. Brown's evaluation also revealed that Penry, who was 22 years old at the time of the crime, had the mental age of a 6 ½-year-old, which means that 'he has the ability to learn and the learning or the knowledge of the average 6 ½-year-old kid.'"[293]

Penry was found competent to stand trial. His counsel objected and had a psychiatrist, Dr. Jose Garcia, testify on his behalf. Garcia stated, among other things, that "Penry was suffering from an organic brain disorder at the time of the offense which made it impossible for him to appreciate the wrongfulness of his conduct or to conform his conduct to the law."[294]

The psychiatric testimony did not end there, however. Two psychiatrists hired by Texas came to different conclusions. They agreed with Dr. Garcia to the point that Penry "was a person of extremely limited mental ability, and that he seemed unable to learn from his mistakes."[295] The agreement, however, ends there. The state's psychiatrists claim "that, although Penry was a person of limited mental ability, he was not suffering from any mental illness or defect at the time of the crime, and that he knew the difference between right and wrong and had the potential to honor the law."[296]

Once again, a Texas jury decides on the appropriate punishment by answering three special issues.

(1) whether the conduct of the defendant that caused the death of the deceased was committed deliberately and with the reasonable expectation that the death of the deceased or another would result;
(2) whether there is a probability that the defendant would commit criminal acts of violence that would constitute a continuing threat to society; and
(3) if raised by the evidence, whether the conduct of the defendant in killing the deceased was unreasonable in response to the provocation, if any, by the deceased.[297]

Defense counsel did object to several aspects of these issues. For example, defense counsel objected to the use of the words deliberately (issue 1) and probability, criminal acts of violence, and continuing threat to society (issue 2), among other defense objections. All objections raised "were overruled by the trial court."[298]

The jury then proceeded to consider the special issues. "The jury answered 'yes' to all three special issues, and Penry was sentenced to death."[299] Penry challenged that sentence as follows: "Among other claims, Penry argued that he was sentenced in violation of the Eighth Amendment because the trial court failed to instruct the jury on how to weigh mitigating factors in answering the special issues, and failed to define the term 'deliberately.' Penry also argued that it was cruel and unusual punishment to execute a mentally retarded person."[300] The District Court and the Court of Appeals for the Fifth Circuit rejected Penry's appeal. Justice O'Connor, for the Court, states the questions that must be addressed in Penry's appeal.

First, was Penry sentenced to death in violation of the Eighth Amendment because the jury was not adequately instructed to take into consideration all of his mitigating evidence and because the terms in the Texas special issues were not defined in such a way that the jury could consider and give effect to his mitigating evidence in answering them? Second, is it cruel and unusual punishment under the Eighth Amendment to execute a mentally retarded person with Penry's reasoning ability?[301]

Justice O'Connor agrees with Penry that the Texas jury was unable to consider all mitigating circumstances that might reduce his punishment from death to life imprisonment. She argues that the jury, by virtue of the three questions it was required to answer, was precluded from considering mitigating evidence that could have resulted in a different sentence.[302] Regarding the failure of Texas to enable the jury to consider all mitigating circumstances, O'Connor concludes, "In this case, in the absence of instructions informing the jury that it could consider and give effect to the mitigating evidence of Penry's mental retardation and abused background by declining to impose the death penalty, we conclude that the jury was not provided with a vehicle for expressing its 'reasoned moral response' to that evidence in rendering its sentencing decision.[303]

Penry's next claim, that executing mentally retarded people constitutes cruel and unusual punishment under the Eighth Amendment, receives a somewhat different response from Justice O'Connor. She presents a brief history about how the law has handled mental retardation. For example, she writes that "[i]t was well settled at common law that 'idiots,' together with 'lunatics,' were not subject to punishment for criminal acts committed under those incapacities."[304] She continues, "There was no one definition of idiocy at common law, but the term 'idiot' was generally used to describe persons who had a total lack of reason or understanding, or an inability to distinguish between good and evil."[305]

Given what has been revealed about Penry, it appears that he could fall into the "idiot" category. Does Penry fall into this category? Not according to Justice O'Connor. Penry, after all, had been found competent to stand trial. "In addition, the jury rejected his insanity defense, which reflected their conclusion that Penry knew that his conduct was wrong, and was capable of conforming his conduct to the requirements of the law."[306]

In *Thompson*, the Court ruled that a defendant who committed murder at fifteen years of age could not be executed and that the execution of individuals less than sixteen years of age constitutes cruel and unusual punishment. Although Penry was twenty-two years of age, he only had the reasoning ability of a seven-year-old at best. Justice O'Connor states the argument as follows:

Penry argues that execution of a mentally retarded person like himself with a reasoning capacity of approximately a 7-year-old would be cruel and unusual because it is disproportionate to his degree of personal culpability. Just as the plurality in *Thompson* reasoned that a juvenile is less culpable than an adult for the same crime, Penry argues that mentally retarded people do not have the judgment, perspective, and self-control of a person of normal intelligence. In essence, Penry argues that, because of his diminished ability to control his impulses, to think in long-range terms, and to learn from his mistakes, he "is not capable of acting with the degree of culpability that can justify the ultimate penalty."[307]

Justice O'Connor rejects Penry's argument. Although mental retardation in some cases merits an insanity defense, that does not mean that it applies in all cases of mental retardation or mental incapacity. Individuals with similar labels applied to them nevertheless differ in their abilities and consequent responsibilities. For O'Connor, cases such as Penry's must be adjudicated on a case-by-case basis since defendants claiming insanity or diminished mental capacity differ in their ability to understand the requirements of the law. "In light of the diverse capacities and life experiences of mentally retarded persons, it cannot be said on the record before us today that all mentally retarded people, by definition, can never act with the level of culpability associated with the death penalty."[308] She concludes:

In sum, mental retardation is a factor that may well lessen a defendant's culpability for a capital offense. But we cannot conclude today that the Eighth Amendment precludes the execution of any mentally retarded person of Penry's ability convicted of a capital offense simply by virtue of his or her mental retardation alone. So long as sentencers can consider and give effect to mitigating evidence of mental retardation in imposing sentence, an individualized determination whether "death is the appropriate punishment" can be made in each particular case. While a national consensus against execution of the mentally retarded may someday emerge reflecting the "evolving standards of decency that mark the progress of a maturing society," there is insufficient evidence of such a consensus today.[309]

There are both concurring (in part) and dissenting (in part) opinions by Justices Brennan, Scalia, and Stevens. Only Brennan's dissent will be noted.

Justice Brennan agrees with the Court that Penry was denied his constitutional rights to advance any mitigating circumstances he would want the Court to hear. Brennan takes exception, however, to the idea that some mentally retarded people can be given the death penalty. It may very well be that, as Justice O'Connor stated, that there are different degrees of mental retardation that reflect different degrees of moral and legal responsibility. Those differences, however, are not relevant differences as far as the Eighth Amendment is concerned. Brennan writes: "Even if mental retardation alone were not invariably associated with a lack of the degree of culpability upon which death as a proportionate punishment is predicated, I would still hold the execution of the mentally retarded to be unconstitutional."[310]

Justice Brennan argues as well that the execution of mentally retarded offenders cannot possibly further the criminal justice goals of retribution and deterrence. Retribution, for example, assumes that offenders must be punished according to their guilt, their moral culpability. Can it be seriously argued that people with diminished mental capacity can appropriately be sentenced to death? How does the death penalty comport with the degree of responsibility of the mentally retarded? As for deterrence, Brennan makes the following observation:

Furthermore, killing mentally retarded offenders does not measurably contribute to the goal of deterrence. It is highly unlikely that the exclusion of the mentally retarded from the class of those eligible to be sentenced to death will lessen any deterrent effect the death penalty may have for nonretarded potential offenders, for they, of course, will under present law remain at risk of execution. And the very factors that make it disproportionate and unjust to execute the mentally retarded also make the death penalty of the most minimal deterrent effect so far as retarded potential offenders are concerned.[311]

In *Penry v. Johnson* (No. 00–6677 [argued 3/27/01; decided 6/4/01]) *(Penry II)*, the Supreme Court overturned Penry's conviction on the basis that the sentencing instructions given by the judge to the jury were flawed. Justice O'Connor wrote the majority opinion in *Penry II* as well. Her position remains consistent with *Penry I* as reflected in the following excerpts from her opinion.

Penry I did not hold that the mere mention of "mitigating circumstances" to a capital sentencing jury satisfies the Eighth Amendment. Nor does it stand for the proposition that it is constitutionally sufficient to inform the jury that it may "consider" mitigating circumstances in deciding the appropriate sentence. Rather, the key under *Penry I* is that the jury be able to "consider and give effect to [a defendant's mitigating] evidence in imposing sentence." . . . For it is only when the jury is given a "vehicle for expressing its 'reasoned moral response' to that evidence in rendering its sentencing decision" that we can be sure that the jury "has treated the defendant as a 'uniquely individual human bein[g],' and has made a reliable determination that death is the appropriate sentence." . . . [312]

Although the supplemental instruction made mention of mitigating evidence, the mechanism it purported to create for the jurors to give effect to that evidence was ineffective and illogical. The comments of the court and counsel accomplished little by way of clarification. Any realistic assessment of the manner in which the supplemental instruction operated would therefore lead to the same conclusion we reached in *Penry I*: [A] reasonable juror could well have believed that there was no vehicle for expressing the view that Penry did not deserve to be sentenced to death based upon his mitigating evidence.[313]

On June 17, 2001, Texas Governor Rick Perry vetoed a Texas bill that would have prohibited the state from executing mentally retarded people. He claimed that Texas had sufficient safeguards built into its criminal justice system to prevent such executions. *Atkins* now serves to prohibit the execution of mentally retarded defendants.

STANFORD V. KENTUCKY

Decided the same day as *Penry*, the Court sustained the constitutionality of the death penalty applied to juveniles sixteen and seventeen years of age. Two cases were combined here, a Kentucky case titled *Stanford v. Kentucky* (492 U.S. 361 [1989] [argued 3/27/89; decided 6/26/89]) that imposed the death penalty on Kevin Stanford, who was seventeen-years-old at the time he murdered, and a Missouri case that imposed the death penalty on Heath Wilkins, who was sixteen-years-old at the time he murdered.

Justice Scalia, for the Court, maintains that the death penalty does not constitute cruel and unusual punishment in these cases. He bases his judgment on two points.

There is no historical support for the claim that the death penalty was considered unconstitutional when the Bill of Rights was passed. Indeed, while in theory seven-year-old children could receive the death penalty, in reality fourteen-year-old children did receive the death penalty.[314]

The defendant's claim, based on *Trop*, that the Eighth Amendment "must draw its meaning from the evolving standards of decency that mark the progress of a maturing society," does not apply to Stanford or Wilkins. The determination of what "evolved" means does not rest solely, if at all, on "the subjective views of individual Justices; judgment should be informed by objective factors to the maximum possible extent."[315] What, then, are those "objective factors" and how are they to be considered? There are three means by which these factors can be identified.

First, over half of the states that have death penalty statutes authorize the death penalty for sixteen- and seventeen-year-olds. That reality, for Justice Scalia, serves to indicate that one of the thresholds used to determine if a specific punishment constitutes cruel and unusual punishment, namely, the widespread opposition to it, has not been reached. "Of the 37 States whose laws permit capital punishment, 15 decline to impose it upon 16-year-old offenders and 12 decline to impose it on 17-year-old offenders. This does not establish the degree of national consensus this Court has previously thought sufficient to label a particular punishment cruel and unusual."[316]

Second, Stanford and Wilkins claim that "the reluctance of juries to impose, and prosecutors to seek" the death penalty demonstrates society's rejection of the death penalty for juveniles under eighteen.[317] Justice Scalia disagrees. He argues that the reluctance to impose the death penalty on juveniles under the age of eighteen reflects only that the death penalty "should *rarely* be imposed." [318]

Third, the defendants argue that legislation prohibiting activities to children under eighteen years of age (e.g., buying cigarettes and voting), should apply as well to the death penalty. That argument, Justice Scalia holds, fails to recognize the difference between general laws that apply to all people under a certain age could cast a sound vote and specific laws, such as found in the criminal justice system, that are used only against individuals who violate them. Scalia explains this distinction as follows: "These laws set the appropriate ages for the operation of a system that makes its determinations in gross, and that does not conduct individualized maturity tests for each driver, drinker, or voter. The criminal justice system, however, does provide individualized testing. In the realm of capital punishment in particular, 'individualized consideration [is] a constitutional requirement,' and one of the individualized mitigating factors that sentencers must be permitted to consider is the defendant's age."[319]

Justice Scalia concludes, "We discern neither a historical nor a modern societal consensus forbidding the imposition of capital punishment on any person who murders at 16 or 17 years of age. Accordingly, we conclude that such punishment does not offend the Eighth Amendment's prohibition against cruel and unusual punishment."[320]

Justice Brennan, joined by Justices Marshall, Blackmun, and Stevens, dissents. He raises numerous points in his dissent. I identify five. First, Brennan maintains that Justice Scalia has miscounted the number of states that support the death penalty. In actuality, according to Brennan, over half the states oppose the death penalty for juveniles under eighteen years of age. He makes this claim based on the fact that thirteen states and the District of Columbia do not have a death penalty, plus the twelve states that do not authorize it for children under seventeen years of age. In short, people obtain the figure they need by counting in a way that enables them to get the result they want. In addition, for Brennan, it is not safe to assume that states that authorize the death penalty but remain silent on its application to those under eighteen would apply it to sixteen- and seventeen-year-olds.

Second, the imposition of the death penalty on juveniles is unusual in that very few judges or juries impose it on those occasions in which they could. "It is certainly true that, in the vast majority of cases, juries have not sentenced juveniles to death, and it seems to me perfectly proper to conclude that a sentence so rarely imposed is 'unusual.'"[321]

Third, the death penalty must be seen as disproportionate for juveniles under eighteen years of age. A principle of proportionality, Justice Brennan argues, has long been held as a guiding principle in the assessment of legal responsibility. That principle "takes account not only of the 'injury to the person and to the public' caused by the crime, but also of the 'moral depravity' of the offender."[322] Brennan continues, "Proportionality analysis requires that we compare 'the gravity of the offense,' understood to include not only the injury caused, but also the defendant's culpability, with 'the harshness of the penalty.' In my view, juveniles so generally lack the degree of responsibility for their crimes that is a predicate for the constitutional imposition of the death penalty that the Eighth Amendment forbids that they receive that punishment."[323]

Fourth, society in general has assumed a responsibility for the well-being of young people it has not assumed for adults. The age of maturity, for whatever reasons, has been set at eighteen, an age "that society has generally drawn, the point at which it is thought reasonable to assume that persons have an ability to make and a duty to bear responsibility for their judgments."[324]

Fifth, the constitutionality of a punishment has at times been determined by whether the punishment serves a social goal, such as deterrence or retribution. Justice Brennan argues that "[u]nless the death penalty applied to persons for offenses under 18 measurably contributes to one of these goals [retribution or deterrence], the Eighth Amendment prohibits it."[325] Retribution is not served by executing a person under eighteen years of age for retribution assumes a person's full accountability for his or her acts, an accountability young people lack. For a very similar reason, deterrence is not served by executing juvenile offenders. Juvenile offenders do not possess the long-term reasoning skills that enable them to make a reasonably informed judgment.[326]

Justice Brennan concludes, "Because imposition of the death penalty on persons for offenses committed under the age of 18 makes no measurable contribution to the goals of either retribution or deterrence, it is 'nothing more than the purposeless and needless imposition of pain and suffering,' and is thus excessive and unconstitutional."[327]

BLYSTONE V. PENNSYLVANIA

In *Blystone v. Pennsylvania* (494 U.S. 299 [1990] [argued 10/10/89; decided 2/28/90]), Blystone was convicted of murder and sentenced to death. He appealed the decision on the basis that, since jurors are required to bring in a sentence of death if there is at least one aggravating circumstance and no mitigating circumstance, Pennsylvania's capital punishment statute essentially mandates the death penalty. Chief Justice Rehnquist finds no merit in Blystone's appeal.

Chief Justice Rehnquist, for the Court, argues that similar appeals have been made, albeit unsuccessfully. For example, in *Jurek* the Court held that the death penalty could not be represented as mandatory since aggravating and mitigating circumstances directed the court's judgment. Because jurors in capital cases in Pennsylvania are allowed to consider all mitigating circumstances, the death penalty meets *Furman* requirements. In addition, the capital punishment statute does not qualify as mandatory. Rehnquist writes:

Nor is the statute impermissibly "mandatory" as that term was understood in *Woodson* or *Roberts*. Death is not automatically imposed upon conviction for certain types of murder. It is imposed only after a determination that the aggravating circumstances outweigh the mitigating circumstances present in the particular crime committed by the particular defendant, or that there are no such mitigating circumstances.[328]

Blystone argued that Pennsylvania's statute was unconstitutional as it applied in his case because "the jury was precluded from considering whether the severity of his aggravating circumstance warranted the death sentence."[329] Chief Justice Rehnquist responds, "We reject this argument. The presence of aggravating circumstances serves the purpose of limiting the class of death-eligible defendants, and the Eighth Amendment does not require that these aggravating circumstances be further refined or weighed by a jury."[330] Blystone claims as well that the jury was precluded from considering all degrees of mitigating circumstances (for example, degrees of mental or emotional disturbance). The jury in Pennsylvania, however, despite the judge's instructions to the jury regarding types of mitigating circumstances, understood that it could consider virtually any mitigating circumstance that might in any way reduce a defendant's sentence. Again, Rehnquist explains:

The requirement of individualized sentencing in capital cases is satisfied by allowing the jury to consider all relevant mitigating evidence. In petitioner's case the jury was specifically instructed to consider, as mitigating evidence, any "matter concerning the character or record of the defendant, or the circumstances of his offense." This was sufficient to satisfy the dictates of the Eighth Amendment.[331]

Justice Brennan, joined by Justice Marshall, and by Justices Blackmun and Stevens in part, dissents. For Brennan, the Pennsylvania statute, for all practical purposes, constitutes a mandatory sentence of death that fails to meet *Furman* requirements. Brennan explains that the state statute requires a jury to bring in the death penalty even if there is only one statutory aggravating circumstance and no mitigating circumstances. But is the finding of one aggravating circumstance sufficient to justify the death penalty? Aggravating circumstances differ not only among states but also within individual differences within states. Each aggravating circumstance cannot possibly count the same. Therefore, for Brennan, a state statute that sets up the possibility for this dilemma cannot be constitutionally sustained. Pennsylvania's capital punishment statute that requires a sentence of death when the jury finds no mitigating circumstance does mean that at least in some cases the death penalty will be mandatory.

Justice Brennan also challenges the Court's claim that the finding of an aggravating circumstance satisfies the constitutional requirement of weighing the aggravating and mitigating circumstances. For example, even if there are no mitigating circumstances, does that mean necessarily that the one aggravating circumstance rises to the degree necessary to impose the death penalty? Brennan insists that the "balance" that *Furman* requires in determining death penalty sentences is not met in *Blystone*. For Brennan, one aggravating circumstance does not necessarily mandate, absent of any mitigating circumstances, the death penalty. A jury must consider as well the weight of that aggravating circumstance. He writes, "The 'weight' of an aggravating circumstance is just as relevant to the propriety of the death penalty as the 'weight' of any mitigating circumstances."[332]

MCKOY V. NORTH CAROLINA

In deciding on whether a convicted first-degree murderer would receive the death penalty, North Carolina juries could not, by statute, take into consideration any mitigating circumstances to which the jury could not unanimously agree. Juries were free to consider any mitigating circumstance, but if even one person on the jury did not agree that that mitigating circumstance was relevant, then the remaining eleven jurors could not consider that circumstance in their deliberations. In *McKoy v. North Carolina* (494 U.S. 433 [1990] [argued 10/10/89; decided 3/5/90]), the jury did unanimously agree on one statutory mitigating circumstance and one nonstatutory mitigating circumstance. Because the jury could not reach unanimous agreement on the remaining mitigating circumstances, the jury weighed the two mitigating circumstances against the two aggravating circumstances it found and held that the mitigating circumstances did not outweigh the aggravating circumstances. *McKoy* is to be decided on the same basis as *Mills*.

Justice Marshall, for the Court, explains the North Carolina sentencing procedure. North Carolina argues that, because the jury must be unanimous with respect to aggravating circumstances, then the same requirement should hold with respect to mitigating circumstances. Marshall disagrees. "A State may not limit a sentencer's consideration of mitigating evidence merely because it places the same limitation on consideration of aggravating circumstances."[333] Marshall, accordingly, overturns the death penalty in McKoy's case: "We conclude that North Carolina's unanimity requirement impermissibly limits jurors' consideration of mitigating evidence and hence is contrary to our decision in *Mills*. We therefore vacate the petitioner's death sentence and remand this case to the North Carolina Supreme Court for further proceedings not inconsistent with this opinion."[334]

Justice Scalia, joined by Chief Justice Rehnquist and Justice O'Connor, dissents. Scalia claims that this case is sufficiently unlike *Mills* that the death penalty should be sustained. For example, two mitigating circumstances were identified unanimously as applying, whereas in *Mills* no mitigating circumstances were unanimously agreed upon. In addition, the aggravating circumstances had to meet the same standard as the mitigating circumstances, namely, the jury must be unanimous in finding aggravating circumstances. Scalia's position is best exemplified in the following passage:

I think this scheme, taken as a whole, satisfies the due process and Eighth Amendment concerns enunciated by this Court. By requiring that the jury find at least one statutory aggravating circumstance, North Carolina has adequately narrowed the class of death-eligible murderers. On the other hand, by permitting the jury to consider evidence of, and find, any mitigating circumstance offered by the defendant, North Carolina has ensured that the jury will "be able to consider and give effect to that evidence in imposing sentence." By requiring both aggravating circumstances to be found unanimously (beyond a reasonable doubt) and mitigating circumstances to be found unanimously (by only a preponderance of the evidence), North Carolina has "reduc[ed] the likelihood that [the jury] will impose a sentence that fairly can be called capricious or arbitrary." Finally, by requiring the jury unanimously to find beyond a reasonable doubt not only that the aggravating circumstances outweigh the mitigating circumstances, but also that they are sufficiently substantial in light of the mitigating circumstances to justify the death penalty, North Carolina has provided even an extra measure of assurance that death will not be lightly or mechanically imposed.[335]

CLEMONS V. MISSISSIPPI

In *Clemons v. Mississippi* (494 U.S. 738 [1990] [argued 11/29/89; decided 3/28/90]), Clemons was given the death penalty in part on the unconstitutional aggravating circumstance as found in *Maynard v. Cartwright* "that the murder was 'especially heinous, atrocious, or cruel.'"[336] Justice White, for the Court, states that state appellate courts can uphold death penalty convictions by either reweighing the aggravating and mitigating circumstances in light of the unconstitutional aggravating circumstance or they can uphold a death sentence on the basis of harmless error, that is, an error that made no difference on the outcome of the case. Unfortunately, White notes, "it is unclear whether the Mississippi Supreme Court correctly employed either of these two methods."[337]

One of Clemons's challenges to the Mississippi Supreme Court's action of upholding his death sentence is that that action negated Clemons's right to have a jury decide his fate. As one of the aggravating circumstances is invalid, the lower court's decision must be overturned and returned to that court for further review by a jury. Justice White disagrees:

Nothing in the Sixth Amendment as construed by our prior decisions indicates that a defendant's right to a jury trial would be infringed where an appellate court invalidates one of two or more aggravating circumstances found by the jury but affirms the death sentence after itself finding that the one or more valid remaining aggravating factors outweigh the mitigating evidence. Any argument that the Constitution requires that a jury impose the sentence of death or make the findings prerequisite to imposition of such a sentence has been soundly rejected by prior decisions of this Court.[338]

Clemons claims as well "that appellate courts are unable to fully consider and give effect to the mitigating evidence presented by defendants at the sentencing phase in a capital case and that it therefore violates the Eighth Amendment for an appellate court to undertake to reweigh aggravating and mitigating circumstances in an attempt to salvage the death sentence imposed by a jury."[339] Justice White disagrees. For him, appellate courts are in a position to consider all relevant evidence, evaluate it fairly, and reweigh it when necessary without doing any disservice to anyone's constitutional rights to a jury trial. The jury has given its ruling, and now the appeals court assesses the merits of that court's finding. In addition, appellate courts have had substantive experience in evaluating lower court rulings. For example, appellate courts can examine a sentence in terms of proportionality that will satisfy the need for "reliability and consistency" in judicial judgments.[340] White summarizes the discussion thus far: "Therefore, we conclude that state appellate courts can and do give each defendant an individualized and reliable sentencing determination based on the defendant's circumstances, his background, and the crime."[341]

The problem with the Mississippi Supreme Court review is that there is no clear and unambiguous indication as to how it proceeded to weigh the aggravating and mitigating circumstances in Clemons's case. For example, Justice White asks if the "especially heinous" condition played any role in weighing the aggravating and mitigating circumstances. White argues that one can find in the Mississippi Supreme Court's review opinions that suggest that it did reweigh the aggravating and mitigating circumstances in an appropriate way, that is, "by applying the proper definition to the 'especially heinous' factor." But White notices the following approach as well: "At other times, however, the opinion indicates the court may have been employing the other approach and disregarding the 'especially heinous' factor entirely."[342] Unfortunately, there is no way the Supreme Court can determine how the Mississippi Supreme Court reached its decision. White draws the following conclusion:

It is perhaps possible, however, that the Mississippi Supreme Court intended to ask whether, beyond reasonable doubt, the result would have been the same had the especially heinous aggravating circumstance been properly defined in the jury instructions; and perhaps on this basis it could have determined that the failure to instruct properly was harmless error. Because we cannot be sure which course was followed in Clemons's case, however, we vacate the judgment insofar as it rested on harmless error, and remand for further proceedings.[343]

WALTON V. ARIZONA

Walton was found guilty of first-degree murder and sentenced to death in *Walton v. Arizona* (497 U.S. 639 [1990] [argued 1/17/90; decided 6/27/90]). In an Arizona capital case, a jury would decide if the defendant was guilty of committing a capital crime and the judge would determine if the death penalty was justifiable. As in most states, aggravating and mitigating circumstances directed the sentencer to a constitutionally sound decision. In *Walton*, the judge found two aggravating circumstances, namely, "(1) the murder was committed 'in an especially heinous, cruel or depraved manner,' and (2) the murder was committed for pecuniary gain."[344] Walton presented mitigating circumstances that included a psychiatrist's opinion that "Walton had a history of drug abuse which impaired his judgment, and that Walton may have been abused sexually as a child."[345] Walton's attorney also noted that Walton was just "20 at the time of sentencing."[346] The judge determined that the mitigating circumstances did not outweigh the aggravating circumstances. Accordingly, Walton was sentenced to death.

The Arizona Supreme Court upheld the lower court's conviction and sentence. Specifically, it agreed with the court judge's judgment that the aggravating circumstances outweighed the mitigating circumstances. The first stated aggravating circumstance was that the murder was "especially heinous, cruel or depraved" by stating that that circumstance occurs when "'the perpetrator inflicts mental anguish or physical abuse before the victim's death,' and that '[m]ental anguish includes a victim's uncertainty as to his ultimate fate.'"[347] The Arizona Supreme Court held not only that "Powell suffered mental anguish prior to his death" but also that "the crime was committed in an especially depraved manner, pointing out that it had defined a depraved manner as one where 'the perpetrator relishes the murder, evidencing debasement or perversion.'"[348] The Arizona

Supreme Court agreed as well that the murder was committed for pecuniary gain. The Arizona Supreme Court concluded as well that the sentence was proportional to sentences meted out in similar cases. Walton challenges his sentence on four grounds.

First, Walton claims that it is unconstitutional for a judge to weigh the aggravating and mitigating circumstances and assess a sentence. In a capital case, Walton claims, the jury should determine the sentence. Justice White, for the Court, notes that the Court has never held that a jury determination of sentence is constitutionally mandated.[349]

Second, Walton challenges Arizona's statute that places "the burden of establishing, by a preponderance of the evidence, the existence of mitigating circumstances sufficiently substantial to call for leniency."[350] Justice White disagrees. "So long as a State's method of allocating the burdens of proof does not lessen the State's burden to prove every element of the offense charged, or in this case to prove the existence of aggravating circumstances, a defendant's constitutional rights are not violated by placing on him the burden of proving mitigating circumstances sufficiently substantial to call for leniency."[351]

Third, Walton maintains that the Arizona capital punishment statute makes the death penalty virtually mandatory when a court determines that the aggravating circumstances outweigh the mitigating circumstances. Walton argues that the statute tacitly implies that the death penalty is the only punishment available once it is determined that aggravating circumstances outweigh mitigating circumstances. Citing *Blystone,* Justice White holds that the death penalty cannot be considered mandatory as long as the death penalty statute permits the submission of all mitigating circumstances. If the sentencer has considered the mitigating circumstances and determined that they do not outweigh the aggravating circumstances, then the defendant has been accorded an individualized sentence consistent with the Eighth and Fourteenth Amendments.[352]

Fourth, Walton claims that the "especially heinous, cruel or depraved" aggravating circumstance violates the Court's position in *Maynard v. Cartwright* and *Godfrey v. Georgia.* Justice White responds by stating that the comparison between Walton's challenge and the decisions in *Maynard* and *Godfrey* are not similar. In *Maynard* and *Godfrey,* for example, the jury determined the meaning of terms such as heinous and depraved. That is not the case in *Walton.* Here a trial judge—a person acutely aware of the nature, meaning, and scope of that aggravating circumstance—can make a more substantial and reasoned judgment about the meaning of those terms due to the judge's greater expertise in understanding and applying the law.[353] Walton's death sentence, accordingly, is sustained.

The dissenting opinions are lengthy and substantive. In one form or another Justices Brennan, Marshall, Blackmun, and Stevens dissent. Only Justices Blackmun's and Stevens's dissents are noted briefly.

Justice Blackmun's dissent challenges the majority opinion virtually on a point by point analysis. His opening paragraph summarizes his position with great clarity.

In my view, two Arizona statutory provisions, pertinent here, run afoul of the established Eighth Amendment principle that a capital defendant is entitled to an individualized sentencing determination which involves the consideration of all relevant mitigating evidence. The first is the requirement that the sentencer may consider only those mitigating circumstances proved by a preponderance of the evidence. The second is the provision that the defendant bears the burden of establishing mitigating circumstances "sufficiently substantial to call for leniency." I also conclude that Arizona's "heinous, cruel or depraved" aggravating circumstance, as construed by the Arizona Supreme Court, provides no meaningful guidance to the sentencing authority and, as a consequence, is unconstitutional.[354]

Justice Stevens holds that a death penalty requires a jury determination. Stevens quotes at length Justice White's opinion from another case on the necessity for jury determinations in criminal trials:

"The guarantees of jury trial in the Federal and State Constitutions reflect a profound judgment about the way in which law should be enforced and justice administered. A right to jury trial is granted to criminal defendants in order to prevent oppression by the Government. Those who wrote our constitutions knew from history and experience that it was necessary to protect against unfounded criminal charges brought to eliminate enemies and against judges too responsive to the voice of higher authority. The framers of the constitutions strove to create an independent judiciary, but insisted upon further protection against arbitrary action. Providing an accused with the right to be tried by a jury of his peers gave him an inestimable safeguard against the corrupt or overzealous prosecutor and against the compliant, biased, or eccentric judge. If the defendant preferred the common-sense judgment of a jury to the more tutored but perhaps less sympathetic reaction of the single judge, he was to have it. Beyond this, the jury trial provisions in the Federal and State Constitutions reflect a fundamental decision about the exercise of official power—a reluctance to entrust plenary powers over the life and liberty of the citizen to one judge or to a group of judges."[355]

The issue of "who decides the appropriate punishment" remained unsettled until June 24, 2002.[356]

LEWIS V. JEFFERS

Lewis v. Jeffers (497 U.S. 764 [1990] [argued 2/21/90; decided 6/27/90]) does not differ from *Walton*. It reinforces the idea that under certain well-defined criteria the phrase "especially heinous, cruel, and depraved" for the death penalty meets constitutional requirements. Arizona's reliance on that phrase sentenced Jeffers to death. Indeed, Justice O'Connor, for the

Court, holds that, for all practical purposes, *Walton* decides Jeffers's sentence. She quotes approvingly from *Walton* as follows:

"Recognizing that the proper degree of definition of an aggravating factor of this nature is not susceptible of mathematical precision, we conclude that the definition given to the 'especially cruel' provision by the Arizona Supreme Court is constitutionally sufficient because it gives meaningful guidance to the sentencer. Nor can we fault the state court's statement that a crime is committed in an especially 'depraved' manner when the perpetrator 'relishes the murder, evidencing debasement or perversion,' or 'shows an indifference to the suffering of the victim and evidences a sense of pleasure' in the killing."[357]

The dissenting opinion remains equally adamant about the unconstitutionality of the "especially heinous, cruel, or depraved" phrase. Justice Blackmun's dissenting opinion, in which he is joined by Justices Brennan, Marshall, and Stevens, explains the minority dissent clearly and specifically. Blackmun writes:

I think it is important that we be frank about what is happening here. The death penalty laws of many States establish aggravating circumstances similar to the one at issue in this case. Since the statutory language defining these factors does not provide constitutionally adequate guidance, the constitutionality of the aggravating circumstances necessarily depends on the construction given by the State's highest court. We have expressed apparent approval of a limiting construction requiring "torture or serious physical abuse." This Court has not held that this is the only permissible construction of an aggravating circumstance of this kind, but, prior to today, we have never suggested that the aggravating factor can permissibly be construed in a manner that does not make reference to the suffering of the victim. The decision today will likely result in the execution of numerous inmates, in Arizona and elsewhere, who would not otherwise be put to death.[358]

PARKER V. DUGGER

Aggravating and mitigating circumstances define *Parker v. Dugger* (498 U.S. 308 [1991] [argued 11/7/90; decided 1/22/91]). Specifically, the jury found that sufficient aggravating and mitigating circumstances existed to recommend a sentence of life imprisonment rather than the death penalty. The trial judge, however, who has the final say in sentence determination in Florida, declared that the aggravating circumstances outweighed the mitigating circumstances in one of the murders Parker committed and sentenced him on that basis to death.

Parker claims that Florida failed to consider adequately the mitigating circumstances in his case, which amounted to an arbitrary and capricious sentence of death. Justice O'Connor, for the Court, explains the process in Florida as follows: "If the jury recommends a life sentence rather than the death penalty, the judge may override that recommendation and impose a sentence of death only where 'the facts suggesting a sentence of death [are] so clear and convincing that virtually no reasonable person could differ.'"[359]

Parker presented several claims of mitigating circumstances, including committing the murders under "large amounts of alcohol and drugs," as a child growing up with "an abusive, alcoholic father," and "a positive adult relationship with his own children and his neighbors."[360]

Florida, as previously noted, is a "weighing" state. That is, juries and judges must weigh the aggravating and mitigating circumstances to reach a decision that reflects a reasoned and balanced judgment. Justice O'Connor argues that in Parker's case, the lower court jury appears to have weighed aggravating and mitigating circumstances, and perhaps the trial judge did as well. The Florida Supreme Court, however, does not appear to have weighed the aggravating and mitigating circumstances. Appeals courts can engage in weighing aggravating and mitigating circumstances, but they cannot do so by accepting without question the finding from the lower court. O'Connor writes, "What the Florida Supreme Court could not do, but what it did, was to ignore the evidence of mitigating circumstances in the record and misread the trial judge's findings regarding mitigating circumstances, and affirm the sentence based on a mischaracterization of the trial judge's findings."[361] Since the Florida Supreme Court did not consider seriously Parker's mitigating circumstances, the sentence "was invalid because it deprived Parker of the individualized treatment to which he is entitled under the Constitution."[362]

Justice White, joined by Chief Justice Rehnquist, and Justices Scalia and Kennedy, dissents. In *Parker*, White argues, the Court went beyond its legitimate oversight domain. White writes, "The Court long ago gave up second-guessing state supreme courts in situations such as the one presented here. Nevertheless, the Court today undertakes and performs that task in a manner that is inconsistent with our precedents and with the Court's role as the final arbiter of federal constitutional issues of great importance. Therefore, I dissent."[363] In addition, White argues that the Court claims that the lower court judge did not properly weigh the aggravating and mitigating circumstances in Parker's case. That claim, however, does not reflect the reality described by the Court itself. White writes: "This is a strange suggestion, particularly in light of the Court's assertion that the judge's statement that 'there are no mitigating circumstances that outweigh the aggravating circumstances' means that the judge found nonstatutory mitigating circumstances but determined that they were outweighed."[364] *Parker* reinforces the strange lengths states and courts must pursue to satisfy the constitutional requirement for individualized sentencing that has become a staple of Supreme Court review in capital cases.

LANKFORD V. IDAHO

Due process requires, among other things, that defendants are made aware of the punishments that can apply if they are convicted.[365] In *Lankford v. Idaho* (500 U.S. 110 [1991] [argued 2/19/91; decided 5/20/91]), "the prosecutor had formally advised the trial judge and the petitioner that the State would not recommend the death penalty."[366] Bryan Lankford, the petitioner, and his older brother Mark, had been charged in two murders. After the arraignment, plea negotiations with the prosecutor began. At no time in those negotiations was the death penalty considered an option. Indeed, the Lankford brothers, along with their counsel, had no reason to believe that the death penalty was even a remote possibility. "At the sentencing hearing on October 12, 1984, there was no discussion of the death penalty as a possible sentence."[367] At the hearing, the prosecutor made sentencing recommendations, as did counsel for the defendants. Again, the prosecuting attorney never mentioned or addressed the death penalty. On sentencing day, however, the judge issued death sentences for both men.

The judge, based on his own findings of aggravating circumstances, held that the murders were committed in the first degree and therefore warranted the death penalty. Justice Stevens, for the Court, overturned the death sentence primarily on the basis that "[t]he issue is one of adequate procedure [due process], rather than of substantive power."[368]

The procedural problem fell equally on the prosecution and the defense. While they were debating on how many years the brothers should spend in prison, the judge was silently debating between life and death. "During the hearing, while both defense counsel and the prosecutor were arguing the merits of concurrent or consecutive, and fixed or indeterminate, terms, the silent judge was the only person in the courtroom who knew that the real issue that they should have been debating was the choice between life or death."[369] Consequently, aggravating and mitigating circumstances were never presented. There was no opportunity, indeed no reason, to raise mitigating circumstances or to challenge aggravating circumstances.

In short, the Supreme Court holds that, if the trial is to be fair, all parties must be made aware of the issues that could be raised. Justice Stevens concludes, "Petitioner's lack of adequate notice that the judge was contemplating the imposition of the death sentence created an impermissible risk that the adversary process may have malfunctioned in this case."[370]

Justice Scalia, joined by Chief Justice Rehnquist and Justices White and Souter, dissents. Scalia argues that, absent information to the contrary, defendants, defendants' attorney, and the prosecuting attorney had to know that in cases of first-degree murder, the death penalty is always an option. The Lankfords and their attorney erroneously believed that death was not an option. That erroneous belief was certainly detrimental to the outcome of their case, but that does not constitute a violation of any due process right. For Scalia, there was no legal or practical basis to believe that the death penalty was not on the table. To assume otherwise undermines the "principle that the capital defendant cannot be presumed to know the law, but must be presumed to have detrimentally relied upon a misunderstanding of the law or a misinterpretation of the judge. I respectfully dissent."[371]

PAYNE V. TENNESSEE

Payne v. Tennessee (501 U.S. 808 [1991] [argued 4/24/91; decided 6/27/91]) effectively overturns *Booth v. Maryland* and *South Carolina v. Gathers*, both of which, as previously explained, held that victim impact statements violate the Eighth Amendment and therefore cannot be introduced at trial. Payne was convicted of first-degree murder. At the sentencing stage of the trial, Payne introduced mitigating circumstances by presenting "the testimony of four witnesses: his mother and father, Bobbie Thomas, and Dr. John T. Hutson, a clinical psychologist specializing in criminal court evaluation work." For example, the clinical psychologist testified that "Payne was 'mentally handicapped.'"[372]

The prosecution presented a VIS by the murdered woman's mother about the continuing impact the deaths of his mother and sister have on the young son, Nicholas. Payne received the death penalty.

Chief Justice Rehnquist, for the Court, held that VISs are not unconstitutional per se. For Rehnquist, the total harm inflicted is relevant to sentencing. He notes that an assessment of the harm done does factor into the determination of guilt and the appropriate degree of punishment. He writes, "Thus, two equally blameworthy criminal defendants may be guilty of different offenses solely because their acts cause differing amounts of harm."[373]

Chief Justice Rehnquist argues further that, regardless of "the prevailing sentencing philosophy, the sentencing authority has always been free to consider a wide range of relevant material."[374] VISs may be new to sentencing philosophy, but that does not render them unconstitutional. Because mitigating circumstances can cover a wide range of individualized considerations, there is no reason to hold that the aggravating circumstances must be limited to the individualized treatment of the guilt of the defendant. VISs are relevant, Rehnquist argues, for they contribute, in a way similar to mitigating circumstances, to the proper assessment of individualized sentencing. VISs acknowledge that the victim was an individual worthy of life.

The challenge to VISs has focused on the fact that such statements can, in theory, make some lives appear more valuable than others. Chief Justice Rehnquist claims that misrepresents the relevance of a VIS. He writes about *Gathers* as follows: "The facts of Gathers are an excellent illustration of this: the evidence showed that the victim was an out-of-work, mentally handicapped individual, perhaps not, in the eyes of most, a significant contributor to society, but nonetheless a murdered human being."[375] In further support of his position, Rehnquist writes, "Victim impact evidence is simply another form or method of informing the sentencing authority about the specific harm caused by the crime in question, evidence of a general type long considered by sentencing authorities."[376] In addition, "[w]e are now of the view that a State may properly conclude that, for the jury to assess meaningfully the defendant's moral culpability and blameworthiness, it should have before it at the sentencing phase evidence of the specific harm caused by the defendant."[377] Rehnquist concludes:

We thus hold that, if the State chooses to permit the admission of victim impact evidence and prosecutorial argument on that subject, the Eighth Amendment erects no *per se* bar. A State may legitimately conclude that evidence about the victim and about the impact of the murder on the victim's family is relevant to the jury's decision as to whether or not the death penalty should be imposed. There is no reason to treat such evidence differently than other relevant evidence is treated.[378]

Justice Marshall, joined by Justice Blackmun, dissents. Marshall maintains that *Gathers* and *Booth* should be upheld. Essentially, victim impact statements, according to Marshall, introduce irrelevant factors into sentencing consideration. If a person is to be judged on the basis of their individual degree of guilt, "admitting evidence of the victim's character and the impact of the murder upon the victim's family predicates the sentencing determination on 'factors . . . wholly unrelated to the blameworthiness of [the] particular defendant.'"[379]

Justice Stevens, joined by Justice Blackmun as well, dissents. Stevens states his disagreement with the Court as follows: "Our cases provide no support whatsoever for the majority's conclusion that the prosecutor may introduce evidence that sheds no light on the defendant's guilt or moral culpability, and thus serves no purpose other than to encourage jurors to decide in favor of death, rather than life, on the basis of their emotions, rather than their reason."[380] He elaborates:

Until today, our capital punishment jurisprudence has required that any decision to impose the death penalty be based solely on evidence that tends to inform the jury about the character of the offense and the character of the defendant. Evidence that serves no purpose other than to appeal to the sympathies or emotions of the jurors has never been considered admissible. Thus, if a defendant, who had murdered a convenience store clerk in cold blood in the course of an armed robbery, offered evidence unknown to him at the time of the crime about the immoral character of his victim, all would recognize immediately that the evidence was irrelevant and inadmissible. Evenhanded justice requires that the same constraint be imposed on the advocate of the death penalty.[381]

STRINGER V. BLACK

The aggravating circumstance "especially heinous, atrocious, or cruel" has been a source of constitutional debate since aggravating and mitigating circumstances became an integral part of capital sentencing decisions.[382] In *Clemons* and *Maynard*, the aggravating circumstance "especially heinous, atrocious, or cruel" was declared unconstitutionally vague.[383] Stringer was convicted of capital murder in *Stringer v. Black* (503 U.S. 222 [1992] [argued 12/9/91; decided 3/9/92]) and received the death penalty, in part, on the basis of the aggravating circumstance "especially, heinous, or cruel."[384] The words heinous, atrocious, and cruel carry enormous yet virtually indefinable weight that can result at times in decisions that appear arbitrary and capricious in violation of *Furman*. The subjective nature of these terms creates the constitutional challenge to this particular aggravating circumstance. The Supreme Court's holding in *Clemons* and *Maynard* provides Stringer his habeas corpus claim against the state of Mississippi.

Mississippi is another weighing state. Once an aggravating circumstance has been determined, the jury must weigh aggravating and mitigating circumstances to determine if the defendant deserves the death penalty. Given Mississippi's weighing process in capital cases, Justice Kennedy, for the Court, argues that aggravating circumstances must be defined "with some degree of precision" to avoid the haphazard imposition of the death penalty.[385] Kennedy argues that state appellate courts can reweigh aggravating and mitigating circumstances that led to the death penalty, but they must conduct "a thorough analysis of the role an invalid aggravating factor played in the sentencing process."[386] In fact, Kennedy argues that "the use of a vague aggravating factor creates the possibility not only of randomness but also of bias in favor of the death penalty" that could require invalidating a death sentence because the weighing process had been contaminated by the invalid aggravating circumstance.[387] Given that no one could know what punishment a jury would have recommended absent the invalid aggravating circumstance, Stringer's death penalty must be vacated.

Justice Souter, joined by Justices Scalia and Thomas, dissents. For Souter, since the Court prior to Stringer's case never required resentencing provided that at least one aggravating circumstance was present, Stringer cannot appeal on the basis of decisions made several years after his conviction and sentence.[388] For Souter, the presence of additional aggravating circumstances in Stringer's case does not qualify for a reweighing of aggravating and mitigating circumstances as constitutionally required.[389]

MORGAN V. ILLINOIS

Morgan v. Illinois (504 U.S. 719 [1992] [argued 1/21/92; decided 6/15/92]) offers an interesting twist on *Witherspoon*. In *Witherspoon* jurors were dismissed from jury duty in capital cases simply because they had some moral or religious doubts or concerns about the death penalty. *Witherspoon* holds that jurors cannot be dismissed for cause in a capital case unless their views on the death penalty would make it impossible for them to return a sentence of death upon a guilty conviction. *Morgan* will be decided on identical grounds.

Justice White, for the Court, explains the issue as follows: "We decide here whether, during *voir dire* for a capital offense, a state trial court may, consistent with the Due Process Clause of the Fourteenth Amendment, refuse inquiry into whether a potential juror would automatically impose the death penalty upon conviction of the defendant."[390]

Following *Witherspoon*, the trial court, during jury selection, asked potential jurors if they would "automatically vote against the death penalty no matter what the facts of the case were."[391] All jurors eventually selected to serve on the jury stated that they could return a sentence of death if the facts so warranted. Morgan's attorney had requested the trial court to ask potential jurors the following question: "'If you found Derrick Morgan guilty, would you automatically vote to impose the death penalty no matter what the facts are?'"[392] The trial court denied the request, "stating that it had 'asked the question in a different vein substantially in that nature.'"[393] Justice White argues to the contrary that Morgan's Fourteenth Amendment due process rights were violated by the trial court's denial of Morgan's attorney's request insofar as that denial created the possibility that a defendant's life could rest on a juror's predetermined belief that a person convicted of murder should receive the death penalty. In other words, just as the state has a right to exclude jurors from capital cases who would never vote for the death penalty, Morgan has a right to exclude jurors who would always vote for the death penalty.[394]

For Justice White, a state has a right to exclude potential jurors who would ignore all aggravating circumstances and vote against a death sentence even if there were no mitigating circumstances. A defendant now has a right to exclude potential jurors who would ignore all mitigating circumstances and vote for a death sentence even if there were no aggravating circumstances.[395]

Justice Scalia, joined by Chief Justice Rehnquist and Justice Thomas, dissents. Scalia argues that there is nothing in the Constitution that entitles a defendant to a defense-favorable jury anymore than a state is entitled to a prosecution-favorable jury. *Witherspoon*, for Scalia, held "that a State may not skew the makeup of the jury *as a whole* by excluding all death-scrupled jurors."[396] Applying his words to *Morgan*, Scalia is saying that a juror predisposed to the death penalty does not necessarily "skew the makeup of the jury *as a whole*" toward the imposition of a death sentence. Scalia writes, "The fact that a particular juror thinks the death penalty proper *whenever* capital murder is established does not disqualify him."[397] Accordingly, Scalia finds that due process is not violated simply because a prospective juror who supports the death penalty would not consider mitigating circumstances in sentence determination. He writes that it is not "'fundamentally unfair' to allow Illinois to make specific inquiries concerning those jurors who will always vote against the death penalty but to preclude the defendant from discovering (and excluding) those jurors who will always vote in favor of death."[398] But why is it not fundamentally unfair to exclude potential jurors who would always vote against and not to exclude potential jurors who would always vote for the death penalty? The difference can be understood as follows.

A juror who would always vote against the death penalty regardless of the aggravating circumstances frustrates the legislative statute that demands the death penalty in response to specific types of murder. In addition, the people of Illinois will have been denied their democratic right to have statutes passed that reflect their will, provided, of course, that there is no violation of fundamental constitutional rights. For example, a legislative statute passed on the basis of a majority of the state's population that denies people the right to vote on the basis of race and gender would not withstand constitutional scrutiny. The death penalty, however, has been declared constitutionally valid in *Gregg*. Accordingly, one juror who would automatically vote against a state's valid death penalty statute frustrates the state, the will of the people, and possibly the eleven other jurors who have voted to impose the death penalty on the basis that the aggravating circumstances outweigh the mitigating circumstances. A juror, however, who would impose the death penalty regardless of any mitigating circumstances does not prevent the remaining eleven jurors from finding that the mitigating circumstances outweigh the aggravating circumstances. Justice Scalia writes that "[a] single death-penalty opponent can block that punishment [the death penalty], but eleven unwavering advocates cannot impose it."[399] However, to rephrase Scalia's point here, a single unwavering death penalty advocate cannot impose the death penalty on eleven jurors who find that the defendant does not qualify for the death penalty. The essential difference between the two cases, then, is that the consequences of the lone death penalty opponent are far greater than the consequences of the lone death penalty proponent.

HERRERA V. COLLINS

In *Herrera v. Collins* (506 U.S. 390 [1993] [argued 10/7/92; decided 1/25/93]), Herrera was convicted of the murders of two police officers and sentenced to death in Texas in 1982. In 1992 he claimed that his brother, now deceased, had actually murdered the two police officers. Chief Justice Rehnquist, for the Court, rejects Herrera's claim of innocence. Rehnquist bases his rejection on the formidable evidence presented at Herrera's trial,[400] the relevance of a conviction (e.g., "[o]nce a defendant has been afforded a fair trial and convicted of the offense for which he was charged, the presumption of innocence disappears"[401]), explains that "the passage of time only diminishes the reliability of criminal adjudications,"[402] and the peculiar offer by Herrera to have the death penalty vacated so "he could spend the rest of his life in prison."[403] Rehnquist examines as well some of the historical and common law practices to determine if Herrera has grounds for any judicial relief.[404] Rehnquist finds none. He holds that Texas has no obligation to consider Herrera's claim of innocence. Denying Herrera's assertion of "newly discovered evidence eight years after his conviction" does not violate "a principle of fundamental fairness 'rooted in the traditions and conscience of our people.'"[405] Is that, then, Herrera's last chance to have his claim of innocence heard? Not exactly.

Herrera, Chief Justice Rehnquist explains, has one final recourse, namely, executive clemency. "This is not to say, however, that petitioner [Herrera] is left without a forum to raise his actual innocence claim. For under Texas law, petitioner may file a request for executive clemency."[406] Rehnquist surveys briefly the history of executive clemency at the federal and state levels and finds that the only legitimate recourse for claims of innocence so long after the conviction and sentence rests in the executive power of clemency. It is that power that provides "the 'fail-safe' in our criminal justice system."[407] Rehnquist acknowledges that "our judicial system, like the human beings who administer it, is fallible."[408] Ample evidence exists, Rehnquist argues, that demonstrates that executive clemency has been quite effective in preventing what otherwise would be miscarriages of justice.[409] Besides, barring the few truly exceptional cases of error, requiring states to reexamine and possibly to retry cases long after the case has been decided will prove too burdensome on states in most cases. Herrera, then, must direct his appeal to the Texas governor.

Justice Blackmun, joined by Justices Stevens and Souter, dissents. Blackmun argues that sufficient ambiguity exists in Herrera's conviction that he should be entitled to a hearing in some court. If a person has evidence of innocence, then, regardless of historical practices or common law traditions, such evidence merits consideration.

Justice Blackmun argues as well that, although the presumption of innocence may no longer hold, "[t]he protection of the Eighth Amendment does not end once a defendant has been validly convicted and sentenced."[410]

As for Chief Justice Rehnquist's claim that a new trial would be less reliable, Justice Blackmun argues that Rehnquist misses the point of Herrera's claim. "The question is not whether a second trial would be more reliable than the first, but whether, in light of new evidence, the result of the first trial is sufficiently reliable for the State to carry out a death sentence."[411] Blackmun does not deny the fact that it is the defendant's burden to present sufficient evidence of the possibility of innocence. "When a defendant seeks to challenge the determination of guilt after he has been validly convicted and sentenced, it is fair to place on him the burden of proving his innocence, not just raising doubts about his guilt."[412] Still, if the defendant presents such evidence, it must be heard so as to avoid the possibility of executing an innocent human being. Blackmun concludes, "Of one thing, however, I am certain. Just as an execution without adequate safeguards is unacceptable, so too is an execution when the condemned prisoner can prove that he is innocent. The execution of a person who can show that he is innocent comes perilously close to simple murder."[413]

ROMANO V. OKLAHOMA

Romano was convicted of a murder committed in 1986 and sentenced to death. Romano was then tried for a different murder committed in 1985. He again received the death penalty. In *Romano v. Oklahoma* (512 U.S. 1 [1994] [argued 3/22/94; decided 6/13/94]), he appealed the second death sentence on the basis that during the sentencing phase the state informed the jury about Romano's conviction and death sentence for the previous trial. *Romano* argues that the introduction of that conviction and sentence undermined the "jury's sense of responsibility for determining the appropriateness of the death penalty, in violation of the Eighth and Fourteenth Amendments."[414] In Oklahoma, the jury, during deliberations on the appropriate punishment, must find at least one statutory aggravating circumstance and then determine if the aggravating circumstances outweigh the mitigating circumstances.

The jury found four aggravating circumstances, including, Chief Justice Rehnquist notes, "two of which are relevant to our discussion: (1) that petitioner had been previously convicted of a violent felony; and (2) that petitioner would constitute a continuing threat to society."[415] Romano introduced seventeen mitigating circumstances.

The jury weighed the aggravating and mitigating circumstances and sentenced Romano to death. While Romano appealed this decision, his previous death sentence was overturned by the Oklahoma Court of Criminal Appeals. Romano claims that the first conviction and sentence was unconstitutionally admitted into the sentencing stage at the second trial when the conviction and sentence in the first trial remained under appeal.

Chief Justice Rehnquist notes that the following question is the one the Court will answer: "Does admission of evidence that a capital defendant already has been sentenced to death in another case impermissibly undermine the sentencing jury's sense of responsibility for determining the appropriateness of the defendant's death, in violation of the Eighth and Fourteenth Amendments?"[416]

The Court majority's answer to that question is "no." Chief Justice Rehnquist writes, "We do not believe that the admission of evidence regarding petitioner's prior death sentence affirmatively misled the jury regarding its role in the sentencing process so as to diminish its sense of responsibility."[417]

Justice Ginsburg, joined by Justices Blackmun, Stevens, and Souter, dissents. Ginsburg, unlike Chief Justice Rehnquist, finds *Caldwell* relevant. Ginsburg writes, "In *Caldwell v. Mississippi*, 472 U.S. 320 (1985), this Court overturned a capital sentence as inadequately reliable because of a statement made by the prosecutor, in closing argument at the penalty phase of the trial."[418] The prosecutor in *Caldwell*, among other things, misrepresented the jury's role in sentencing. For Ginsburg, the same kind of result occurs here, namely, a jury may have been led to decide a sentence in part by misinformation. For Ginsburg, "the jury's consideration of evidence at the capital sentencing phase of petitioner Romano's trial, that a prior jury had already sentenced Romano to death, infected the jury's life-or-death deliberations."[419] Ginsburg "would vacate the death sentence imposed upon Romano and remand for a new sentencing hearing."[420]

SIMMONS V. SOUTH CAROLINA

The question before the Court in *Simmons v. South Carolina* (512 U.S. 154 [1994] [argued 1/18/94; decided 6/17/94]) focuses again on a due process issue, namely, if a "defendant's future dangerousness is at issue," must the jury be made aware that, in addition to the death penalty, the defendant could receive life imprisonment without the possibility of parole? Justice Blackmun, for the Court, answers affirmatively.

Simmons was on trial for the murder of "an elderly woman, Josie Lamb."[421] Before he went to trial, "he pleaded guilty to first degree burglary and two counts of criminal sexual conduct in connection with two prior assaults on elderly women."[422] He was convicted of the murder of Josie Lamb. At the sentencing hearing, Simmons's counsel introduced "mitigating evidence tending to show that petitioner's violent behavior reflected serious mental disorders that stemmed from years of neglect and extreme sexual and physical abuse petitioner endured as an adolescent."[423] The prosecution ended its presentation to the jury as follows:

In its closing argument, the prosecution argued that petitioner's future danger-ousness was a factor for the jury to consider when fixing the appropriate punish-ment. The question for the jury, said the prosecution, was "what to do with [petitioner] now that he is in our midst." The prosecution further urged that a ver-dict for death would be "a response of society to someone who is a threat. Your verdict will be an act of self-defense."[424]

The judge, when asked by the jury whether a life sentence carried the possibility of parole, refused to inform the jury that life imprisonment meant life imprisonment without the possibility of parole. For Justice Blackmun, the failure to inform the jury about sentencing options and what those options entailed violated Simmons's due process rights. The jury, for example, may have believed that a life sentence carried the possibility for parole. The jury made a decision based on information they were denied. The verdict, accordingly, is constitutionally infirm.

Justice Scalia, joined by Justice Thomas, dissents. Scalia argues that there is no constitutional foundation for the Court's holding. Information about parole, Scalia claims, typically is withheld from jury consideration. More than likely, Scalia argues, the jury sentenced Simmons to death because he deserved it. Reviewing the brutal murder and previous crimes of the defendant, Scalia is "sure it was the sheer depravity of those crimes, rather than any specific fear for the future, which induced the South Carolina jury to conclude that the death penalty was justice."[425]

HARRIS V. ALABAMA

How are aggravating and mitigating circumstances to be weighed? Can one statutory aggravating circumstance outweigh three mitigating circumstances? How should juries weigh aggravating and mitigating circumstances? To what extent is it constitutional to allow a judge to override a jury's sentence recommendation?

In Alabama, judges have the final word in sentence determination. The judge, however, must consider the jury's sentence recommendation. In *Harris v. Alabama* (513 U.S. 504 [1995] [argued 12/5/94; decided 2/22/95]), the jury recommended a life sentence without the possibility of parole. The judge ruled that the aggravating circumstances outweighed the mitigating circumstances and sentenced Harris to death. Justice O'Connor, for the Court, explains the issue as follows: "We granted certiorari to consider petitioner's argument that Alabama's capital sentencing statute is unconstitutional because it does not specify the weight the judge must give to the jury's recommendation, and thus permits arbitrary imposition of the death penalty."[426]

In Alabama, judges in capital cases need only to "'consider' the jury's recommendation."[427] Harris appeals on the basis that such judicial discretion makes it more likely that a death penalty will be handed out in an arbitrary and haphazard manner in violation of *Furman* requirements. Justice O'Connor defers here to states to determine how their punishments are to be determined, provided that there is no clear constitutional infringement. On several occasions Justices have argued that, given the finality of the death penalty, juries, not judges, should be responsible for sentence determination. O'Connor disagrees. The Supreme Court's role in criminal justice matters, according to O'Connor, "extends only to determine whether the policy choices of the community, expressed through its legislative enactments, comport with the Constitution."[428]

Justice O'Connor argues that there are no constitutional requirements that judges, rather than juries, determine the final punishment. A sentencing judge, all other things being equal, must be trusted to make a balanced judgment, which means, when necessary, to overrule a jury's recommendation.

Justice Stevens writes a stinging dissent. He argues "that the complete absence of standards to guide the judge's consideration of the jury's verdict renders the statute invalid under the Eighth Amendment and the Due Process Clause of the Fourteenth Amendment."[429] He maintains that juries, especially in Alabama, have standards that provide some direction in sentencing, whereas judges can too easily dismiss a jury's verdict. He writes, "In my opinion, total reliance on judges to pronounce sentences of death is constitutionally unacceptable."[430] His conclusion cannot be stated more eloquently and forcefully:

The Court today casts a cloud over the legitimacy of our capital sentencing jurisprudence. The most credible justification for the death penalty is its expression of the community's outrage. To permit the state to execute a woman in spite of the community's considered judgment that she should not die is to sever the death penalty from its only legitimate mooring. The absence of any rudder on a judge's free-floating power to negate the community's will, in my judgment, renders Alabama's capital sentencing scheme fundamentally unfair and results in cruel and unusual punishment. I therefore respectfully dissent.[431]

BUCHANAN V. ANGELONE

Buchanan had been tried for and convicted of murdering his father, stepmother, and two brothers in *Buchanan v. Angelone* (522 U.S. 269 [1998] [argued 11/3/97; decided 1/21/98]). Based on the Virginia aggravating circumstance of "vileness," the jury returned the death penalty despite several mitigating circumstances, including "his mother's early death from breast cancer, his father's subsequent remarriage, and his parents' attempts to prevent him from seeing his maternal relatives."[432]

The jury had been informed that it could not sentence Buchanan to death if Virginia failed to establish the aggravating circumstance of vileness. If the jurors did believe that the murders were vile, they were told that they must weigh that aggravating circumstance against the mitigating circumstances and return a verdict of life imprisonment if the evidence did not warrant the death penalty. No additional clarification was made.

Buchanan argues that the jury should have been instructed on each specific mitigating factor, followed by a statement that if that mitigating factor was present, "then that is a fact which mitigates against imposing the death penalty, and you shall consider that fact in deciding whether to impose a sentence of death or life imprisonment."[433] Buchanan proposed the following instruction as well: "In addition to the mitigating factors specified in other instruction, you shall consider the circumstances surrounding the offense, the history and background of [Buchanan] and any other facts in mitigation of the offense."[434]

The Virginia court refused to present these qualifying statements. Buchanan contends that the failure of the court to "to provide the jury with express guidance on the concept of mitigation, and to instruct the jury on particular statutorily defined mitigating factors" resulted in an unconstitutional application of the death penalty.[435] Specifically, without such guidance, Buchanan argues that the imposition of the death penalty can only be arbitrary and capricious.

Chief Justice Rehnquist, for the Court, maintains that such detailed instruction is not necessary to preserve the constitutional integrity of a jury's decision. The only instruction that juries need relative to mitigating circumstances is that they are to consider all mitigating circumstances presented by defense. States "may shape and structure the jury's consideration of mitigation so long as it does not preclude the jury from giving effect to any relevant mitigating evidence."[436] But there is no constitutional requirement that states "must affirmatively structure in a particular way the manner in which juries consider mitigating evidence."[437] Given the fact that there were two days of testimony regarding mitigating circumstances, along with the instruction that the jury was "to consider 'all the [mitigating] evidence,'" there is no basis to claim that the jury needs more specific direction and definition as it considers the appropriate punishment.[438] Rehnquist concludes, "The absence of an instruction on the concept of mitigation and of instructions on particular statutorily defined mitigating factors did not violate the Eighth and Fourteenth Amendments to the United States Constitution."[439]

Justice Breyer, joined by Justices Stevens and Ginsburg, dissents. In essence, Breyer argues that the additional instructions requested by Buchanan were necessary to guarantee that the jury considered seriously the mitigating circumstances. Breyer argues that the failure to provide the jury with more specific, clear, and coherent instructions on the relationship between aggravating and mitigating circumstances, and specifically how mitigating circumstances are to be weighed, does jeopardize a defendant's constitutional rights at sentencing. The instructions given the jury focus on the aggravating circumstances rather than the mitigating circumstances, thereby possibly tilting sentence determination toward death, a practice that cannot be constitutionally sustained.[440]

RING V. ARIZONA

In 2002 the Supreme Court decided two cases that constitute a sea change regarding death penalty cases. The first major departure from previous decisions occurred in *Atkins* when the Supreme Court ruled that it is unconstitutional to sentence mentally retarded criminals to the death penalty. The second major departure occurred in *Ring v. Arizona* (2002) (No. 01-488 [2002]) [argued 4/22/02; decided 6/24/02]) when the Supreme Court ruled that a death penalty must be handed down by a jury rather than by a judge. The decision in *Ring* could impact some 529 prisoners on death row in nine states: Arizona, Colorado, Idaho, Montana, Nebraska, Alabama, Delaware, Florida, and Indiana.[441] In one form or another, these nine states left the final determination of sentence to a judge or a three-judge panel. That determination is now suspect constitutionally, and several of those states have started the process of reviewing the cases of those on death row to determine if their sentence fails because of *Ring*.[442] While the full ramifications of *Ring* remain uncertain, there is no question but that at least nine states will have to change their capital punishment statutes.

Justice Ginsberg, for the Court, wrote that "[c]apital defendants, no less than non-capital defendants . . . are entitled to a jury determination of any fact on which the legislature conditions an increase in their maximum punishment."[443] Ginsburg explains, "In Arizona, following a jury adjudication of a defendant's guilt of first-degree murder, the trial judge, sitting alone, determines the presence or absence of the aggravating factors required by Arizona law for imposition of the death penalty."[444] Ring was convicted by the lower court of felony murder but not premeditated murder. Based on the information and facts presented at trial, there was no evidence that Ring participated in the crime, much less murder the victim. Ring certainly was connected to the money the robbery netted but not directly to the robbery or the murder. In order to sentence a criminal to the death penalty, a judge would have to find at least one aggravating circumstance. In this case, it would be an aggravating circumstance that the jury never heard and considered. Had that information been available, the jury might well have convicted Ring of premeditated murder. While the judge would still set the punishment, at least the jury's verdict would have enabled the trial judge to follow Arizona law relating to a verdict of premeditated murder and sentenced Ring to death, a punishment consistent with the jury's premeditated murder verdict. The relevance of this legal drama drew attention to the reality that a judge and not a jury would be solely responsible for assessing a death penalty. It is that reality that *Ring* addresses.

Justice Ginsburg identifies the constitutional issue as follows: "The question presented is whether [an] aggravating factor may be found by the judge, as Arizona law specifies, or whether the Sixth Amendment's jury trial guarantee, made applicable to the States by the Fourteenth Amendment [selective incorporation], requires that the aggravating factor determination be entrusted to the jury."[445] In other words, can capital sentencing decisions rest solely with a judge rather than a jury?

In a 1989 Florida case, *Hildwin v. Florida*,[446] in a per curiam opinion,[447] the Supreme Court held that the Constitution does not require capital sentences to be determined solely by a jury. In *Walton*,[448] the Court upheld Walton's death sentence against the claim that a jury and not a judge should be required to make the sentencing determination. In response to that claim, Justice White maintained that it was never the case that the Constitution mandated sentencing determinations by juries. If *Ring's* argument receives Supreme Court support, *Walton* and *Hildwin* are effectively overturned. That is exactly what occurred in Ring. In overturning *Walton*, Justice Ginsburg writes, "[W]e overrule Walton to the extent that it allows a sentencing judge, sitting without a jury, to find an aggravating circumstance necessary for imposition of the death penalty." In speaking about the importance of a jury trial, Ginsburg quotes from a 1968 case as follows: "'The guarantees of jury trial in the Federal and State Constitutions reflect a profound judgment about the way in which law should be enforced and justice administered. . . . If the defendant preferred the common-sense judgment of a jury to the more tutored but perhaps less sympathetic reaction of the single judge, he was to have it.'"[449]

Justice Scalia writes a concurring opinion. He states his position succinctly: "I believe that the fundamental meaning of the jury-trial guarantee of the Sixth Amendment is that all facts essential to imposition of the level of punishment that the defendant receives . . . must be found by the jury beyond a reasonable doubt."

Justice Scalia believes as well that Supreme Court decisions, "over the past 12 years," have come perilously close to sacrificing the fundamental right of trial by jury. Scalia writes that

[M]y observing over the past 12 years the accelerating propensity of both state and federal legislators to adopt "sentencing factors" determined by judges that increase punishment beyond what is authorized by the jury's verdict . . . cause[s] me to believe that our people's traditional belief in the right of trial by jury is in perilous decline. That decline is bound to be confirmed, and indeed accelerated, by the repeated spectacle of a man's going to his death because *a judge* [and not a jury] found that an aggravating factor existed. We cannot preserve our veneration for the protection of the jury in criminal cases if we render ourselves callous to the need for that protection by regularly imposing the death penalty without it.[450]

Justice Breyer writes a concurring opinion as well, although one that is not based on same principles as articulated by Justice Ginsburg and Scalia. His decision rests solely on the claim that he "believe[s] that jury sentencing in capital cases is mandated by the Eighth Amendment."[451] His position is based on two claims. First, "retribution provides the main justification for capital punishment" and, second, that a jury has a "comparative advantage in determining, in a particular case, whether capital punishment will serve that end."[452] Each point merits brief attention.

Justice Breyer's support of retribution is based on the belief that a jury has a better sense of a community's position on the death penalty than does a judge and that other justifications for the death penalty—deterrence, incapacitation, and rehabilitation—are without substantial foundation. First, Breyer notes that "[s]tudies of deterrence are, at most, inconclusive." Second, while "fewer offenders sentenced to life without parole (as an alternative to death) commit further crimes," as long as the convicted murderer remains alive, there remains as well the potential for the murderer to commit additional crimes. Third, "rehabilitation, obviously, is beside the point."[453] In acknowledging the legitimacy of retribution and the competency of juries, Breyer writes:

In respect to retribution, jurors possess an important comparative advantage over judges. In principle, they are more attuned to "the community's moral sensibility" . . . because they "reflect more accurately the composition and experiences of the community as a whole." . . . Hence they are more likely to "express the conscience of the community on the ultimate question of life or death," . . . and better able to determine in the particular case the need for retribution, namely, "an expression of the community's belief that certain crimes are themselves so grievous an affront to humanity that the only adequate response may be the penalty of death."[454]

Justice Breyer notes as well that even democratically elected judges are unlikely "to change the jury's comparative advantage [since] the jury remains uniquely capable of determining whether, given the community's views, capital punishment is appropriate in the particular case at hand."[455] For Breyer, "the Eighth Amendment requires individual jurors to make, and to take responsibility for, a decision to sentence a person to death."[456]

Justice O'Connor, joined by Chief Justice Rehnquist, dissents. Primarily she does not accept the majority's claim that Walton should be overturned. She sees no reason why a judge cannot make a final sentencing determination. In addition, the majority's ruling in *Ring* will more than likely prove disastrous for the courts. She writes:

The Court effectively declares five States' capital sentencing schemes unconstitutional. . . . There are 168 prisoners on death row in these States [Arizona, Colorado,

Idaho, Montana, and Nebraska], each of whom is now likely to challenge his or her death sentence. . . . [T]he need to evaluate these claims will greatly burden the courts in these five States. In addition, I fear that the prisoners on death row in Alabama, Delaware, Florida, and Indiana, which the Court identifies as having hybrid sentencing schemes in which the jury renders an advisory verdict but the judge makes the ultimate sentencing determination, may also seize on today's decision to challenge their sentences. There are 529 prisoners on death row in these States.[457]

The cases considered here reflect the variety of opinion and discord that exists among the Justices regarding the constitutionality of the death penalty. The positions on both sides are articulated carefully and reflectively. The Justices address the meaning of the death penalty historically, its justification philosophically, and its legal standing constitutionally. There is no unanimity of opinion among the Justices, nor should there be, given a social issue as sensitive and complex as the death penalty. It should be clear that the predominant position of the Court in 2002 sustains the constitutionality of the death penalty. That does not mean, however, that the Justices are moving in a direction that is constitutionally sound or defensible. Based on the range of opinion that has been encountered in these cases, chapters 5 and 6 focus on concerns I do not think can be addressed satisfactorily so as to meet the requirements set forth in *Furman* necessary to sustain capital punishment.

CHAPTER 5

The Ongoing Constitutional Debate

When a federal court is asked to review a state court's application of an individual statutory aggravating or mitigating circumstance in a particular case, it must first determine whether the statutory language defining the circumstance is itself too vague to provide any guidance to the sentencer. If so, then the federal court must attempt to determine whether the state courts have further defined the vague terms, and, if they have done so, whether those definitions are constitutionally sufficient, i.e., whether they provide some guidance to the sentencer. In this case, there is no serious argument that Arizona's "especially heinous, cruel or depraved" aggravating factor is not facially vague. But the Arizona Supreme Court has sought to give substance to the operative terms, and we find that its construction meets constitutional requirements.

Justice Sandra Day O'Connor, *Walton v. Arizona*

In my view, two Arizona statutory provisions, pertinent here, run afoul of the established Eighth Amendment principle that a capital defendant is entitled to an individualized sentencing determination which involves the consideration of all relevant mitigating evidence. The first is the requirement that the sentencer may consider only those mitigating circumstances proved by a preponderance of the evidence. The second is the provision that the defendant bears the burden of establishing mitigating circumstances "sufficiently substantial to call for leniency." I also conclude that Arizona's "heinous, cruel or depraved" aggravating circumstance, as construed by the Arizona Supreme Court, provides no meaningful guidance to the sentencing authority and, as a consequence, is unconstitutional.

Justice Blackmun, *Walton v. Arizona*

In 2002, the Supreme Court does not have one voice that argued that the death penalty by its very nature constitutes a cruel and unusual punishment in violation of the Eighth Amendment. The retirements of Justices Brennan, Marshall, and Blackmun silenced the voices that had held the death penalty, in one form or another, unconstitutional. That does not mean that the current Justices support the death penalty unequivocally. It does mean, however, that states will have to violate some very fundamental constitutional right before the Supreme Court will overturn a death sentence. Even then, the likelihood is that the case will be returned to the original court for a retrial that results once again in the imposition of the death penalty.

Individuals who support the death penalty (retentionists) find their position currently politically popular and constitutionally strong. One source of dissatisfaction retentionists have with the death penalty is that it takes too long to impose. Individuals who oppose the death penalty (abolitionists) find their position currently politically unpopular and constitutionally weak. One source of gratification abolitionists have with the death penalty is that some states are calling for a moratorium on capital punishment while the moral and constitutional problems that their criminal justice systems have encountered are examined. Certainly, from a political or constitutional perspective, the abolitionists are substantively outnumbered. That does not mean, however, that the death penalty will remain constitutionally irrevocable. The sole purpose of this chapter is to identify some concerns that will continue to follow the Court as it weaves its way around the labyrinthian death penalty minefield.

The arguments for and against the death penalty's constitutionality are found in the cases examined in chapters 3 and 4. In this chapter I focus on some of the dissenting opinions in those cases that have been decided since post-*Furman* statutes have been legislated. In fact, the dissenting opinions in those cases that sustained a sentence of death provide a good sense of the constitutional difficulties inherent in the determination of guilt and innocence and, if guilty, the determination of the appropriate punishment. The constitutional difficulties with the death penalty raised here may one day be resolved in favor of the death penalty, but I doubt it. These difficulties, when considered collectively, present a formidable challenge to the death penalty's continued use, despite popular opinion and perceived constitutional strength. A word of caution, however, is in order.

In chapters 3 and 4 I presented the plurality and dissenting opinions without any evaluative comments. That was intentional. In this chapter I ignore, for the most part, the plurality opinions in support of the death penalty. I will not weigh the arguments for and against the death penalty as judges and juries weigh aggravating and mitigating circumstances to determine a defendant's sentence. But it is important to keep in mind that the following concerns are dissenting in nature. Do not underestimate, however, the strengths of the plurality opinions. For example, I disagree with most of the death penalty votes cast by Chief Justice Rehnquist and Justice Scalia. Nonetheless, I have great respect for their positions and the means by which they reason to those positions. In short, there are good arguments for the death penalty. Many of those arguments were presented in chapter 4. My goal in this chapter is to offer some critical reflection on concerns that I think cannot be resolved in favor of the death penalty. That does not mean that the death penalty is about to be legislated out of existence. It is easy to forget the social appeal of the death penalty. In 1989, for example, David Gottlieb, a professor at the University of Kansas School of Law, wrote optimistically about Kansas rejecting death penalty legislation in 1987 and 1989. While he acknowledged that "it would be a mistake to try to make too much out of these developments," he did think that "one might suspect that capital punishment will command less and less attention as our years as an abolitionist state continue to increase."[1] Gottlieb was wise not to make too much of those legislative victories. Kansas reinstated the death penalty in 1994. My position on the death penalty focuses on seven issues relative to the determination of sentence.

First, and foremost, the use of aggravating and mitigating circumstances as the means to avoid the arbitrary and capricious implementation of the death penalty has failed, and will always fail. More specifically, aggravating circumstances fail to distinguish between convicted murderers who should receive the death penalty from those who should not receive the death penalty in a manner that meets the Fourteenth Amendment's requirement "nor shall any state deprive any person of life, liberty, or property, without due process of law; nor deny to any person within its jurisdiction the equal protection of the laws."[2] Second, the appointment of incompetent or inexperienced counsel to defend indigent capital offenders runs an enormous risk that such defendants will be more likely to end up on death row. Third, the selection of jurors in capital cases risks the distinct possibility of a conviction-prone jury. Fourth, it is logically impossible to provide juries with "guided discretion" while requiring that they make "individualized sentencing" determinations. Fifth, victim impact statements introduce information at the sentencing stage that serves only to make more subjective a process that must avoid arbitrary and capricious judgments. Sixth, prosecutors contribute to the haphazard use of the death penalty by determining what defendants shall be charged with a capital crime. I begin with what I consider the most egregious aspect of death penalty determination, the use of aggravating circumstances as the means by which death penalties allegedly overcome charges of arbitrary and capricious death penalty judgments.

I maintain that aggravating circumstances enable us to cloak a highly subjective and necessarily arbitrary punishment under a guise of moral and legal objectivity. Aggravating circumstances relieve capital jurors, and the people they represent, from confronting the reality of the capital decision they are called on to make. Aggravating circumstances are all the more problematic because they enable jurors to believe that they were "just doing their job." Aggravating circumstances are among the most serious flaws in capital sentencing schemes. I have several problems with these circumstances, both theoretical and practical.

To begin theoretically, what does the use of aggravating circumstances suggest? What reality, if any, do these circumstances hide? For example, aggravating circumstances suggest to me that some murders are not as "bad" as other murders, and therefore are less deserving of the death penalty. Do aggravating circumstances offer members of society some psychological security by taking only the lives of the worst people in it? Do these circumstances lull people into a false sense of moral accountability? Are people less likely to question the moral legitimacy of taking the lives of really monstrous people if they can appeal to a process that distinguishes between terrible murderers and not-so-terrible murderers? Consider the following hypothetical example.

Regarding a not-so-terrible murderer, a murderer who *just* takes a life, do people, perhaps subconsciously, think as follows: "Well, yes, he murdered his girlfriend, but at least he did not torture her or mutilate her body. He *just* killed her." Has just killing becomes less offensive and less punishable than aggravated murder? When did that happen? And on whose authority? Why am I not entitled to answer: "Hey, that was my daughter he murdered. It was not *just* a killing. Granted, he's not a rapist/murderer as was Ted Bundy, but he murdered my daughter. He too deserves the death penalty."

Why is it that someone needs to commit a vile and depraved murder to be eligible for the death penalty? The Bible states that in matters of harm a person "shall give life for life, tooth for tooth, hand for hand, foot for foot, burn for burn, wound for wound, stripe for stripe."[3] The Bible does not state "an eye for an eye only if an ice pick is used." There are no qualifications to the punishments for these offenses; no aggravating circumstances offer grounds for a reduction in the seriousness of the offense or the severity of the punishment. The Bible states as well that "[w]hoever sheds the blood of man, by man shall his blood be shed."[4] My point in selecting these two brief biblical passages is not to argue in support of abolishing aggravating and mitigating circumstances and mandating the death penalty for any first-degree murderer. My point here is to demonstrate part of the folly that results from legislative and judicial efforts to make the death penalty as "objective" as possible.

The use of aggravating circumstances lead people to think that some murders are more offensive, that is, "aggravating," than others and therefore that it is only those murderers who deserve to die. That claim, however, at least retributively, does not make sense. Several Supreme Court Justices, as noted in chapters 3 and 4, argued that retribution is a valid justification for punishment. The retributive philosophy holds that the punishment must fit the crime. In cases of murder, people who murder forfeit their lives. But when aggravating circumstances are necessary to justify capital punishment, does that not lessen the value of all murder victims who were *just* murdered? Efforts to differentiate between heinous and not-so-heinous murders disturb me. The efforts of legislators and judges to make those subtle nuances serve only to blur the law and to confuse the public. Do I mean, then, that society should put all guilty murderers to death since they, on retributive grounds, deserve to die? Not exactly.

From a retributive perspective, the punishment must fit the crime. The death penalty, in theory, "fits" only those who *do not commit* vile and vicious murders, those who do not meet any of the aggravating circumstances categories. The "suitable" retributive punishment for murder is death. What, then, is the suitable punishment for rape and murder? Should society find a way to rape and kill a convicted rapist/murderer? What should society do to those felons who have done even more despicable acts than murder, such as desecrating the body, setting the body on fire, or cutting the victim's body into parts? Did the Court error when it ruled in *Coker* that the death penalty was disproportionate to the crime of rape? For example, would it be reasonable to hold that while the death penalty is disproportionate in the rape of an adult, it is quite appropriate for the rape of a child?[5] These questions require a reevaluation of aggravating circumstances. But before any discussion about the constitutionality of aggravating circumstances occurs, people should ask themselves what they want punishments to signify. For example, if only despicable (aggravated) murderers are sentenced to death, what does that say about nondespicable murderers? Aggravating circumstances require society to say about some murders something like the following: "Well, she's not so bad. She just killed her husband with one clean shot to the heart. He never suffered. He never even knew what hit him." The use of aggravating circumstances brings society perilously close to making very similar kinds of statements. For example, not desecrating a victim's body does not strike me as a charitable, kind, or virtuous act. I find the entire concept of aggravating circumstances disturbing as their existence implies that some murders are not really that offensive (i.e., not violent or aggravating). But I find that implication unacceptable, for it implies that relatives of a murder victim should derive some peace knowing that their loved one was not brutally murdered. I agree that some murders are more heinous than others, but that does not change the degree of the murder. I find that the aggravating circumstances measuring rod raises an unanswered question, namely, why should a not-so-bad murderer be less deserving of death, either in terms of retribution, deterrence, or the Constitution? That theoretical concern aside, however, there are practical issues to consider.

Since the Supreme Court has supported unequivocally aggravating circumstances, the next question must be, do aggravating circumstances really satisfy *Furman* demands that the death penalty not be arbitrarily and capriciously imposed?

The use of aggravating circumstances by judges and juries has narrowed the field of death-eligible defendants. The most heinous acts imaginable have been committed, and those truly guilty of such acts have been met with a justifiable, constitutional response, namely, the death penalty. But aggravating circumstances do not adequately address the *Furman* concerns that the death penalty be implemented in a nonarbitrary and noncapricious manner. Although aggravating circumstances may narrow the class of death-eligible felons and provide some guided discretion to juries and judges as they deliberate between the death penalty and life imprisonment with or without parole, they do not prevent the death penalty from arbitrary and capricious implementation.

Aggravating circumstances, as noted in *Zant*, are designed to achieve two objectives, namely, to "narrow the class of persons eligible for the death penalty and [to] reasonably justify the imposition of a more severe sentence on the defendant compared to others found guilty of murder."[6] But do they do that? Even if it is assumed that aggravating and mitigating circumstances provide the constitutional foundation for legitimate death sentences, their application does not necessarily guarantee that arbitrary and capricious death penalty sentences will not be handed down. Aggravating circumstances alone fail to meet *Furman* and *Gregg* requirements of individualized sentencing and guided discretion. The aggravating circumstance identified by terms such as wantonly vile, depravity of mind, heinous, atrocious, depraved, cruel, and utter disregard for human life, identify part of the difficulty in achieving these twin objectives. By the very definitions of these terms, jurors must use subjective judgments in applying these terms. Intentionally or unintentionally, such judgments can prove arbitrary and capricious.

In *Godfrey*, one of Georgia's aggravating circumstances was that the murder "was outrageously or wantonly vile, horrible, or inhuman in that it involved torture, depravity of mind, or an aggravated battery to the victim."[7] In *Gregg*, the Supreme Court did not identify this aggravating circumstance as unconstitutional. In *Godfrey*, the Court reconsidered its decision in *Gregg* partly on the basis that the justices did not think that Georgia would apply that statutory aggravating factor so broadly. Justice Stewart, for the Court, maintained that these aggravating circumstances could be used provided that the judge explains their scope. In *Godfrey*, Stewart argued that the lower court failed to provide any clarification of these terms in such as way that a jury could understand the nature and scope of their application. Stewart, for example, states that "[p]art of a State's responsibility in this regard is to define the crimes for which death may be the sentence in a way that obviates 'standardless [sentencing] discretion.' It must channel the sentencer's discretion by 'clear and objective standards' that provide 'specific and detailed guidance,' and that 'make rationally reviewable the process for imposing a sentence of death.'"[8] The problem in *Godfrey*, for Justice Stewart, occurs because, without clear and substantial explanation of the aggravating circumstance, "[t]here is no principled way to distinguish this case, in which the death penalty was imposed, from the many cases in which it was not."[9] In short, the failure to explain this aggravating circumstance made it impossible to guide the jury's discretion.

Chief Justice Burger and Justice White, however, wrote separate dissenting opinions.[10] White explains his position in terms of the obviously heinous nature of the murders:

As described earlier, petitioner, in a cold-blooded executioner's style, murdered his wife and his mother-in-law and, in passing, struck his young daughter on the head with the barrel of his gun. The weapon, a shotgun, is hardly known for the surgical precision with which it perforates its target. The murder scene, in consequence, can only be described in the most unpleasant terms. Petitioner's wife lay prone on the floor. Mrs. Godfrey's head had a hole described as "[a]pproximately the size of a silver dollar" on the side where the shot entered, and much less decipherable and more extensive damage on the side where the shot exited. Pellets that had passed through Mrs. Godfrey's head were found embedded in the kitchen cabinet.

It will be remembered that, after petitioner inflicted this much damage, he took out time not only to strike his daughter on the head, but also to reload his single-shot shotgun and to enter the house. Only then did he get around to shooting his mother-in-law, Mrs. Wilkerson, whose last several moments as a sentient being must have been as terrifying as the human mind can imagine. The police eventually found her face-down on the floor with a substantial portion of her head missing and her brain, no longer cabined by her skull, protruding for some distance onto the floor. Blood not only covered the floor and table, but dripped from the ceiling as well.[11]

Justice White finds the Court's judgment, as did Chief Justice Burger, unjustifiable. Both maintain that the Court has overstepped its proper role in judicial oversight of a state capital statute that does meet *Furman* and *Gregg* requirements. Given White's description of the murders, however, how can the Court hold that the murders were not "outrageously vile, horrible, or inhuman"? What kind of definition must the sentencing court offer that can guide juries to a constitutionally sound punishment? The *Godfrey* confusion continues.

In *Barclay v. Florida*,[12] the Court accepts the Florida aggravating circumstance of "especially heinous, atrocious, or cruel." The judge, in sentencing Barclay, compared World War II Nazi concentration camps with the race war that Barclay and his cohorts sought to start. Chief Justice Rehnquist, for the Court, explains the Court's position as follows:

The United States Constitution does not prohibit a trial judge from taking into account the elements of racial hatred in this murder. The judge in this case found Barclay's desire to start a race war relevant to several statutory aggravating factors. The judge's discussion is neither irrational nor arbitrary. In particular, the comparison between this case and the Nazi concentration camps does not offend the United States Constitution. Such a comparison is not an inappropriate way of weighing the "especially heinous, atrocious, or cruel" statutory aggravating circumstance in an attempt to determine whether it warrants imposition of the death penalty.[13]

Chief Justice Rehnquist explains as well that sentencing judgments cannot be made mechanically, as if devoid of human experience. He writes:

We have never suggested that the United States Constitution requires that the sentencing process should be transformed into a rigid and mechanical parsing of statutory aggravating factors. But to attempt to separate the sentencer's decision from his experiences would inevitably do precisely that. It is entirely fitting for the moral, factual, and legal judgment of judges and juries to play a meaningful role in sentencing. We expect that sentencers will exercise their discretion in their own way and to the best of their ability. As long as that discretion is guided in a constitutionally adequate way, and as long as the decision is not so wholly arbitrary as to offend the Constitution, the Eighth Amendment cannot and should not demand more.[14]

The language in *Godfrey*, then, that a murder was "outrageously or wantonly vile," must be less directive than the language "especially heinous, atrocious, or cruel" in *Barclay*. I fail to see the subtle difference between the two aggravating circumstances in these two cases. How can "heinous, atrocious, or cruel" clarify grisly murders in a way that "outrageously or wantonly vile" does not? Is it that a comparison to a Nazi concentration camp provides clearer direction to the jury? The Court, however, seemingly unable to draw a clear line between similarly stated aggravating circumstances, continues to face the problems these aggravating circumstances create. But the confusion does not end there.

In *Poland v. Arizona*,[15] the judge sentenced the Poland brothers to the death penalty on the basis of the aggravating circumstance "especially heinous, cruel, or depraved."[16] It was the Arizona Supreme Court, however, that ruled, consistent with *Godfrey*, that that standard does not meet the constitutional requirements for a valid aggravating circumstance. The Polands, however, were convicted and sentenced to death on a different aggravating circumstance. Accordingly, the Supreme Court did not have to draw a line between "especially heinous, atrocious, or cruel" and "especially heinous, atrocious, cruel, or depraved." Still, the Arizona Supreme Court merely applied what it understood to be a constitutional line that the United States Supreme Court had established in *Godfrey*. Fortunately for the Arizona Supreme Court, but not for the Polands (Michael Poland was executed on June 17, 1999; his brother remains on death row), other valid aggravating circumstances sustained the death penalties.

In *Maynard*[17] the Supreme Court rejected the aggravating circumstance "heinous, atrocious, or cruel" as constitutional. The Court found no obvious indication that the terms were given any specificity that would direct the judge or jury in deciding Cartwright's sentence. Justice White, for the Court, offers the following summation of Cartwright's crimes:

On May 4, 1982, after eating their evening meal in their Muskogee County, Oklahoma, home, Hugh and Charma Riddle watched television in their living room. At some point, Mrs. Riddle left the living room and was proceeding towards the bathroom when she encountered respondent Cartwright standing in the hall holding a shotgun. She struggled for the gun, and was shot twice in the legs. The man, whom she recognized as a disgruntled ex-employee, then proceeded to the living room, where he shot and killed Hugh Riddle. Mrs. Riddle dragged herself down the hall to a bedroom, where she tried to use a telephone. Respondent, however, entered the bedroom, slit Mrs. Riddle's throat, stabbed her twice with a hunting knife the Riddles had given him for Christmas, and then left the house. Mrs. Riddle survived, and called the police. Respondent was arrested two days later, and charged with first-degree murder.[18]

Superficially it appears that these acts were indeed "especially heinous, atrocious, or cruel." Justice White disagrees. There is no effort on the part of the legislature or the court to clarify these terms in any way that would enable a sentencer to distinguish Cartwright's acts from those that might not be "especially heinous, atrocious, or cruel." For White, these terms are no more clearly articulated in *Maynard* than they were in *Godfrey*. He explains the problem, in part, as follows:

The Oklahoma court relied on the facts that Cartwright had a motive of getting even with the victims, that he lay in wait for them, that the murder victim heard the blast that wounded his wife, that he again brutally attacked the surviving wife, that he attempted to conceal his deeds, and that he attempted to steal the victims' belongings. Its conclusion that, on these facts, the jury's verdict that the murder was especially heinous, atrocious, or cruel was supportable did not cure the constitutional infirmity of the aggravating circumstance.[19]

Accordingly, for the Court, the aggravating circumstance of "especially heinous, atrocious, or cruel" fails to meet *Furman* requirements insofar as it offers no explanation as to how those terms apply. Once again, however, I remain confused. If the clarification of "especially heinous, atrocious, or cruel" in terms of the description of the murder and attempted murder fails to direct a jury's sentencing discretion, I want to know what kind of description or clarification would direct satisfactorily that discretion.

In *Walton*[20] the Court affirmed the aggravating circumstance of "especially heinous, cruel or depraved manner." While additional aggravating circumstances applied in *Walton* as well, Justice White, for the Court, argued that *Walton* does differ substantively and relevantly from *Maynard* and *Godfrey.* In *Walton,* for example, a judge determined the meaning of the terms, heinous and depraved, not a jury. Judges, so White reasons, are better situated, given their education and experience, to understand and apply the law. Here, on review, the Arizona Supreme Court provided the review of the terms in such a way that the terms do have meaning not established in similar cases. White writes:

> Recognizing that the proper degree of definition of an aggravating factor of this nature is not susceptible of mathematical precision, we conclude that the definition given to the "especially cruel" provision by the Arizona Supreme Court is constitutionally sufficient because it gives meaningful guidance to the sentencer. Nor can we fault the state court's statement that a crime is committed in an especially "depraved" manner when the perpetrator "relishes the murder, evidencing debasement or perversion," or "shows an indifference to the suffering of the victim and evidences a sense of pleasure" in the killing.[21]

For this and other reasons, Walton's death penalty was sustained.

In *Stringer,*[22] a Mississippi case, the aggravating circumstance "especially heinous, atrocious, or cruel" is challenged in light of *Clemons* and *Maynard* where the aggravating circumstance "especially heinous, atrocious, or cruel" was declared unconstitutionally vague.[23] Stringer was convicted of capital murder and received the death penalty, in part, on the basis of the aggravating circumstance "especially heinous, atrocious, or cruel,"[24] the identical aggravating circumstance declared invalid by the Supreme Court in *Clemons* and *Maynard.* Stringer's sentence, however, had been decided before the Supreme Court's holding in *Clemons* and *Maynard.* On the basis of those two cases Stringer appeals his conviction, an appeal that appears consistent with the judgments in *Clemons* and *Maynard.* Did Stringer have a legitimate claim?

Mississippi is another weighing state. Once an aggravating circumstance has been determined, the jury must "weigh" aggravating and mitigating circumstances to determine if the defendant deserves the death penalty. Given Mississippi's weighing process in capital cases, Justice Kennedy, for the Court, argued that aggravating circumstances must be defined "with some degree of precision" to avoid the haphazard imposition of the death penalty.[25] Kennedy argued that state appellate courts can reweigh aggravating and mitigating circumstances that led to the death penalty, but they must conduct "a thorough analysis of the role an invalid aggravating factor played in the sentencing process."[26] In fact, Kennedy argues that "the use of a vague aggravating factor creates the possibility not only of randomness but also of bias in favor of the death penalty" that could require invalidating a death sentence because the "weighing process" had been contaminated by the invalid aggravating circumstance.[27] Given that no one could know what punishment a jury would have recommended absent the invalid aggravating circumstance, Stringer's death penalty was vacated.

In *Sochor v. Florida*,[28] Sochor challenged two of the four aggravating circumstances used to sentence him to death, namely, "the crime for which the defendant is to be sentenced was especially wicked, evil, atrocious or cruel, and [that] the crime for which the defendant is to be sentenced was committed in a cold, calculated and premeditated manner, without any pretense of moral or legal justification."[29]

The Florida Supreme Court rejected Sochor's claim that the "especially wicked, evil, atrocious or cruel" circumstance was constitutionally unsound. The Florida Supreme Court, however, agreed with Sochor that the evidence to support the "cold, calculated and premeditated manner" circumstance had not been established. Nonetheless, the Florida Supreme Court sustained the death penalty on the basis that the three aggravating circumstances sufficed to uphold the death sentence, especially since no mitigating circumstances existed that would require the aggravating and mitigating circumstances to be reweighed.

Justice Souter, for the Court, held that the Florida Supreme Court did not err in upholding the "especially wicked, evil, atrocious or cruel" circumstance. Souter agreed with the Florida Supreme Court that the second aggravating circumstance ("cold, calculated and premeditated manner") was not supported by the evidence. Souter, however, did not agree with the Florida Supreme Court that the invalidity of the second circumstance constituted harmless error. Accordingly, Souter vacates Sochor's death penalty. Souter explains as follows:

In sum, Eighth Amendment error occurred when the trial judge weighed the coldness factor. Since the Supreme Court of Florida did not explain or even "declare a belief that" this error "was harmless beyond a reasonable doubt" in that "it did not contribute to the [sentence] obtained," the error cannot be taken as cured by the State Supreme Court's consideration of the case. It follows that Sochor's sentence cannot stand on the existing record of appellate review. We vacate the judgment of the Supreme Court of Florida, and remand the case for proceedings not inconsistent with this opinion.[30]

Chief Justice Rehnquist and Justices White, Thomas, and Scalia concur in the Court's rejection of Sochor's claim that the heinous factor violated his constitutional rights. They agreed as well that the trial judge erred when he "weighed the invalid 'coldness' factor in imposing Sochor's death sentence."[31] They dissent, however, in the Court's overturning the death penalty because they maintain "that the Supreme Court of Florida cured this sentencing error by finding it harmless."[32] They would sustain Sochor's death sentence.

In *Richmond v. Lewis*, [33] the heinous factor again enters the death penalty debate. Richmond challenges his death sentence on the basis "that the 'especially heinous, cruel or depraved' aggravating factor . . . upon which the sentencing judge relied, was unconstitutionally vague."[34] Consistent with the numerous Supreme Court cases that have rejected as unconstitutionally vague the heinous factor, Justice O'Connor, for the Court, holds Richmond's death sentence invalid. She writes, "Petitioner's death sentence was tainted by Eighth Amendment error when the sentencing judge gave weight to an unconstitutionally vague aggravating factor. The Supreme Court of Arizona did not cure this error, because the two justices who concurred in affirming the sentence did not actually perform a new sentencing calculus. Thus, the sentence, as it stands, violates the Eighth Amendment."[35]

In the 1993 Supreme Court case *Arave v. Creech*,[36] the Court accepted an aggravating circumstance similar to "heinous, atrocious and cruel." Thomas Creech pled guilty of murdering a fellow inmate at the Idaho State Penitentiary and sentenced to death. The aggravating circumstance used to help sentence him to death was that he "exhibited utter disregard for human life."[37] Creech was serving life sentences for twenty-six murders he either committed or participated in. The trial judge at the sentencing hearing acknowledged the mitigating circumstance that Creech did not start the fight that led to the inmate's death. However, the judge found the aggravating circumstance that Creech went far beyond doing what was necessary to defend himself. Indeed, the judge wrote, "The murder, once commenced, appears to have been an intentional, calculated act."[38] The Idaho Supreme Court affirmed the death sentence on that basis that the standard—"utter disregard for human life"—does help distinguish between those who should receive the death penalty and those who should not. The phrase itself, according to the Idaho Supreme Court, does offer a sufficient standard to evaluate whether a death penalty should be imposed. The Idaho Supreme Court wrote: " 'We conclude instead that the phrase is meant to be reflective of acts or circumstances surrounding the crime which exhibit the highest, the utmost, callous disregard for human life, i.e., the cold-blooded, pitiless slayer.' "[39] Justice O'Connor, for the Court, states the constitutional issue in *Arave* as follows: "The sole question we must decide is whether the 'utter disregard' circumstance, as interpreted by the Idaho Supreme Court, adequately channels sentencing discretion as required by the Eighth and Fourteenth Amendments."[40]

Justice O'Connor argued that the Idaho standard does provide the content necessary to make the aggravating circumstance of "utter disregard for human life" consistent with constitutional sentencing requirements in capital cases. She noted, for example, that states must " 'channel the sentencer's discretion by clear and objective standards that provide specific and detailed guidance, and that make rationally reviewable the process for imposing a sentence of death.' "[41] She wrote that "the phrase 'cold-blooded pitiless slayer' is not without content." She noted that *Webster's Third New International Dictionary* "defines 'pitiless' to mean devoid of, or unmoved by, mercy or compassion." Cold-blooded refers to " 'marked by absence of warm feelings: without consideration, compunction, or clemency.' "[42]

Justice O'Connor acknowledges that the words—pitiless and cold-blooded—could loosely apply to all murders. In reality, they do not. She writes:

Given the statutory scheme, however, we believe that a sentencing judge reasonably could find that not all Idaho capital defendants are "cold-blooded." That is because some within the broad class of first-degree murderers do exhibit feeling. Some, for example, kill with anger, jealousy, revenge, or a variety of other emotions. In *Walton*, we held that Arizona could treat capital defendants who take pleasure in killing as more deserving of the death penalty than those who do not. Idaho similarly has identified the subclass of defendants who kill without feeling or sympathy as more deserving of death. By doing so, it has narrowed in a meaningful way the category of defendants upon whom capital punishment may be imposed.[43]

Responding to the concern that utter disregard for human life and cold-blooded do not appear to differ significantly from the unconstitutional use of heinous, atrocious, or cruel, Justice O'Connor writes, "In light of the consistent narrowing definition given the 'utter disregard' circumstance by the Idaho Supreme Court, we are satisfied that the circumstance, on its face, meets constitutional standards."[44] Two Justices, however, do not see it her way.

Justice Blackmun, joined by Justice Stevens, dissents. Blackmun does not mince words.

Confronted with an insupportable limiting construction of an unconstitutionally vague statute, the majority in turn concocts its own limiting construction of the state court's formulation. Like "nonsense upon stilts," however, the majority's reconstruction only highlights the deficient character of the nebulous formulation that it seeks to advance. Because the metaphor "cold-blooded" by which Idaho defines its "utter disregard" circumstance is both vague and unenlightening, and because the majority's recasting of that metaphor is not dictated by common usage, legal usage, or the usage of the Idaho courts, the statute fails to provide meaningful guidance to the sentencer, as required by the Constitution. Accordingly, I dissent.[45]

Justice Blackmun argues that the Court has deviated here from the constitutional requirement that standards be articulated that distinguish between defendants who deserve the death penalty and those who do not. The Court's majority, for Blackmun, has failed to explain that standard relative to pitiless and cold-blooded. Blackmun grants that the facts in this case were particularly brutal and gruesome, but that does not alter the constitutional requirement for clear and coherent sentencing guidelines. Quoting *Maynard*, Blackmun writes, "We have 'plainly rejected the submission that a particular set of facts surrounding a murder, however shocking they might be, were enough in themselves, and without some narrowing principle to apply to those facts, to warrant the imposition of the death penalty.'"[46]

Justice Blackmun argues that "[e]very first-degree murder will demonstrate a lack of regard for human life, and there is no cause to believe that some murders somehow demonstrate only partial, rather than 'utter' disregard."[47] Blackmun focuses throughout his dissent on the futility to make verbal distinctions by reference to other verbal ambiguities. Ultimately, if the terms utter disregard and cold-blooded can be constitutionally applied to *Creech*, then they can be applied to virtually all capital cases, if for no other reason than that all murders demonstrate an utter disregard for human life. Blackmun writes, "If Creech somehow is covered by the 'utter disregard' factor as understood by the majority, then there can be no doubt that the factor is so broad as to cover any case."[48]

This limited review of some of the cases that raise concerns about aggravating circumstances such as heinous, depraved, utter disregard for human life, depraved, outrageously or wantonly vile, and atrocious constitutes, for me, an example of the failure of post-*Furman* statutes to overcome the charge that death penalties are imposed in an arbitrary and haphazard manner. Aggravating circumstances were designed to distinguish between murderers who should be executed and murderers who should not. In my opinion, these circumstances fail miserably to make constitutional distinctions that reflect "equal justice under law." In this context it should be remembered that the Supreme Court only hears on average about four to six death penalty cases each year out of the countless death penalty cases decided in lower courts each year. What about the over 3,800 people who sit on death row as a result of an aggravating circumstance that appears, at least to me, as subjective as any criteria pre-*Furman* capital punishment statutes offered? From my perspective, legislators and judges are engaged in a futile effort to address *Furman* concerns. On that basis alone, and at the very least, a moratorium on executions is warranted. I want to note, however, an additional practical concern raised by the use of aggravating and mitigating circumstances to determine death-eligible defendants.

If jurors are to balance aggravating and mitigating circumstances, how will they do it? James R. Acker and Charles S. Lanier, among others, have raised these issues.[49] As Acker and Lanier note, "[t]he most widely used sentencing model requires the judge or jury to identify the aggravating and mitigating factors associated with the offense and offender, to balance or weigh those factors against one another, and to make a punishment decision on the comparative assessment."[50] But what does that mean in practice?

In general, Acker and Lanier summarize the various options states have used to help judges and juries to return a responsible verdict. States can be found that require that one statutory aggravating circumstance must be cited before any nonstatutory aggravating circumstances can be cited. In addition, some states do not permit any nonstatutory aggravating circumstances to be cited. All states are required as well to permit all relevant mitigating circumstances. Of course, what is relevant remains less than clearly defined or in any way limited. Then there are the judge's instructions to the jury about how to balance aggravating and mitigating circumstances. But no instruction exists to state clearly, much less to guide clearly, a jury's deliberations.[51] To repeat a previous question, can one statutory aggravating circumstance outweigh three mitigating circumstances? Acker and Lanier raise another issue in this context. For example, what is to be done if only one statutory aggravating circumstance is identified and no mitigating circumstances are identified? Does that system then not constitute a kind of mandatory death sentence in violation of *Woodson* and *Roberts*? Not according to the Court in *Blystone v. Pennsylvania*. The Court there upheld a death sentence imposed on a convicted murderer who was unable to list any mitigating circumstances. But should that mean that the convicted murderer automatically (mandatorily) gets the death penalty? What if the jury believes that the statutory aggravating circumstance was not that aggravating? "For example, the sentencer has no opportunity to assess the moral significance of the aggravating factor(s) at issue, nor to consider directly whether the offender's conduct is so condemnable that capital punishment is appropriate under the facts of a particular case."[52] Again, these issues only begin to depict the constitutional quagmire that aggravating and mitigating circumstances have created. The constitutional concerns, however, do not end here.

My second concern, the presence of incompetent or inexperienced counsel in capital cases, receives clear articulation from Stephen Bright. He reveals judicial practices that render "the right to counsel all but meaningless."[53] For example, on at least three occasions "the defendant's lawyer slept during trial." In one case, the presiding judge "permitted the trial to continue on the theory that '[t]he Constitution doesn't say the lawyer has to be awake.'"[54] Bright cites numerous examples of sleeping defense attorneys whose clients were executed. One defense attorney known for sleeping through trials had ten defendants receive the death penalty, one of whom has been executed. David D. Langfitt and Billy H. Nolas offer additional examples that reinforce Bright's claims of incompetent defense attorneys.[55] In one case the defense attorney did not present any mitigating circumstances. Fortunately, a federal district court ruled that the defendant had not received effective sentence of counsel.[56] In another case, two attorneys failed to defend their client on the basis that the defendant had informed them that he wanted to die. His defense attorneys "apparently accepted his statement at face value: They did not investigate his background or mental health. When the court-appointed psychiatrist testified that the defendant was competent to stand trial, they did not cross-examine." Langfitt and Nolas continue, "Both attorneys later testified that they believed they had no duty to represent the defendant, given his desire to die. They conducted no investigation, did not interview his family or friends, and did not obtain any medical or other records. In fact, they did nothing to defend a client who was facing the death penalty."[57] Langfitt and Nolas detail attorney incompetence in capital trials. One case is particularly noteworthy.

In another case, the defense lawyer met his client the day before the jury was selected. Not surprisingly, he prepared no defense. When new counsel raised a claim of ineffective assistance, the defense lawyer testified that it was his practice not to meet clients until just before the trial began so that he would not be prejudiced in listening to the prosecution's evidence when developing a defense. He also testified that he would ask his client to testify without preparation in the capital penalty phase so that he could hear the evidence just as the jury heard it—fresh and for the first time—before making his summation.[58]

For Lanffitt and Nolas, "these cases reflect the arbitrariness of the death penalty. Although every case involved grossly deficient lawyering, some of the defendants were executed, and some were not."[59] In short, over twenty-five years of post-*Furman* review has, in many cases, not changed the reality found unacceptable in *Furman*. There is, however, another element to consider in this context.

The old saying "you get what you pay for" accurately describes the plight of defendants who cannot afford to hire the best counsel. For example, in one of the cases identified by Bright, the "court-appointed attorney [was] paid $11.84/hour."[60] Langfitt and Nolas offer the following fictional description of a "typical scenario" of court-appointed counsel.

A man whom you [an attorney] have never met is arrested for a brutal murder. The court that will preside at trial appoints your firm to represent him. The defendant never graduated from high school, never held a steady job, and is a poor communicator. He has no prior relationship with your firm.

Your new client is indigent and cannot pay anything. Instead, the firm will be compensated by the same court that will preside at both trial and sentencing. There is no retainer. Payment will be a *fraction* of what the firm could expect for equivalent hourly fee work. In fact, the firm will receive a flat fee of $8,000 for the entire case. The court will give you a limit of just $2,000 to cover experts and an investigator.[61]

For many people, the $8,000 may appear lucrative. But it does not begin to cover the costs necessary to receive a fair trial in a capital case. Indigent defendants, the condition of most defendants in capital trials, will continue to receive inadequate counsel for several reasons; one is that the court-appointed defense attorneys or public defenders cannot put in the kinds of hours necessary to defend a defendant adequately in a capital case. And they cannot put in the necessary hours in part because they are insufficiently compensated. Langfitt and Nolas offer a vivid example of the costs involved in a capital defense.

Investigations and interviews . . . are not done for an indigent capital defendant because there simply is not enough money to do the work. Likewise, counsel simply cannot afford to retain the consultants and testifying experts who would be hired for a well-heeled client. It should come as no surprise that appointed counsel in capital cases often fail to investigate every defense and prepare every promising witness, particularly in cases that seem hopeless because of the strong evidence of guilt.[62]

For Langfitt and Nolas, "[t]he more closely one looks at our current system of capital punishment, the more one sees just how arbitrary it really is."[63]

Bright's summation about Texas justice paints the same picture. He writes, "Texas has neither an independent judiciary nor an adequate system for providing representation to the poor. As a result, the process by which poor people are condemned to death is often a farce, a mockery, and a disgrace to the legal system and the legal profession."[64] Texas, however, is an extreme example. Bright notes that Texas, since *Gregg*, executed 200 convicted murderers "before any other state executed seventy-five."[65] What occurs in Texas, however, occurs in most other states as well, only on a smaller scale. Bright notes that "other states lack independent judiciaries and inadequate indigent defense systems. Judges are elected in thirty-two of the thirty-eight states that have the death penalty. The removal of judges perceived as 'soft on crime' has made it clear to those remaining on the bench that upholding the law in capital cases comes at their own peril."[66] If poor legal representation were the only problem with the system, many of those conditions could be more adequately challenged and changed. Unfortunately, that does not happen to be the case.

My third concern focuses on jury selection in capital cases. *Witherspoon* held that potential jurors could not be excluded from jury duty simply because they had some misgivings about the morality of the death penalty. Potential jurors can be excluded only if their beliefs would prevent them from either finding a defendant guilty of a capital crime if the evidence so warranted or if they could not bring in a sentence of death if the evidence so warranted. But does the exclusion of potential jurors opposed to the death penalty create juries that are conviction-prone? Justices Brennan and Marshall believe so. Brennan argued that jurors selected in part on the basis that they can bring in a sentence of death if the evidence warrants automatically placed the defendant at a disadvantage. "If the presently prevailing view of the Constitution is to permit the State to exact the awesome punishment of taking a life, then basic justice demands that juries with the power to decide whether a capital defendant lives or dies not be poisoned against the defendant."[67] For Brennan, "[b]road death-qualification threatens the requirement that juries be drawn from a fair cross-section of the community and thus undermines both the defendant's interest in a representative body and society's interest in full community participation in capital sentencing."[68] He believes that the Court, in *Wainwright,* acted as little more than a rubber stamp for state imposition of the death penalty. "Like the death-qualified juries that the prosecution can now mold to its will to enhance the chances of victory, this Court increasingly acts as the adjunct of the State and its prosecutors in facilitating efficient and expedient conviction and execution irrespective of the Constitution's fundamental guarantees. One can only hope that this day too will soon pass."[69] Since little has changed since 1985, it does not appear that "this day will soon pass." This is not the only context, however, in which the objectivity of jurors can be challenged.

Jurors, as much as we honor and value them, are not necessarily pillars of justice. Joseph L. Hoffman offers some insight into the nature of how juries function in capital cases.[70] Hoffman reports some initial findings by one of the most extensive research projects undertaken—the "Capital Jury Project"—to study how juries function in capital cases. He focuses on two general questions. First, how do different factors affect jury deliberation? Among the factors he identifies, one of the most important factors a jury considers "is whether the defendant, if he is allowed to live, is likely to pose a danger to society in the future."[71] A death sentence, then, in some cases, may depend more on what the jury projects the future to hold—an incredibly arbitrary and capricious judgment—than on what it in reality might be. For example, oftentimes juries are confused about the alternatives to the death penalty. If juries understood more clearly that life imprisonment without the possibility of parole in reality actually meant life imprisonment without the possibility of parole, would they bring in a death sentence? In many states life imprisonment without the possibility of parole is a genuine sentencing option, "[y]et 31.9 percent of the jurors we interviewed said that, based on their understanding of the judge's instructions, the law 'required' a death sentence if the defendant would be 'dangerous in the future.'"[72]

A fourth issue concerns statutory efforts to universalize and individualize death penalty judgments. Post-*Furman* capital punishment statutes try to balance individualized sentencing procedures with guided discretion. Stephen R. McAllister states that "the Supreme Court identified and applied two primary principles that now form the core of the Court's Eighth Amendment capital jurisprudence. These principles are that (1) the sentencer must be given specific guidance regarding how to determine when death is an appropriate sentence (the 'guided discretion' principle) and (2) in making that determination, the sentencer must be permitted to consider each defendant's situation on an individual basis (the 'individualized sentencing' principle)."[73] Logically, these two principles are incompatible. The more guided discretion a state has, the less applicable is individualized sentencing; the more individualized sentencing a state has, the less guided discretion a state has. According to McAllister, however, the need to balance the two principles has not been achieved and may never be achieved.[74] "Neither principle can be extended except at the expense of the other. The Supreme Court largely has ignored the conflict and purported to decide capital cases as if the principles coexist in harmony. Unless and until the full Court acknowledges the dilemma, no solution will be forthcoming."[75]

A fifth concern is based on the use of VISs as debated in *Booth v. Maryland*, *South Carolina v. Gathers*, and *Payne v. Tennessee*. At issue in these three cases was the constitutionality of using victim impact statements at the sentencing stage of the trial, a statement that could more easily result in a sentence of death. In *Booth* and *Gathers*, the Court rejected any attempt by prosecutors to use either VISs or to find a means to introduce information about the victim that might tilt the scales of justice toward the death penalty. In both cases, the Court reasoned that VISs were unconstitutional on the basis that information irrelevant to the crime, and therefore to the punishment, prejudiced the defendant's case and punishment by directing jury attention away from what is relevant about the crime and the defendant's participation in it. In *Payne v. Tennessee*, however, the Court reversed itself and held VISs constitutional. Now the victim's family can present, at the sentencing phase of a capital trial, what the death of this beloved family member meant. Are VISs constitutional?

On the surface, such considerations appear logical. Chief Justice Rehnquist, in *Payne,* argued that VISs constituted one more piece of relevant information that permitted juries to consider the harm the defendant caused. After all, if the defendant has an opportunity to present evidence in mitigation, why should the victim's family not be permitted to testify to what that murder has done to the victim's family? Despite Rehnquist's claim that such information guides juries and judges as they consider the individualized sentence to inflict, there are at least three problems with these statements.

First, the death penalty would be based in part on highly subjective criteria, a situation the Supreme Court tried to minimize in capital cases. Juries already have numerous considerations to weigh in reaching a defensible decision. Aggravating and mitigating circumstances alone require careful scrutiny. The addition of victim impact statements can only serve to make the decision-making process more complicated and hence more likely to result in arbitrary and capricious sentences.

Second, VISs elevate the victim's social worth at the expense of the defendant's trial, a trial that is supposed to be about crimes committed, not people victimized. For example, a man convicted on rape charges should be sentenced according to statutes prescribing sentencing options. The sentence must not be based on whether the victim was a popular or an unpopular professor. To state the obvious, a rape is a rape. It does not become less of a rape because the person raped was unpopular.

Third, and following directly from the second, criminals will be sentenced on the importance of the victim, not the seriousness of the crime. Amy K. Phillips explains this third point rather vividly. In fact, the title of her article captures the problem in seven words: "Thou Shalt Not Kill Any Nice People."[76] VISs inform judges and juries about the social worth and importance of the victim. That is what they are designed to do. What do these statements ultimately imply? They imply that some lives are more important than others. If an obscure professor of philosophy (e.g., me) and a well-known and highly respected neurosurgeon are murdered, which of the two will have the better chance that his or her murderer will receive the death penalty? Phillips writes, for example, that "victim impact evidence invites the jury to evaluate the victim's characteristics, such as wealth, class, and family characteristics, and to value the victim's worth accordingly."[77] In addition, "[b]ecause prosecutors are aware of the power of victim evidence on capital sentencers, prosecutors will become more likely to seek the death penalty in cases where there is an attractive victim."[78] Since 1991, VISs have added another element to the trial that only can serve to reinforce the prosecuting attorney's story. VISs constitute a kind of prosecutorial trump card. They can tip the balance of victory

toward the prosecutor's position by continuing and reinforcing the prosecutor's charges.

In her conclusion, Phillips reiterates one of the major liabilities of a VIS,
namely, it "risks the imposition of the death penalty according to the perceived 'social worth' of the victim."[79] Rather than contributing to the difficult task of evaluating an appropriate punishment, VISs could present
"juries with an easy, although improper, way out of a difficult decision."[80]
Because it appears that VISs are politically popular, Phillips makes one
specific recommendation. "Because victim impact statements are likely to
encourage the imposition of the death penalty according to the 'worth' of
the victim, and because legislators are unlikely to repeal victim impact
laws in the current political environment, judges should exercise their discretion to limit victim impact statements to the degree allowed by law in
capital sentencing hearings."[81]

Phillips's position finds reinforcement in Joshua D. Greenberg's arguments against the Court's position in *Payne*.[82] As he notes in his introduction, "*Payne* is constitutionally infirm not because it injected a new
element of randomness into the capital sentencing process, but rather
because it permits negligently caused harm to make the difference
between life and death and because it rests on the Justices' misplaced
desire to 'balance' victims' position at sentencing with that of defendants."[83] Greenberg has the same misgivings as Phillips regarding the
socially, politically, and legally popular VISs.

Until *Payne*, the Court had never held that negligently caused harm could, consistent with the Eighth Amendment, make the difference between life and death. . . .
Clearly the Court will not revisit the relevance of victim-impact evidence to capital sentencing hearings for the foreseeable future. Thus, Payne stands as yet
another monument to the Court's confused conception of culpability and its evi-
dent desire to take any means necessary to exit the business of monitoring the
States' implementation of capital punishment.[84]

VISs, in short, contribute to the arbitrary imposition of the death penalty;
they contribute to the failure of courts to meet *Furman* requirements necessary to avoid the charge that capital punishment is imposed arbitrarily
and capriciously. The following observation on VISs has been made:

Surely chief in significance among the many recent victim-oriented changes
within the criminal justice system is the use of "victim impact evidence," an emotionally potent brand of evidence modestly designed to provide "a quick glimpse"
of the "unique" life taken by the convicted murderer. Eight years after *Payne v. Tennessee* permitted the use of impact evidence in capital trials, however, it is obvious
that far more than a mere "quick glimpse" is being offered jurors. Capital juries
now regularly absorb extensive, highly inflammatory victim impact evidence,
and, receive precious little in the way of guidance as to its purpose and function in

death decisions. Compounding these problems, appellate courts have effectively disavowed any meaningful role in the review of the emotionally potent evidence, making the permissible bounds of impact evidence all the more uncertain.[85]

Victim-impact evidence seems to have a life of its own. There is no clear means to control it so as to guarantee that defendants convicted of murder will have the remotest chance of receiving "equal justice under law." The problems with such statements, however, do not end here.

An additional problem in this connection is that VISs reinforce the views of those who oppose retributive justifications of punishment on the basis that retribution constitutes little more than revenge. Austin Sarat, the William Nelson Cromwell professor of jurisprudence and political science at Amherst College, for example, argues that attempts to distinguish between retribution and revenge end, necessarily, with the collapse of one into the other.[86] I maintain, contrary to Sarat, that retribution and revenge are totally separate and distinguishable concepts. Yet I must agree with him that the introduction of VISs can blur the line between retribution and revenge. Sarat writes, "Victim impact evidence is valuable precisely because it is not abstract and impersonal. It insists that punishment respond to real pain. The jury is asked to hear that pain and to avenge it, to repay death with death to end the victimization. The unmasking of the retribution-revenge distinction, as well as the return of revenge, is now complete as the victim is given both a voice and a champion."[87] VISs carry undeniably emotional issues that must be controlled to avoid a legitimate charge that death penalties have more to do with revenge than they do with retribution or deterrence. Thus far, courts have exercised little control of VISs. It is doubtful that they can.

Finally, VISs serve to nullify mitigating circumstances. The jurors, or the judge in a bench trial, hear from the victim's family and loved ones. The Supreme Court has not established any clear limits on VISs (anymore than states have set limits on prosecutorial discretion). The prosecutor, of course, can argue that the Court has not placed any meaningful limits on mitigating circumstances either. For example, what is the legal relevance of a prison guard's statement in mitigation that the defendant had been a model prisoner while awaiting trial? Immanuel Kant, a retributivist, argued that the only consideration permitted in the determination of punishment is the law of retribution, the law that prescribes the retributive principle that the punishment must fit the crime. Kant writes, "But it should be understood that only the law of retribution can determine exactly what quality and quantity of punishment is required, and it must do so in court, not within your private judgment. All other criteria are inconstant; they cannot be reconciled with the findings of pure and strict justice, because they introduce other outside considerations."[88] VISs introduce outside considerations that can corrupt the legal process. Prior to

VISs, the prosecutor and the defense attorney played, to some extent, on a level playing field. That parity, with the advent of VISs, no longer exists.

A sixth issue is raised by the fact that prosecutors determine whether to seek a death penalty in the first place. Before any trial begins, a prosecutor has the discretion not only to bring charges but also what charges, if any, to bring. Prosecutorial discretion exists at all levels in the criminal justice system. District attorneys determine what cases to prosecute and to what extent they are to be prosecuted. Indeed, plea-bargaining itself can take the death penalty off the sentencing table. While that discretion exists with respect to all criminal prosecutions, it becomes more problematic in death penalty cases for the simple and often repeated reason that death is different. "Equal justice under law" may be compromised from the start. For example, if a first-degree murderer has some worthwhile information with which to bargain, a first-degree murder charge could be reduced to second-degree murder. The following comment focuses specifically on prosecutorial discretion in New York:

Under the terms of the [New York] death penalty statute, the People, acting through individual juries, may impose the penalty of death only if the prosecutor chooses to charge, and has given prior notice of the intention to pursue such a punishment. Because the statute is silent as to the scope or limits of the prosecutor's discretion in this matter, a prosecutor's decision may be based upon a variety of factors, including personal beliefs or opinions and political consideration, instead of upon objective legal considerations as to whether certain conditions are present which justify implementation of the statute. . . .

Consequently, charging the death penalty may depend on arbitrary decision-making processes reflective of an individual prosecutor's moral or ideological position on the death penalty, or on his or her notion of justice.[89]

It must be remembered as well that prosecutors differ from one county to the next regarding these personal considerations. The capital punishment process, then, almost by definition, involves arbitrary, because subjectively discretionary, decisions that affect all potential capital defendants. Should death depend on such discretionary power?

The issues raised here are not by any means the only concerns that can be articulated regarding the use of the death penalty. For example, now that juries must decide between life or death, a defendant's fate rests on his or her community's moral, religious, or political beliefs, among others, as theoretically represented by a jury of one's peers. Such a realization indicates just how difficult it will be to set forth any standards or conditions that will satisfy *Furman* requirements. How, for example, should juries be selected? Should a person's life depend on whether a juror is Catholic, Methodist, Muslim, or Mormon? Would an atheistic or agnostic juror sentence differently? Would university professors make good jurors? Perhaps what capital defendants need is a jury composed of philosophy teachers. Or perhaps what *Furman* and all post-*Furman* cases indicate is that it is virtually impossible to sentence people to death in a way that meets constitutional requirements. The death penalty should be rejected, perhaps, not because it does not deter or because retributive principles are difficult to meet, but because every death sentence is based on situations and conditions that must, by definition, be subjective and therefore arbitrary and capricious. True, all criminal cases carry the same limitations. Prisons cannot be closed because some subjective elements of the criminal justice system exist. But the death penalty can be rejected because *death is different*.

CHAPTER 6

Reflections and Conclusions

Cases such as these provide for me an excruciating agony of the spirit. I yield to no one in the depth of my distaste, antipathy, and indeed, abhorrence, for the death penalty, with all its aspects of physical distress and fear and moral judgment exercised by finite minds. That distaste is buttressed by a belief that capital punishment serves no useful purpose that can be demonstrated. For me, it violates childhood's training and life experiences, and is not compatible with the philosophical convictions I have been able to develop. It is antagonistic to any sense of "reverence for life." Were I a legislator, I would vote against the death penalty.

> Justice Harry Blackmun, dissenting, *Furman v. Georgia*

From this date forward, I no longer shall tinker with the machinery of death. For more than twenty years I have endeavored—indeed, I have struggled—along with a majority of this Court, to develop procedural and substantive rules that would lend more than the mere appearance of fairness to the death penalty endeavor. Rather than continue to coddle the Court's delusion that the desired level of fairness has been achieved and the need for regulation eviscerated, I feel morally and intellectually obligated simply to concede that the death penalty experience has failed. It is virtually self-evident to me now that no combination of procedural rules or substantive regulations ever can save the death penalty from its inherent constitutional deficiencies.

> Justice Harry Blackmun, dissenting, *Callins v. Collins*

Justice Blackmun's journey from 1972 to 1994, through hundreds of death penalty cases heard and not heard,[1] represents the struggle all people should have with a punishment that, by its finality alone, raises questions about what a nation must do with citizens who murder. For Blackmun, twenty-two years of effort to make the death penalty constitutionally palatable proved in vain. Ultimately, for Blackmun, the judicial system, regardless of the fail-safe mechanisms built into it, such as bifurcated trials, aggravating and mitigating circumstances, and guaranteed appellate review, cannot end completely the arbitrary and capricious infliction of the death penalty. That is not to say that the judicial system is otherwise perfect. Erroneous convictions occur throughout the criminal justice system.[2] But there is a clear difference between a death and a nondeath sentence. The difference, obviously, is death. Arbitrary and capricious nondeath sentences can, to some extent, be rectified. But, as Supreme Court Justices have noted on numerous occasions, "death is different." Wrongful deaths cannot be undone. Blackmun realized that tinkering "with the machinery of death" could never change the substantive constitutional hurdles necessary to avoid the problems with the death penalty defined so clearly and coherently in the plurality opinions in *Furman*.

Reflecting on these cases leaves me, more often than not, with mixed emotions. As I read about some of the gruesome, inhuman, barbaric, and savage acts that have been committed against others, the death penalty does not even begin to compensate for the evil done. I cannot imagine a punishment that could be inflicted on some of these murderers that would satisfy either retributive or deterrent justifications for punishment without that punishment reflecting negatively on society. To recall an earlier question, what can be done to people who rape, torture, and then murder their victims? What punishment would be necessary to achieve retribution in such cases? What punishment could deter such people? Even if there was a punishment for the most heinous crimes committed that would meet both retributive and deterrent justifications, should that punishment be used?

For a moment, and for illustrative purpose, let us suspend the cruel and unusual punishment clause of the Eighth Amendment. What punishment, then, could be inflicted that might satisfy either or both social goals of retribution and deterrence for serial rapists/murderers? Shall serial rapists/murderers be boiled alive, axed to death, or burned at the stake? How about being flayed alive? There is precedent for each. According to Geoffrey Abbott, a person flayed alive "was first castrated then endured the removal of his entire skin while still alive."[3] Does that sound about right retributively for the rapist/murderer? I cannot imagine that it would not serve as a deterrent. Of course, to achieve the desired effect, the punishment (being flayed alive) might need to be televised. Mass murderers, on the other hand, would not be castrated, but could be made to suffer "under the scalpel-like blade as their skins were peeled away, strip by strip, dying as their flesh was laid bloodily bare."[4] But what retributive punishment corresponds with a crime that includes rape, murder, and bodily mutilation? What retributive punishment corresponds to someone who hacks off a person's arms? Could hacking off a person's arms serve to deter such abominable acts? If deterrence is the primary social goal of punishment, and the Eighth Amendment remains suspended, should drunk drivers be summarily executed, that is, executed on the spot, without any trial or defense attorney? What if the summary execution of drunk drivers reduced drunk driving incidents by 95 percent? Would people want to live in a society in which a drunk driver could be summarily executed on the basis of a failed sobriety test at a sobriety checkpoint? I believe that the announcement that seventeen drunk drivers were summarily executed on a Monday would have a dramatic impact on drinking and driving on Tuesday. And I believe that some people in society would support that police action. If the policy worked, that is, if it did indeed serve as a deterrent, would the execution be justified? If someone steals, why not cut off that person's hands? At least that person will not steal again, at least with his or her hands. Were it not for the cruel and unusual punishment clause, such actions could be used. But would members of society accept these draconian forms of punishment? I want to think not. I know some people would not object, but I believe that the vast majority would. But if the vast majority of members of society accepted those punishments, what would that say about that society? My point here is simple, but unfortunately, controversial. In the end, neither retributive nor deterrent philosophies ultimately drive the punishment machine, for if they did, society would have to bring back centuries-old punishments. The rack, the iron maiden, the nail through the ear, and being torn apart by horses would be viable punishments[5] that would, in my opinion, degrade and corrupt all members of society. Indeed, one argument against the death penalty is that it has a brutalizing effect on society. William J. Bowers and Glenn L. Pierce describe the effect as follows:

The lesson of the execution, then, may be to devalue life by the example of human sacrifice. Executions demonstrate that it is correct and appropriate to kill those who have gravely offended us. The fact that such killings are to be performed only by duly appointed officials on duly convicted offenders is a detail that may get obscured by the message that some such offenders deserve to die. If the typical murderer is someone who feels that he has been betrayed, dishonored, or disgraced by another person—and we suggest that such feelings are far more characteristic of those who commit murder than a rational evaluation of costs and benefits—then it is not hard to imagine that the example executions provided may inspire a potential murderer to kill the person who has greatly offended him. In effect, the message of the execution may be lethal vengeance, not deterrence.[6]

Bowers and Pierce may exaggerate the possible effect about which they speculate, but the idea, for me, moves in the right direction. What messages do punishments send? Are those the messages society wants to send? Could they be sent in a more creative way? Are there any moral limits to the means by which the messages are sent? For example, Timothy McVeigh was executed by lethal injection for his role in the devastating bombing of the Alfred P. Murrah Federal Building in Oklahoma City, Oklahoma, that claimed 168 lives and permanently injured, physically and psychologically, many more. I read four newspaper reports of his execution and what that execution meant to those who had lost loved ones.[7] Among the families who lost loved ones in the fiendish bombing, few experienced any shared feelings. Some reported relief; some felt unappeased; some described a feeling of emptiness; some maintained that "death" was too easy for the mass murderer. What available punishment could satisfy all of these individually unique wants and needs? And now, after September 11, if we could apprehend, try, and convict those still living who are responsible for over 3,000 deaths, what punishment would serve retributive and deterrent purposes? I do not believe that we have any punishment that would serve either of these purposes. What, then, should society do to people like McVeigh and those who plotted the murders of innocent people in New York City, at the Pentagon, and in Pennsylvania?

The general alternative recommended to the death penalty is life imprisonment without the possibility of parole. I cannot accept that alternative. I maintain that life imprisonment with the possibility of parole after having served twenty-five years in prison would satisfy most retributive and deterrent needs. Parole boards, however, must review seriously the crimes of the defendant under parole consideration. For example, McVeigh, had he received my recommended sentence, would never be granted parole. In addition, a life sentence would accomplish another social goal as well, namely, the most fiscally sound punishment available. As a nation that embraces capitalism, McVeigh's execution constitutes a temporary lapse of sound economic judgment. The costs associated with capital trials and capital punishments are beyond the scope of my inquiry. Those costs, however, must be recognized.[8] When moral and constitutional arguments fail, the revelation of the fiscally unsound death penalty might change some minds. (If we want to end the capital punishment game, all arguments must be used. It is not crass to oppose the death penalty solely for economic reasons; indeed, it is myopic to ignore such costs.) McVeigh's trial has cost the government, at the very minimum, $15 million. "The taxpayer's tab for defending Oklahoma City bomber Timothy McVeigh stood at an estimated $15 million even before his futile appeals—and now will probably go much higher. Under federal rules for death penalty cases, the government paid the fees and expenses for McVeigh's two main defense lawyers at his trial and for three others during the appeals process."[9] Had the government sought life imprisonment without parole or with very limited parole possibility, the costs would have dropped dramatically, perhaps by as much as $14 million. As noted, I doubt that McVeigh would ever be granted parole, if for no other reason than to prevent him from being murdered. The money saved could have been used instead to help the affected families receive the counseling they will surely need and to pay for the physical and psychological therapy the injured survivors clearly need. McVeigh would be sitting in a nine-by-six cell at an estimated cost of $30,000/year. Assuming that he would live fifty years, it would cost only $1.5 million at today's prices to ensure that he never again sees the light of day. In short, the death penalty constitutes the worst kind of financial investment.

In general, then, I am not convinced that any punishment offers any final answer. Punishments are absolutely essential until society devises better methods to reduce crime dramatically. The only justification that makes sense in the short run is incapacitation. The more felons can be removed from society, the fewer crimes those individuals can commit. In the long run, however, improving on the methods of punishment, including capital punishment, will not solve the crime problem. Still, until society understands more about the causes of crime and the best means to reduce or to minimize those causes, should the death penalty continue to serve as the punishment for those who commit aggravated murders? I believe that society, while it must punish, does not need the death penalty in its arsenal of punishment options. Some murders, however, are so horrific that the death penalty seems to be not only constitutional but also absolutely necessary. Consider the following two cases.

In *Baldwin v. Alabama*, Brian Baldwin was on trial for the following:

The facts are sordid, but a brief recital of them must be made. Petitioner Brian Keith Baldwin, then 18 years of age, escaped from a North Carolina prison camp on Saturday, March 12, 1977. That evening, he and a fellow escapee, Edward Horsley, came upon 16-year-old Naomi Rolon, who was having trouble with her automobile. The two forcibly took over her car and drove her to Charlotte, N.C. There, both men attempted to rape her, petitioner sodomized her, and the two attempted to choke her to death. They then ran over her with the car, locked her in its trunk, and left her there while they drove through Georgia and Alabama. Twice, when they heard the young woman cry out, they stopped the car, opened the trunk, and stabbed her repeatedly. On Monday afternoon, they stole a pickup truck, drove both vehicles to a secluded spot, and, after again using the car to run over the victim, cut her throat with a hatchet. She died after this 40-hour ordeal.[10]

Justice Scalia addresses Justice Blackmun's concern in *Callins v. Collins* as follows:

Convictions in opposition to the death penalty are often passionate and deeply held. That would be no excuse for reading them into a Constitution that does not contain them, even if they represented the convictions of a majority of Americans. Much less is there any excuse for using that course to thrust a minority's views upon the people. JUSTICE BLACKMUN begins his statement by describing with poignancy the death of a convicted murderer by lethal injection. He chooses, as the case in which to make that statement, one of the less brutal of the murders that regularly come before us—the murder of a man ripped by a bullet suddenly and unexpectedly, with no opportunity to prepare himself and his affairs, and left to bleed to death on the floor of a tavern. The death-by-injection which JUSTICE BLACKMUN describes looks pretty desirable next to that. It looks even better next to some of the other cases currently before us which JUSTICE BLACKMUN did not select as the vehicle for his announcement that the death penalty is always unconstitutional—for example, the case of the 11-year-old girl raped by four men and then killed by stuffing her panties down her throat. How enviable a quiet death by lethal injection compared with that! If the people conclude that such more brutal deaths may be deterred by capital punishment; indeed, if they merely conclude that justice requires such brutal deaths to be avenged by capital punishment; the creation of false, untextual and unhistorical contradictions within "the Court's Eighth Amendment jurisprudence" should not prevent them.[11]

That the defendants in these two cases received the death penalty does not make me morally uneasy about their situation on death row. Contrary to popular belief and opinion, death row is not a fun place to spend one's life.[12] However, it is precisely cases such as these that test the fundamental strength of constitutional democracies. Initially, I want "an eye for an eye" for these two incredibly vicious and detestable acts. I even like the idea of boiling alive. I want, not retribution, but good, old-fashioned revenge.[13] But one reason societies establish laws is to provide a venue to control these highly emotional, albeit not necessarily irrational, feelings.[14] John Locke, for example, in his Second Treatise of Government, argued that people without a government of laws could impose any punishment, regardless of severity, on someone who violated the law of nature, which for Locke states that "no one ought to harm another in his life, health, liberty, or possessions."[15] Without a formal government, someone who violates the law of nature "may be punished to that degree, and with so much severity, as will suffice to make it an ill bargain to the offender, give him cause to repent, and terrify others from doing the like."[16] Upon hearing about such vile and despicable acts, then, some social institution (such as a formal criminal justice system) must prevent these feelings from serving as the basis for legitimate social action. That something, in the United States, is the Constitution.

As I read about the procedures and courtroom practices that jeopardize defendants' rights, I become convinced that the death penalty goes too far when one considers the myriad possibilities for the arbitrary and capricious infliction of it, not to mention the possibility that an innocent person will be executed.[17] I think, for example, of Leonel Herrera, who was executed in Texas by lethal injection on May 12, 1993. Ten years after his conviction, he appealed his sentence on the basis that new evidence indicated that he was innocent. The Supreme Court held that unless some specific constitutional violation had occurred in the trial court, there was no valid support for the Supreme Court to consider evidence that might possibly establish a defendant's innocence. Justice Blackmun, however, found the Court's decision little more than a very narrow ruling designed to avoid constitutional complications. If there is even a remote possibility that a defendant is innocent based on new evidence, that defendant has a constitutional right to have that evidence reviewed. Blackmun writes, "Nothing could be more contrary to contemporary standards of decency, or more shocking to the conscience, than to execute a person who is actually innocent."[18] He challenges both the Court's majority holding and the State of Texas.

The Court's enumeration of the constitutional rights of criminal defendants surely is entirely beside the point. These protections sometimes fail. We really are being asked to decide whether the Constitution forbids the execution of a person who has been validly convicted and sentenced, but who, nonetheless, can prove his innocence with newly discovered evidence. Despite the State of Texas' astonishing protestation to the contrary, I do not see how the answer can be anything but "yes."[19]

As we read these cases, we must remember that we are reflecting on some 100 death penalty cases from a death row population of over 3,800. What kinds of constitutional violations sit there undetected or unheard? What kinds of murders have been perpetrated by those convicted? I know that many of the acts of those on death row would nauseate me. Indeed, after reading some of these cases, I feel as if I am the one who has been victimized. The only difference between a murder victim and me could be nothing more than being in the wrong place at the wrong time. But, in a way, defendants are often in the wrong place at the wrong time. Regardless of what anyone feels about society's most heinous criminals, and, I believe, the hatred felt can be quite rational, no person's life should be based on happenstance. Granted, the clerk's life at the convenience store that was ended suddenly by a robber's bullet lost his or her life by what could be described as a lottery. The clerk was in the wrong place at the wrong time. But that does not mean that society needs to use a lottery to select guilty murderers at random to execute. Just as the clerk's life was unjustly taken, so is the murderer's life unjustly taken because the death penalty will be imposed inevitably in a metaphorical lottery that will be determined in violation of the "equal protection of the laws." Where does this leave me?

Since Justice Douglas, in 1972 in *Furman*, stated that the death penalty cannot be inflicted in an unequal and arbitrary manner, the death penalty continues to be inflicted in an unequal and arbitrary manner. It is time to move to other punishment alternatives.

What would happen, for example, if we handed down life sentences with the possibility of parole after twenty-five years? What happens if members of society were to choose that sentence for those who commit the most heinous crimes imaginable? Does that choice imply that the victim's life is less important than the defendant's? In *The Killing of Bonnie Garland*, Willard Gaylin describes accurately one element that had been missing from murder trials, namely, the victim. Bonnie Garland's boyfriend had viciously murdered her in her parents' home. Yet much of the trial focused more on the defendant than on the victim. Gaylin writes, "A system of justice cannot forget Bonnie Garland, because it was designed originally to protect her and to serve her needs. It was designed to serve the purposes of the law-abiding, not the offender."[20] Told meticulously and movingly, Gaylin describes, in part, Bonnie's noticeable absence from her own murder trial. He notes that several people identified more with the murderer than the victim, in part because nothing could be done to help Bonnie now that she was dead. The act terminated, the boyfriend's life was still salvageable. The major legal concern appeared to be what should happen to the defendant. Gaylin writes, "Obviously for these people there exists a specific concept of justice that only looks forward; it is concerned with what purpose would be served by punishment in the future. It starts with the death of the victim, and looks forward from there."[21] I believe most people, however, would find that response unacceptable. It is unacceptable precisely because it is a response that ignores "justice" altogether. Regarding such a response, Gaylin writes, "This is an incomplete and imperfect consideration of the concept of justice. A worthy concept of justice would demand that we look backward [to the act] as well as forward. This concept of justice would require a respectful consideration of punishment."[22] Written in 1982, *The Killing of Bonnie Garland* does not address fully, and could not have addressed fully, the influence the victims' rights movement would have between 1982 and 2002. During that period the victims' rights movement was very successful in ensuring that victims, especially in capital trials, would be present in the courtroom. I think victims, or, in the case of murder, the families and loved ones, must be there. But to what extent? Without the death penalty, does society lose a sense of justice? Without the death penalty, does society forget the victim? Just what, exactly, does the choice of a death penalty prove or establish? What social ill does it make right or correct? And does it satisfy every feeling experienced by those affected by the murder?

The punishment choices of which any society avails itself reflects something about that society's moral, political, emotional, and spiritual nature. But what do those choices imply? I believe that ultimately they speak to the soul, to the heart, of a nation. Is society compassionate? Does it seek to understand before it acts to condemn? Is it a reflective, contemplative, and philosophical society? Does it act or react? Does revenge or justice drive it? Does it seek to create or to destroy?

If the death penalty is rejected, however, that does not make society necessarily more compassionate or kindhearted. Neither death row nor prison is a delightful place to spend one's life.[23] John Stuart Mill, the nineteenth-century English philosopher, argued in support of capital punishment in part because it was more humane than life imprisonment.[24] The death penalty and life imprisonment without the possibility of parole constitute, for me, the Scylla and Charybdis of punishment options in murder cases. There is no question but that some murderers can never again live free in society. The mass murderer Charles Manson serves a life sentence with the possibility of parole. While it is in theory possible that he might one day be released from prison, it is highly unlikely. As previously noted, McVeigh never would have been paroled. I would also argue that the state should err on the side of safety in parole considerations. That is, when in doubt, do not grant parole. While I have difficulty with aggravating and mitigating circumstances in the sentencing process, I do not have the same concern in parole board hearings. The murdered victim's family members and loved ones should play a role in any parole consideration for the murderer. Might that mean that some murderers will remain in prison because they just happened to murder someone with a family that wants complete retribution (either the death penalty or life imprisonment without parole)? Yes it does. But it also keeps open windows of opportunity in case of mistake or reconciliation. Reconciliation is a word not often heard in murder cases, yet there is a group of individuals who, in capital cases, seek just that.[25] They do not want the death penalty. They do not need retribution, or, if they do, life imprisonment satisfies that need. I am not sure I would belong to such a group if someone murdered a member of my family. I would argue, however, for a life sentence with the possibility of parole no sooner than after twenty-five years. I do not base that figure on any objective assessment. But we are not in a land of objective assessments when it comes to the most vicious crimes perpetrated against law-abiding citizens. Absolute answers to the question of what punishments are justified for heinous crimes do not immediately come to mind. We are, however, in a land of feelings, a most dangerous land in which to make life and death judgments. In this context, while I do not forget the victims of the vicious murders that have been committed, I can never forget as well reading the case of Willie Francis.[26] The botched electric chair execution attempt of Willie Francis by the state of Louisiana in 1946 continues to disturb me. Of course, the electric chair will soon be relegated to history as states and the federal government adopt lethal injection as the method of execution. One day, perhaps, a method completely free from any pain might be adopted.[27] There is a good chance, however, that Willie Francis was innocent. But one day soon we may have the perfect instrument to determine guilt unequivocally.[28] So had the perfect test for guilt found Willie guilty, and had the perfect painless method for execution been used, would I be as troubled by Willie's execution? Perhaps not. However, if Willie had been guilty unequivocally of first-degree murder, and had the execution been painless, no one would have even written about his case. I would have never known about Willie Francis. But because I know about the naked brutality of Willie's execution, and his case is not an isolated botched execution attempt,[29] I cannot imagine the death penalty to offer a solution to any social ills. At best, the death penalty lulls us into a false sense of security by sending the message that we are "tough" on crime.

I have one final thought about Willie. The Supreme Court decided to put Willie in an electric chair for a second time by a 5–4 vote. Many of the cases that I have cited here have been decided by 5–4 votes. Some life and death decisions come down to one vote. A change of one vote for Willie would have left him imprisoned but alive. New evidence could have freed him. Once dead, how many people want to continue to investigate? That life comes down to a best-of-nine vote strikes me as macabre. Facetiously, I think of convicted capital defendants spinning a giant wheel of fortune with three possible outcomes: life imprisonment without the possibility of parole, life imprisonment with the possibility of parole, and the death penalty. At 7:00 each evening we could turn on the TV to see the most recently convicted murderer spin the punishment wheel. I can hear the announcer now: "Oh, Dave, you just missed life imprisonment with the possibility of parole. Too bad about that death penalty. But now it's time to move to the next wheel to determine your execution date, at which time we will meet the lucky recipients who wait for your vital organs for transplant.[30] For the viewing audience, don't go away. We'll be right back after a commercial message."

I must agree with Justice Blackmun. It is, and will remain, impossible to end the discriminatory manner in which the death penalty is imposed. More important, the death penalty debate has climaxed. There is little new to say about it. I do not believe that the death penalty debate will ever be resolved morally, philosophically, or constitutionally, at least not to everyone's satisfaction. It will be resolved only by the maturity of the society that will no longer tinker with the "machinery of death" and by the maturity of the society that discovers that its heart is greater than its hate.

Notes

CHAPTER 1

1. *Wilkerson v. Utah*, 99 U.S. 130 (1878).
2. *In re Kemmler*, 136 U.S. 436 (1890).
3. Bryan Vila and Cynthia Morris, eds., *Capital Punishment in the United States* (Westport, Conn.: Greenwood Press, 1997), 127–28.
4. *Furman v. Georgia*, 408 U.S. 238 (1972).
5. These words are the inscription, in bold letters, found on the front of the United States Supreme Court building in Washington, D.C. The words represent the ideals of equality and justice for all people.
6. U.S. Const. amend. XIV, § 1: "No State shall make or enforce any law which shall abridge the privileges or immunities of citizens of the United States; nor shall any State deprive any person of life, liberty, or property, without due process of law; nor deny to any person within its jurisdiction the equal protection of the laws."
7. See Raoul Berger, *Death Penalties* (Cambridge, Mass.: Harvard University Press, 1982).
8. U.S. Const. amend. VIII.
9. *Woodson v. North Carolina*, 428 U.S. 280 (1976) (bold print in original).
10. *Coker v. Georgia*, 433 U.S. 584 (1977).
11. Steven H. Gifis, *Law Dictionary* (Hauppauge, N.Y.: Barron's Educational Series, Inc., 1996), 462–63.
12. Ellen Alderman and Caroline Kennedy, *In Our Defense: The Bill of Rights in Action* (New York: William Morrow and Company, 1991), 16–17. Alderman and Kennedy note as well those rights that have not been incorporated. "As of now, the few rights not incorporated against the states include the Second Amendment right to keep and bear arms, the Fifth Amendment right to a grand jury indictment, the Sixth Amendment requirement of twelve jurors on a criminal jury, and the Seventh Amendment right to a civil jury. The Supreme Court has held various state proce-

dures adequate to protect the values inherent in those constitutional rights. All the rest of the fundamental freedoms in the Bill of Rights have been incorporated and may not be infringed by the federal government or by the states" (17).

13. "Congress shall make no law respecting an establishment of religion, or prohibiting the free exercise thereof; or abridging the freedom of speech, or of the press, or the right of the people peaceably to assemble, and to petition the Government for a redress of grievances." U.S. Const. amend. I.

14. U.S. Const. amend. XIV, § 1.

15. U.S. Const. amend. XIV, § 1.

16. It is important to qualify this claim about what states cannot do to their citizens because states and the federal government have violated those constitutional guarantees. There is a critical philosophical distinction, beyond the scope of this inquiry, between having a right and exercising that right. The point here, however, is less substantive, namely, people cannot legitimately be denied these rights. These rights will continue on occasions to be abridged. Ultimately, it is "the people" who must demand their rights against illegitimate government encroachments.

17. See, for example, *Powell v. Alabama*, 287 U.S. 45 (1932) and *Norris v. Alabama*, 294 U.S. 587 (1935). These cases are examined in chapter 2.

18. *Betts v. Brady*, 316 U.S. 455 (1942). Justice Roberts, for the Court, concluded *Betts* as follows: "As we have said, the Fourteenth Amendment prohibits the conviction and incarceration of one whose trial is offensive to the common and fundamental ideas of fairness and right, and, while want of counsel in a particular case may result in a conviction lacking in such fundamental fairness, we cannot say that the Amendment embodies an inexorable command that no trial for any offense, or in any court, can be fairly conducted and justice accorded a defendant who is not represented by counsel."

19. *Gideon v. Wainwright*, 372 U.S. 335 (1963).

20. That does not mean, however, that all people are happy with incorporation. It remains a point of debate among constitutional scholars. But, beyond its relevance to legal scholarship, the issue of incorporation is moot.

21. See note 14 above.

22. Jeremy Bentham, *The Principles of Morals and Legislation* (Amherst, N.Y.: Prometheus Books, 1988), 171.

23. If, however, a criminal writes a novel totally unrelated to his or her criminal activity, that criminal, in theory, should receive the resulting profit.

24. An examination of these two fundamental philosophies will show that one of the major differences between them is that retributivism focuses substantively on *desert* while deterrence focuses substantively on what is *necessary* to reduce criminal behavior.

25. Immanuel Kant, *Lectures on Ethics*, trans. Louis Infield (Indianapolis, Ind.: Hackett Publishing Company, 1963), 55.

26. See, for example, Susan Jacoby, *Wild Justice: The Evolution of Revenge* (New York: Harper & Row, 1983); and Herbert L. Packer, *The Limits of the Criminal Sanction* (Stanford, Calif.: Stanford University Press, 1968). Packer makes clear his rejection of retributivism as rooted in revenge throughout the first three chapters. In addition, Supreme Court Justices Brennan and Marshall, in several Supreme Court cases I examine, maintain that retribution is nothing more than revenge.

27. Jacoby, *Wild Justice*, 4.

28. David Lyons, *Ethics and the Rule of Law* (New York: Cambridge University Press, 1984), 142.

29. Immanuel Kant, *Ethical Philosophy*, 2d ed., *Metaphysical Principles of Virtue*, trans. James Ellington (Indianapolis, Ind.: Hackett Publishing Company, 1994), 125.

30. Ibid., 126 (italics added). I argue in my conclusion in chapter 6 that a mature society will be one that does not act on the basis of hate.

31. See John Kaplan, *The Problem of Capital Punishment*, 1983 University of Illinois Law Review, 555–77, reprinted in *A Capital Punishment Anthology*, ed. Victor Streib (Cincinnati, Ohio: Anderson Publishing Company, 1993), 4.

32. It is in this context as well that most retributivists justify the death penalty, namely, respect for the victim requires that the perpetrator be put to death.

33. Henrik Stangerup, *The Man Who Wanted to Be Guilty* (New York: Marion Boyars, Ltd., 1982).

34. Ibid., 56.

35. See *Kant's Political Writings*, ed. with an introduction and notes by Hans Reiss (London: Cambridge University Press, 1970), 155.

36. *Furman v. Georgia*, 408 U.S. 238 (1972).

37. *Coker v. Georgia*, 433 U.S. 584 (1977).

38. In this context, the death penalty will certainly nullify any advantage the criminal accrued as a result of committing murder. But the death penalty is not necessarily the only way in which an advantage can be nullified.

39. For a more detailed treatment, see Herbert L. Packer, *The Limits of the Criminal Sanction* (Stanford, Calif.: Stanford University Press, 1968), 39–48.

40. Bentham, *Principles*, 179.

41. Ibid., 181.

42. Ibid.

43. Ibid., 182.

44. See, for example, Kent S. Miller and Michael L. Radelet, *Executing the Mentally Ill* (Newbury Park, Calif.: Sage Publications, 1993).

45. *Penry v. Lynaugh*, 492 U.S. 302 (1989).

46. On June 4, 2001, the Supreme Court did overturn Penry's death sentence, but not on the ground that the execution of a mentally ill defendant violates the Constitution. The sentence was overturned on a procedural matter.

47. *Atkins v. Virginia*, slip op. at 1–2 (United States Supreme Court, June 20, 2002).

48. *Id.* at 2.

49. *Id.* at 2–3.

50. *Id.* at 4.

51. *Gregg v. Georgia*, 428 U.S. 153 (1976). This case is examined in chapter 4.

52. *Atkins v. Virginia*, slip op. at 14.

53. *Id.*

54. *Id.* at 15.

55. *Id.*

56. *Atkins v. Virginia*, slip op. at 14 (United States Supreme Court, June 20, 2002; Justice Scalia dissenting).

57. *Id.* at 15.

58. If we must execute, however, the victim's family may want to celebrate. That is a matter independent from the social response.

59. For an excellent example of such insensitivity read Willard Gaylin, *The Killing of Bonnie Garland* (New York: Simon & Schuster, 1982).

60. *Furman v. Georgia*, 408 U.S. 238 (1972).

CHAPTER 2

1. *Weems v. United States*, 217 U.S. 349 (1910); and *Trop v. Dulles*, 356 U.S. 86 (1958).

2. *Wilkerson v. Utah*, 99 U.S. 130 (1878) at 132.

3. *Id.*

4. *Id.* at 134–35.

5. Torture would include such things as a prisoner being "dragged to the place of execution," "to be embowelled alive, beheaded, and quartered," "public dissection," and "burning alive." *Wilkerson* at 135.

6. *Id.* at 135–36.

7. *In re Kemmler*, 136 U.S. 442 (1890).

8. *Id.* at 442–43.

9. *Id.*, at 443 (1890). It is important to note that that assumption has proven less than reasonable. In the case of *State of Louisiana ex rel. Francis v. Resweber*, 459 U.S. 459 (1947), we encounter the administration of the death penalty as "death by installment." In addition, in 1997, in Florida, something went wrong with the electric chair and flames began bursting out from behind the mask. How that does not constitute cruel and unusual punishment bewilders me.

10. *In re Kemmler*, 136 U.S. 444 (1890). The move to lethal injection is quite consistent with this reasoning, namely, that there exists a more humane means of taking a person's life.

11. *Id.* at 446.

12. *Id.* at 447.

13. *Id.*

14. *Id.*

15. *Id.* at 448.

16. Gifis, *Law Dictionary*, 72.

17. *Logan v. United States*, 144 U.S. 298 (1892).

18. See particularly *Witherspoon v. Illinois*, 391 U.S. 510 (1968).

19. Jethro K. Lieberman, *A Practical Companion to the Constitution* (Berkeley: University of California Press, 1999), 253.

20. Ibid.

21. *Weems v. United States*, 217 U.S. 349 (1910) at 373 (italics added).

22. *Id.*

23. *Id.* at 368–73.

24. *Id.* at 349. We are talking here of 204 pesos and 408 pesos, not exactly a major act of fraud. The amount, however, is irrelevant. Indeed, it is not relevant that no one was injured or was supposed to be injured, or whether the falsification succeeded or failed. The only relevant concern under this provision of Philippine law at the time was an intent to commit fraud. Justice McKenna quotes from the Philippine court in this case as follows: "It is not necessary that there be any fraud

nor even the desire to defraud, nor intention of personal gain on the part of the person committing it, that a falsification of a public document be punishable; it is sufficient that the one who committed it had the intention to pervert the truth and to falsify the document, and that by it damage might result to a third party." *Id.* at 362.

25. *Id.* at 366. This description makes clear the severity of the punishment, but it fails to capture the total draconian nature of what would have happened to Weems had the Supreme Court not considered his writ of error.

26. *Id.* at 367. That we as a nation have punished not only excessively but also foolishly cannot be gainsaid; still, in light of our own history and compared with some practices around the world, we are moving toward more enlightened responses to crime, although that development has not been necessarily smooth and continuous.

27. *Id.* at 367–82.

28. *Id.* at 383.

29. *Id.* at 383–385.

30. *Id.* at 386–387.

31. *Id.* at 387.

32. *Id.* at 388–389.

33. The 1689 English Bill of Rights reads, in part, "That excessive bail ought not to be required, nor excessive fines imposed; nor cruel and unusual punishments inflicted."

34. *Weems,* 217 U.S. at 409.

35. This case has been referred to as the case of the "Scottsboro boys" because they were called "the boys" throughout the trial. For a detailed examination of this mockery of justice, see Dan T. Carter, *Scottsboro: A Tragedy of the American South,* rev. ed. (Baton Rouge: Louisiana State University Press, 1979).

36. In 1977 the Supreme Court would rule, in *Coker v. Georgia,* 433 U.S. 584 (1977), that the death penalty for the crime of rape is disproportionate to the crime and therefore a violation of the Eight Amendment's prohibition against cruel and unusual punishment. *Coker* is examined in chapter 4.

37. *Norris v. Alabama,* 294 U.S. 587 (1935) at 588.

38. *Powell v. Alabama,* 287 U.S. 52 (1932)

39. *Id.* at 52–53.

40. *Id.* at 57.

41. *Id.* at 58.

42. *Id.* at 59.

43. U.S. Const. amend. XIV, § 1.

44. *Powell,* 287 U.S. at 59–60.

45. *Id.* at 67.

46. *Id.* at 67–68.

47. *Id.* at 69.

48. *Id.* at 71.

49. *Gideon v. Wainwright,* 372 U.S. 335 (1963).

50. *Powell,* 287 U.S. at 76.

51. *Id.* at 77.

52. U.S. Const. amend. XIV, § 1.

53. *Norris,* 294 U.S. at 589.

54. *Id.* at 589–593.

55. *Id.* at 593–94.

56. *Id.* at 596.

57. See *Id.* at 599.

58. *Louisiana ex rel. Francis v. Resweber,* 329 U.S. 459 (1947) at 460–61.

59. U.S. Const. amend. V.

60. *Francis,* 329 U.S. at 462.

61. *Id.* at 463.

62. *Id.,* fn. 4.

63. *Id.* at 464.

64. *Id.* at 465.

65. *Id.*

66. *Id.*

67. *Id.*

68. *Id.* at 465–66.

69. Justice Burton's dissenting opinion follows.

70. *Francis,* 329 U.S. at 470–71.

71. *Id.* at 469.

72. *Id.* at 471.

73. U.S. Const. amend. XIV, § 1: No State shall make or enforce any law which shall abridge the privileges or immunities of citizens of the United States; nor shall any State deprive any person of life, liberty, or property, without due process of law; nor deny to any person within its jurisdiction the equal protection of the laws.

74. *Francis,* 329 U.S. at 467.

75. *Id.* at 466.

76. *Id.* at 469.

77. *Id.* at 467.

78. *Id.* at 472.

79. Justice Burton's dissenting opinion is joined by Justices Douglas, Murphy, and Rutledge.

80. 329 U.S. 459 at 474. "Death by installments" has been highlighted to draw attention to the superb book on the Francis case by Arthur S. Miller and Jeffrey H. Bowman, *Death by Installments* (New York: Greenwood Press, 1988).

81. *Francis,* 329 U.S. at 474.

82. *Id.* at 479.

83. *Id.* at 477.

84. For a few examples, see Sister Helen Prejean, *Dead Man Walking* (New York: Vintage Books, 1993), 19–20.

85. In 2002, the Court will hold that a jury, and not a judge, must make a death penalty sentencing decision.

86. *Williams v. New York,* 337 U.S. 241 (1949) at 245.

87. *Id.*

88. *Id.* at 247.

89. *Id.* at 252.

90. *Id.*

91. *Id.* at 253.

92. *Id.*

93. *Id.*

94. *Trop v. Dulles*, 356 U.S. 86 (1958); argued 5/2/57; reargued 10/28–29/57; decided 3/31/58.

95. *Id.* at 88.

96. *Id.*

97. *Id.* at 92.

98. In *Perez v. Brownell*, 356 U.S. 44 (1958), for example, the Supreme Court held that anyone who votes in a foreign political election loses citizenship. The decision in this case, interestingly enough, was decided on the same day as *Trop*, and was decided as well by a 5–4 vote. Chief Justice Warren's argument for the plurality in *Trop* was the dissenting opinion in Perez. Indeed, the only person to change his position on this issue was Justice William Brennan, who was in the majority for both cases.

99. *Trop*, 356 U.S. at 92–93.

100. *Id.* at 99.

101. *Id.*

102. See *Weems*.

103. *Trop*, 356 U.S. at 99–101 (italics added).

104. *Id.*

105. *Id.* at 101–2. Chief Justice Warren spends the next two pages elaborating on the meaning of denial of citizenship. Although his carefully structured response is unnecessary for my purpose, those pages merit reading.

106. *Id.* at 103–4.

107. *Id.* at 105.

108. *Furman v. Georgia*, 438 U.S. 238 (1972).

109. See Alan I. Bigel, *Justices William J. Brennan, Jr. and Thurgood Marshall on Capital Punishment* (Lanham, Md.: University Press of America, 1997).

110. *Trop*, 356 U.S. at 111–12.

111. *Id.* at 121.

112. *Id.* at 121–22.

113. *Id.* at 126.

114. *Id.* at 128.

115. A venireman is a person who has been summoned to appear before a court as a potential member of a jury.

116. *Witherspoon v. State of Illinois*, 391 U.S. 524 (1968).

117. *Id.* at 514.

118. *Id.* at 520–21.

119. *Id.* at 537.

120. *Id.* at 537–38.

121. *Id.* at 538.

122. *Id.* at 542.

123. *Id.*

124. *Id.* at 520, fn. 16.

125. *Id.* at 519–20. Of course, in light of the fact that current polls indicate strong support for the death penalty, would it then be more constitutionally permissible to exclude those potential jurors who have reservations about the death penalty? After all, if it is important to maintain a balance when there is a balance, is it also important to maintain an imbalance when there exists such a clear imbalance?

126. *Id.* at 521–23.

127. *Id.* at 532.

128. *Fay v. New York,* 332 U.S. 261 (1947).

129. Justice Murphy, as quoted by Justice Douglas in *Witherspoon v. Illinois,* 391 U.S. at 524.

130. *Witherspoon,* 391 U.S. at 524–25.

131. For example, there will be no constitutional problem with excluding members from the Ku Klux Klan or the neo-Nazis in those cases where those beliefs threaten the constitutional rights of a defendant.

132. *Witherspoon,* 391 U.S. at 530.

133. *Id.* at 531.

134. *Furman v. Georgia,* 408 U.S. 238 (1972).

135. *McGautha v. California,* 402 U.S. 183 (1971) at 185.

136. *Id.* at 186

137. *Id.* at 187.

138. *Id.* at 187–89.

139. *Id.* at 189–90 (italics added).

140. *Id.* at 192.

141. U.S. Const. amend. V. The details of the crime for which Crampton was found guilty and sentenced to death can be found in *McGautha,* 402 U.S. at 191–95.

142. *McGautha,* 402 U.S. at 194.

143. *Id.*

144. *Id.* at 195–96.

145. *Id.* at 196.

146. *Id.* at 197–203.

147. Jury nullification has been defined as follows: "A jury's knowing and deliberate rejection of the evidence or refusal to apply the law either because the jury wants to send a message about some social issue that is larger then the case itself or because the result dictated by law is contrary to the jury's sense of justice, morality, or fairness." *Black's Law Dictionary,* 7th ed., 862.

148. In current practice in capital cases juries are directed to consider aggravating and mitigating circumstances regarding the act or the defendant. Depending on the situation, a jury that finds that mitigating circumstances outweigh aggravating circumstance can bring in a penalty short of death. "Jury nullification" can be understood as a jury recognizing mitigating circumstances before such circumstances were formally established in capital cases.

149. *McGautha,* 402 U.S. at 199.

150. *Id.* at 202.

151. *Id.* at 203.

152. *Id.* at 195.

153. *Id.* at 204.

154. Ernst van den Haag offers a similar argument in defense of the death penalty despite the lack of consistent sentencing guidelines. He argues that just because some who do deserve the death penalty do not get it does not mean that those who deserve it and who do get it have been treated unjustly. The injustice is that those who do deserve it do not get it. See Ernest van den Haag, *The Death Penalty Once More,* 18 U.C. Davis L. Rev. 957 (1085).

155. Harlan quotes as follows: "No formula is possible that would provide a reasonable criterion for the infinite variety of circumstances that may affect the

gravity of the crime of murder. Discretionary judgment on the facts of each case is the only way in which they can be equitably distinguished. This conclusion is borne out by American experience: there the experiment of degrees of murder, introduced long ago, has had to be supplemented by giving to the courts a discretion that in effect supersedes it." *McGautha* at 205. Justice Brennan, as we will see, responds to Harlan on this point.

156. *McGautha*, 402 U.S. at 205.

157. *Id.* at 206.

158. *Id.* at 207 (italics added).

159. *Id.* at 207–8. As we will see, there may be some very good reasons why states should not trust the sentencing discretion of juries.

160. *Malloy v. Hogan*, 378 U.S. 1 (1964).

161. *McGautha*, 402 U.S. at 210–11.

162. *Id.* at 211.

163. *McGautha*, 402 U.S. at 215.

164. *Id.*

165. *Id.* It is worth noting, yet should come as no surprise, that Harlan was one of just two dissents in *Malloy*.

166. *Id.* at 218–19.

167. *Id.* at 220.

168. *Id.* at 221.

169. *Id.*

170. *Id.* at 225. In *Furman*, the Court's majority will use Black's language to hold that the death penalty, as then implemented, constituted cruel and unusual punishment.

171. *Id.* at 226.

172. *Id.* at 228.

173. The Supreme Court, as noted in chapter 1, began to apply the provisions of the Bill of Rights to the states in the twentieth century through the Fourteenth Amendment. Thus, the Fifth Amendment, which had originally applied only to the federal government, came to be applied to state governments through a process of incorporation. To make this point somewhat differently, we could say that the Supreme Court incorporated the provisions of the Bill of Rights through the Fourteenth Amendment and thereby were able to apply provisions such as the right against self-incrimination to the states. Needless to say, some people felt that the Court had usurped state power illegitimately. Some still maintain that perspective.

174. *McGautha*, 402 U.S. at 229–30.

175. As we will see, the two-stage or bifurcated trial does become the means by which states came to have their death penalty statutes constitutionally sustained.

176. *McGautha*, 402 U.S. at 235.

177. *Id.*

178. *Id.* at 236–38.

179. *Id.* at 238.

180. *Id.* at 239.

181. This opinion can be seen as somewhat pivotal in Brennan's development into one of the two most outspoken critics of the death penalty, the other being Justice Thurgood Marshall. In *McGautha*, Brennan's argument can be understood as

supporting the constitutionality of the death penalty. This will be the last case in which Brennan shows some support, at least constitutionally, for capital punishment.

182. *McGautha*, 402 U.S. at 249.

183. *Id.* at 251–52. This passage indicates as well that at this point in time Brennan would support capital punishment provided states had established some standards to guide jury decision making.

184. *Id.* at 255–56.

185. *Id.* at 256.

186. *Id.*

187. *Id.*

188. *Id.* at 254.

189. *Id.* at 270.

190. *Id.* at 282.

191. *Id.* at 283–84.

192. *Id.* at 284–85.

193. *Id.* at 287.

194. *Id.* at 287–309.

CHAPTER 3

1. *Furman v. Georgia*, 408 U.S. 238 (1972) at 240–58.

2. *Id.* at 242.

3. Arthur J. Goldberg and Alan M. Dershowitz, "Declaring the Death Penalty Unconstitutional," 83 *Harv. L. Rev.* 1773 (1970). At the time this article was written, Alan Dershowitz, now Professor Dershowitz, was Justice Goldberg's law clerk.

4. *Furman*, 408 U.S. at 249.

5. *Id.* at 249–50.

6. *Id.* at 251.

7. *Id.* at 255–57.

8. *Id.* at 256–57.

9. *Furman*, 408 U.S. at 258–64.

10. *Id.* at 263.

11. *Id.* at 267. This power, incidentally, is not one readily acknowledged by other Supreme Court Justices or by many constitutional scholars. The dissenting opinions challenge Brennan's interpretive theory of constitutional decision making.

12. Again we are confronted with questions of constitutional interpretation. Principles of judicial restraint hold that courts should not overturn lightly legislative judgments about how the people of the state want to be governed. Principles of judicial activism hold that judges need not be guided, for example, by election returns. Brennan is building a case for judicial activism, perhaps a limited judicial activism, regarding judicial interpretations of the cruel and unusual punishment clause. Again, the dissenting opinion will contribute to this discussion about constitutional interpretation.

13. See especially *Furman*, 408 U.S. at 268–69. Quoting from *Weems*, Brennan writes that judicial restraint would reduce the Court's "'efficacy and power,'" and

quoting from *Trop*, Brennan notes that under judicial restraint the cruel and unusual punishment clause "would become, in short, 'little more than good advice.' "

14. *Id.* at 279. Brennan does not consider what principle would govern if society's standards took a turn for the worst. Logically, Brennan, if faced with such a scenario, would be placed in a most awkward position.

15. *Id.* at 270.

16. *Id.* at 271.

17. *Id.* at 272–73.

18. *Id.* at 273.

19. *Id.* Brennan uses the examples of mental illness, leprosy, or drug addiction.

20. *Id.* at 273–74.

21. *Id.* at 274.

22. *Id.* at 274–77.

23. *Id.* at 277 (italics added).

24. *Id.*

25. *Id.* at 279.

26. Brennan advances a view here of constitutional democracy inconsistent with the practice of a constitutional democracy. In a democracy, people are elected theoretically to represent the interests of members of society. But Brennan seems willing to substitute his opinion for society's based on a finding that since society does not bring in death verdicts often, society therefore finds them repugnant.

27. *Furman*, 408 U.S. at 279.

28. *Id.*

29. *Id.* at 282.

30. *Id.*

31. *Id.* at 283–84.

32. *Id.* at 297–88.

33. *Id.* at 288.

34. *Id.* at 288–89.

35. *Id.* at 291.

36. *Id.* at 292–92.

37. At the time of *Furman*, the death penalty was a punishment option for rape in nine states.

38. *Furman*, 408 U.S. at 293.

39. *Id.* at 294–95.

40. *Id.* at 295.

41. *Id.*

42. *Id.*

43. *Id.*

44. *Id.*

45. *Id.*

46. *Id.* at 300.

47. *Id.*

48. *Id.* at 302.

49. *Id.*

50. *Id.* at 304–5.

51. *Id.* at 305.

52. The old adage about good things coming in small packages is applicable here. Stewart's opinion is short, but contains an insight that may prove as important as any argument against the death penalty.

53. *Furman,* 408 U.S. at 309–10 (italics added).

54. *Id.* at 310–11.

55. *Id.* at 313.

56. *Id.* at 311–12.

57. *Id.* at 312.

58. *Id.*

59. *Id.*

60. *Id.* at 314–74.

61. *Id.* at 315. The relationship between self-respect and cruel and unusual punishment is less than clear and constitutes, one could argue, judicial legislative decision making. There is no Eighth Amendment history to indicate that self-respect, however defined, was relevant to the debate on the Eighth Amendment.

62. *Id.* at 329.

63. *Id.* at 330–32.

64. *Id.*

65. *Id.*

66. *Id.* at 342–43.

67. John Rawls makes essentially the same distinction in his article, "Two Concepts of Rules." His distinction in this context is "between justifying a practice and justifying a particular action falling under it." For example, although punishment in general can be justified, specific punishments might not be justifiable. John Rawls, "Two Concepts of Rules," in H. B. Acton, ed., *The Philosophy of Punishment* (London: Macmillan and Co. Ltd., 1969), 105–14.

68. *Furman,* 408 U.S. 343. As noted previously, retribution has not been universally condemned. Marshall's claims in this context are less than sound.

69. For Marshall, retribution is a euphemism for retaliation and vengeance, both of which are baser qualities, primitive qualities, of human beings. Accordingly, for Marshall, retribution cannot serve as a legitimate justification for any specific punishment.

70. *Furman,* 408 U.S. at 344.

71. *Id.* Again, Marshall's claims about retribution are contestable. "Retributivists" always try to match the punishment with the seriousness of the crimes committed. A retributive justification for punishment would never allow legislatures to invoke any penalty for any crime.

72. *Furman,* 408 U.S. at 344–45.

73. *Id.* at 345.

74. *Id.*

75. *Id.* at 346–47.

76. *Id.* at 354. The "massive amount of evidence" existed more in Marshall's mind than in any factual or statistical certitude.

77. *Id.* at 355.

78. *Id.*

79. *Id.*

80. *Id.*

81. *Id.* at 356. Although beyond the scope of my analysis, it is worth pondering Marshall's claim about one's Sixth Amendment right to a jury trial with respect to any condition involving plea bargaining. For example, doesn't plea bargaining in general compromise a person's Sixth Amendment right to a jury trial by offering the suspect a "deal" that is difficult to turn down?

82. *Id.* at 357.

83. *Id.* at 358. The economics of the death penalty are examined briefly in chapter 6.

84. *Id.* at 358–59.

85. *Id.* at 360.

86. *Id.*

87. *Id.* at 361. Marshall's argument here sounds as if it begs the question or makes illicit assumptions. There is no question but that he is saying that if a person thinks as Marshall thinks, that person will draw the same conclusions as Marshall has drawn. That certainly does not establish Marshall's opinion as sound.

88. *Id.* at 362.

89. *Id.* at 362–63.

90. *Id.* at 364.

91. *Id.* at 369.

92. *Id.* at 371.

93. *Id.* at 375.

94. U.S. Const. amend. V.

95. *Id.*

96. *Id.*

97. *Furman,* 408 U.S. at 380.

98. *Id.*

99. *Id.* at 382.

100. *Id.* at 383–84.

101. *Id.* at 385.

102. *Id.*

103. *Id.* Burger's example is designed to demonstrate that there are indeed certain kinds of punishments of which most Americans would disapprove. "Burning at the stake," for example, would be morally and constitutionally unacceptable. The death penalty, however, does not pose the same moral dilemma, at least it does not seem so legislatively.

104. *Id.* at 385–86.

105. *Id.* at 387.

106. *Id.* at 387–88.

107. *Id.* at 388.

108. *Id.* at 389.

109. *Id.* at 393–94.

110. *Id.* at 394.

111. *Id.*

112. *Id.* at 395.

113. *Id.* at 396.

114. *Id.* at 404–5.

115. *Id.* at 405–6.

116. *Id.* at 406.

117. *Id.* at 408.
118. *Id.* at 410.
119. *Id.* at 420.
120. *Id.* at 410.
121. *Id.* at 413.
122. *Id.* at 410–11.
123. *Id.* at 413–14.
124. *Id.* at 414.
125. *Id.*
126. *Id.* at 418.
127. *Id.* at 419. For an extended defense of this statement, see Berger's *Death Penalties.*
128. Of course, it is also inconceivable that a legislative body would adopt these draconian punishments.
129. *Furman,* 408 U.S. at 431.
130. *Id.* at 434–35.
131. *Id.* at 436.
132. *Id.*
133. *Id.* at 437.
134. *Id.* at 437–39.
135. *Id.* at 439–40.
136. *Id.* at 441.
137. *Id.* at 442.
138. *Id.* at 447.
139. *Id.* at 447–48.
140. *Id.*
141. *Id.* at 448–49.
142. *Id.* at 450.
143. *Id.* at 451.
144. *Id.*
145. *Id.*
146. *Id.*
147. *Id.* at 452.
148. *Id.* at 454.
149. *Id.* at 454–56.
150. *Id.* at 456.
151. *Id.* at 461–62.
152. *Id.* at 465.
153. *Id.* at 466.
154. John Locke, *Two Treatises of Government* (Cambridge, Mass.: Cambridge University Press, 1988), 355–63.
155. *Furman,* 408 U.S. at 467.
156. *Id.* at 466.
157. *Id.* at 467.
158. *Id.* at 468.
159. *Id.*
160. *Id.*
161. *Id.* at 470.

162. See Michael Meltsner, *Cruel and Unusual* (New York: Random House, 1973).

CHAPTER 4

1. Six capital punishment decisions were issued on July 2, 1976. While Justices Stewart, Powell, and Stevens wrote the majority opinion, Justice Stewart announced the decision from the bench. For purposes of brevity, all references to the lead opinion (what Justice White, in dissent, refers to as "the plurality") will cite only Justice Stewart.

2. *Gregg v. Georgia*, 428 U.S. 153 (1976), at 158.

3. *Id.* at 163–64. On June 24, 2002, the Court ruled that a death sentence cannot be determined by a judge. A jury, not a judge, must determine if a death penalty is warranted.

4. *Id.* at 165–66. The aggravating circumstances are

(1) The offense of murder, rape, armed robbery, or kidnapping was committed by a person with a prior record of conviction for a capital felony, or the offense of murder was committed by a person who has a substantial history of serious assaultive criminal convictions.

(2) The offense of murder, rape, armed robbery, or kidnapping was committed while the offender was engaged in the commission of another capital felony or aggravated battery, or the offense of murder was committed while the offender was engaged in the commission of burglary or arson in the first degree.

(3) The offender by his act of murder, armed robbery, or kidnapping knowingly created a great risk of death to more than one person in a public place by means of a weapon or device which would normally be hazardous to the lives of more than one person.

(4) The offender committed the offense of murder for himself or another, for the purpose of receiving money or any other thing of monetary value.

(5) The murder of a judicial officer, former judicial officer, district attorney or solicitor or former district attorney or solicitor during or because of the exercise of his official duty.

(6) The offender caused or directed another to commit murder or committed murder as an agent or employee of another person.

(7) The offense of murder, rape, armed robbery, or kidnapping was outrageously or wantonly vile, horrible or inhuman in that it involved torture, depravity of mind, or an aggravated battery to the victim.

(8) The offense of murder was committed against any peace officer, corrections employee or fireman while engaged in the performance of his official duties.

(9) The offense of murder was committed by a person in, or who has escaped from, the lawful custody of a peace officer or place of lawful confinement.

(10) The murder was committed for the purpose of avoiding, interfering with, or preventing a lawful arrest or custody in a place of lawful confinement, of himself or another. [428 U.S. 153 (1976) at 209–11.]

5. *Id.* at 166.

6. *Id.* at 166–67.

7. In death penalty cases the following requirements must be met as well. "A transcript and complete record of the trial, as well as a separate report by the trial

judge, are transmitted to the court for its use in reviewing the sentence. The report is in the form of a 6 1/2-page questionnaire designed to elicit information about the defendant, the crime, and the circumstances of the trial. It requires the trial judge to characterize the trial in several ways designed to test for arbitrariness and disproportionality of sentence. Included in the report are responses to detailed questions concerning the quality of the defendant's representation, whether race played a role in the trial, and, whether, in the trial court's judgment, there was any doubt about the defendant' guilt or the appropriateness of the sentence. A copy of the report is served upon defense counsel. Under its special review authority, the court may either affirm the death sentence or remand the case for resentencing. In cases in which the death sentence is affirmed, there remains the possibility of executive clemency." [428 U.S. 158 (1976) at 167–68.]

8. *Id.* at 169.

9. *Id.* at 170.

10. *Id.* at 175.

11. *Id.* at 180–81.

12. *Id.* at 181.

13. *Id.*

14. *Id.* at 182.

15. *Id.* at 183.

16. *Id.* (italics added).

17. *Id.*

18. *Id.* The Justices cite *Furman* at this point as follows: "The instinct for retribution is part of the nature of man, and channeling that instinct in the administration of criminal justice serves an important purpose in promoting the stability of a society governed by law. When people begin to believe that organized society is unwilling or unable to impose upon criminal offenders the punishment they 'deserve,' then there are sown the seeds of anarchy—of self-help, vigilante justice, and lynch law."

19. *Id.* at 184.

20. *Id.* at 186–87.

21. *Id.* at 187.

22. *Id.* at 189.

23. *Id.* at 191–92.

24. *Id.* at 192.

25. The following list of aggravating and mitigating circumstances have been recommended by the Model Penal Code:

Aggravating Circumstances.

(a) The murder was committed by a convict under sentence of imprisonment.

(b) The defendant was previously convicted of another murder or of a felony involving the use or threat of violence to the person.

(c) At the time the murder was committed the defendant also committed another murder.

(d) The defendant knowingly created a great risk of death to many persons.

(e) The murder was committed while the defendant was engaged or was an accomplice in the commission of, or an attempt to commit, or flight after committing or attempting to commit robbery, rape or deviate sexual intercourse by force or threat of force, arson, burglary or kidnapping.

(f) The murder was committed for the purpose of avoiding or preventing a lawful arrest or effecting an escape from lawful custody.

(g) The murder was committed for pecuniary gain.

(h) The murder was especially heinous, atrocious or cruel, manifesting exceptional depravity.

Mitigating Circumstances.

(a) The defendant has no significant history of prior criminal activity.

(b) The murder was committed while the defendant was under the influence of extreme mental or emotional disturbance.

(c) The victim was a participant in the defendant's homicidal conduct or consented to the homicidal act.

(d) The murder was committed under circumstances which the defendant believed to provide a moral justification or extenuation for his conduct.

(e) The defendant was an accomplice in a murder committed by another person and his participation in the homicidal act was relatively minor.

(f) The defendant acted under duress or under the domination of another person.

(g) At the time of the murder, the capacity of the defendant to appreciate the criminality [wrongfulness] of his conduct or to conform his conduct to the requirements of law was impaired as a result of mental disease or defect or intoxication.

(h) The youth of the defendant at the time of the crime.

Gregg at 193.

26. *Id.* at 195.

27. Justices Stewart, Powell, and Stevens note that the procedure just explained does not have to be the only way in which the objections of *Furman* are overcome. It has turned out to be the case, however, that this practice has become the generally accepted means to meet the *Furman* conditions.

28. *Id.* at 229.

29. *Id.* at 232. Marshall refers here to the 1976 article by Sarat and Vidmar, "Public Opinion, the Death Penalty, and the Eighth Amendment: Testing the Marshall Hypothesis," 1976 *Wis.L.Rev. 171.*

30. *Id.* at 236.

31. *Id.* at 238.

32. *Id.*

33. *Id.* at 240.

34. *Id.* at 240–41.

35. *Id.* at 241.

36. The logic of a mandatory death penalty appeared reasonable to North Carolina legislators. If people commit a capital offense, and the death penalty is mandatory, there cannot be any possibility that the death penalty has been arbitrarily and capriciously imposed. Because juries and judges would be barred legislatively from penalty determination in capital sentencing, no discrimination in

the sentencing process could occur. But would discrimination and discretion then shift to the guilt phase of the trial?

37. *Woodson v. North Carolina*, 428 U.S. 280 (1976) at 286. This case raises another issue regarding the imposition of the death penalty even if the death penalty is constitutionally sound, namely, is the death penalty for felony murder constitutionally justifiable. The felony murder doctrine has been defined as follows: "The doctrine holding that any death resulting from the commission or attempted commission of a felony is murder." The rule is further clarified as follows: "Most states restrict this rule to inherently dangerous felonies such as rape, arson, robbery, or burglary." *Black's Law Dictionary*, 7th ed., 633. Of course, North Carolina could be asked how a person can receive more than life imprisonment (murder in the second degree shall be punished no "more than life imprisonment"). Yes, some states have given some criminals multiple life sentences to be served *consecutively*, a punishment that makes no sense from either a retributive or deterrent perspective.

38. Again, for brevity's sake, only Justice Stewart will be cited.

39. 428 U.S. at 288.

40. The reader must consider that these arguments, and the facts they purport to claim, are not without contention, as Justice Rehnquist's dissenting opinion makes clear.

41. 428 U.S. at 289.

42. *Id.*

43. *Id.* at 290.

44. *Id.* at 291.

45. 428 U.S. 295 (1976). The brief historical review can be found at 428 U.S. 289–96 (1976).

46. *Id.* at 295–96 (1976).

47. *Id.* at 301

48. *Id* at 299.

49. *Id.* at 303.

50. *Id.*

51. *Id.*

52. *Id.* at 305.

53. *Id.* at 304.

54. See *Furman*.

55. *Id.* at 311.

56. *Id.*

57. See especially *Id.* at 311–14.

58. *Id.* at 313–14.

59. Jury nullification has been defined as "the power, and occasional practice, of a jury in a criminal case to ignore the judge's instructions on the law and acquit a defendant despite overwhelming evidence of guilt and absence of reasonable doubt." James E. Clapp, *Dictionary of the Law* (New York: Random House, 2000), 258.

60. Ibid. at 324.

61. *Proffitt v. Florida*, 428 U.S. 242 (1976) at 252.

62. *Id.*

63. *Id.* at 253. I do, however, have a problem with these convictions if fully 33 percent of death sentences had to be overturned. It does look as if the system works. On the other hand, isn't it somewhat disconcerting that the Florida Supreme Court at that point had to intervene in eight of twenty-one death sentences?

64. *Id.* at 255.

65. *Id.* at 258.

66. *Id.*

67. *Id.* at 259.

68. *Jurek v. Texas,* 428 U.S. 262 (1976) at 268.

69. *Id.* at 269.

70. *Id.* at 272.

71. *Id.*

72. *Id.* at 276.

73. *Gardner v. Florida,* 430 U.S. 349 (1977) at 352, fn. 3.

74. *Id.* at 353. *Black's Law Dictionary* defines a presentence investigation report as follows: "A probation officer's detailed account of a convicted defendant's educational, criminal, family, and social background, conducted at the court's request as an aid in passing sentence." *Black's Law Dictionary,* 7th edition, 1202.

75. *Id.*

76. *Id.*

77. *Id.* at 359.

78. *Id.*

79. *Id.* at 360.

80. *Id.*

81. *Id.*

82. *Id.*

83. *Id.* at 362.

84. *Coker v. Georgia,* 433 U.S. 584 (1977) at 592.

85. *Id.* at 593.

86. *Id.* at 594.

87. *Id.* at 596. White is quoting *Gregg* here.

88. *Id.* at 596–97. Of course, White does not make clear what would constitute an "extreme" case of rape as opposed to a "non-extreme" case.

89. *Id.* at 595–96. White notes that "two other jurisdictions provide capital punishment when the victim is a child."

90. *Id.* at 597.

91. *Id.* at 601.

92. *Id.* at 603.

93. *Id.*

94. *Id.*

95. *Id.* at 606–7.

96. *Id.* at 607.

97. *Id.* at 607–8.

98. *Id.* at 622.

99. Three challenges obviously failed. First, the prosecuting attorney's remarks to the jury that the evidence in the case stood "unrefuted" and "uncontradicted" did not violate Lockett's Fifth and Fourteenth Amendment right not to

testify in her own case, especially after her counsel had earlier informed the jury that she would testify. Second, the exclusion of four potential jurors on the basis that their opposition to the death penalty might compromise their ability to judge did not violate the *Witherspoon* holding. Three, under the "fair warning" principle she claimed that she could not have known what to expect in case she and her cohorts were caught. The Court dismissed all three claims relating to her conviction. *Lockett v. Ohio*, 438 U.S. 586 (1978) at 594–97.

100. *Id.* at 597.
101. *Id.* at 604.
102. *Id.* at 605.
103. *Id.*
104. *Id.* at 619–20.
105. *Id.* at 620–21.
106. *Id.* at 629.
107. *Id.* at 631.
108. *Id.* at 635–36.
109. *Godfrey v. Georgia*, 446 U.S. 420 (1980) at 422.
110. *Id.* at 423.
111. *Id.*
112. *Id.*
113. *Id.* at 426. Godfrey had used a shotgun to kill his wife and mother-in-law.
114. *Id.* at 427.
115. *Id.* at 428.
116. *Id.* at 429–30.
117. *Id.* at 431–32.
118. *Id.* at 532.
119. *Id.* at 433.
120. *Id.*
121. *Id.* at 443.
122. *Id.*
123. *Id.* at 443–44.
124. A "lesser included offense" is defined as follows: "A crime that is composed of some, but not all, of the elements of a more serious crime and that is necessarily committed in carrying out the crime, battery is a lesser included offense of murder." *Black's Law Dictionary*, 7th edition, 1109.
125. *Beck v. Alabama*, 447 U.S. 625 (1980) at 627.
126. *Id.* at 637.
127. *Id.* at 638.
128. For more on the Adams case, see Randall Adams, with William Hoffer and Marilyn Mona Hoffer, *Adams v. Texas* (New York: St. Martin's Press, 1991). Adams was innocent, yet came close to losing his life.
129. *Adams v. Texas*, 448 U.S. 38 (1980) at 45.
130. *Id.* at 50.
131. *Id.* at 50–51.
132. *Bullington v. Missouri*, 451 U.S. 430 (1981).
133. *Id.* at 435.
134. *Id.* at 436.
135. *Id.*

136. *Id.* at 437.
137. *Id.* at 438.
138. *Id.*
139. *Id.* at 451.
140. *Estelle v. Smith,* 451 U.S. 454 (1981) at 456.
141. *Id.* at 456–57. In a footnote Burger writes: "This psychiatric evaluation was ordered even though defense counsel had not put into issue Smith's competency to stand trial or his sanity at the time of the offense. The trial judge later explained: 'In all cases where the State has sought the death penalty, I have ordered a mental evaluation of the defendant to determine his competency to stand trial. I have done this for my benefit, because I do not intend to be a participant in a case where the defendant receives the death penalty and his mental competency remains in doubt.' "
142. *Estelle v. Smith,* 451 U.S. 454 (1981) at 459–60.
143. *Id.* at 462.
144. *Id.*
145. *Id.* at 463.
146. *Id.*
147. *Id.* at 467–68.
148. *Id.* at 469.
149. *Id.* at 471.
150. *Id.* at 473.
151. *Eddings v. Oklahoma,* 455 U.S. 104 (1982) at 106–7.
152. *Id.* at 107.
153. *Id.*
154. *Id.*
155. *Id.*
156. *Id.* at 109.
157. *Id.* at 110.
158. *Id.* at 114–15.
159. *Id.* at 120.
160. *Id.* at 123–25.
161. *Id.* at 122.
162. *Enmund v. Florida,* 458 U.S. 782 (1982) at 788.
163. *Id.* at 788–93.
164. *Id.* at 794.
165. *Id.* at 797.
166. *Id.*
167. *Id.* at 800.
168. *Id.* at 801.
169. *Id.* at 806.
170. *Id.* at 808.
171. *Zant v. Stephens,* 462 U.S. 862 (1983) at 867.
172. *Id.*
173. *Id.* at 885.
174. *Id.* at 888–90.
175. *Id.* at 905.
176. *Id.* at 912–13.

177. *Barclay v. Florida,* 463 U.S. 939 (1983) at 941–42.

178. *Id.* at 946.

179. *Id.* at 954.

180. *Id.* at 956.

181. *Id.* at 958.

182. *Id.*

183. *Id.* at 984.

184. *Id.* at 986–87.

185. *Pulley v. Harris,* 465 U.S. 37 (1984) at 39–40.

186. *Id.* at 43.

187. *Id.*

188. *Id.* at 54.

189. *Id.* at 67–68.

190. *Wainwright v. Witt,* 469 U.S. 412 (1985) at 416.

191. *Id.* at 418.

192. *Id.* at 423.

193. *Id.* at 424.

194. *Id.* at 442.

195. *Caldwell v. Mississippi,* 472 U.S. 320 (1985) at 329.

196. *Id.* at 331–32.

197. *Id.* at 349.

198. *Id.* at 350.

199. *Skipper v. South Carolina,* 476 U.S. 1 (1986) at 3.

200. *Id.* at 4.

201. *Id.* at 3.

202. *Id.* at 7.

203. That such a fact needs to be stated reflects a social reality that should embarrass all people. The facts should be nothing more than that a man, Turner, murdered another man, W. Jack Smith Jr. As a society, unfortunately, we are not there yet. In just a few lines I note that there were eight whites and four blacks on the jury. Of what possible interest could that fact be if there is "equal justice under law"?

204. *Turner v. Murray,* 476 U.S. 28 (1986) at 30.

205. Are there nonwhite Caucasians?

206. *Turner v. Murray,* 476 U.S. 28 (1986) at 30–31.

207. *Id.* at 31.

208. *Id.*

209. *Id.*

210. *Id.* at 34.

211. *Id.* at 36–37.

212. *Id.* at 42–43.

213. These very general remarks are not easily sustainable in theory. A more specific explanation of these two claims is beyond the scope of this book.

214. *Ford v. Wainwright,* 477 U.S. 399 (1986) at 402.

215. *Id.* at 402–3.

216. *Id.* at 405.

217. *Id.* at 410–16.

218. *Id.* at 417.

219. *Id.* at 435.

220. Justice O'Connor provides the "facts" of the case in *Tison v. Arizona,* 481 U.S. 137 (1987) at 139–41.

221. *Id.* at 142.

222. *Id.* at 142–43. The aggravating circumstances were that "the Tisons had created a grave risk of death to others," that "the murders had been committed for pecuniary gain," and that "the murders were especially heinous." The mitigating circumstances focused on the boys' youth (20 and 19), no prior criminal record, and that "each had been convicted of the murders under the felony-murder rule."

223. See especially *id.* at 144–45.

224. *Id.* at 148.

225. *Id.* at 154.

226. *Id.* at 157–58.

227. *Id.* at 160.

228. *Id.* at 164–68.

229. *Id.* at 168–70.

230. *Id.* at 173.

231. That assumes, of course, that people will agree on what reasonable doubt means.

232. *McCleskey v. Kemp,* 481 U.S. 279 (1987) at 286. The study cited by Justice Powell is that of David C. Baldus, George Woodworth, Charles A. Pulaski Jr., *Equal Justice and the Death Penalty* (Boston, Mass.: Northeastern University Press, 1990). See especially pp. 306–93.

233. *McCleskey v. Kemp,* 481 U.S. 279 (1987) at 286–87.

234. *Id.* at 292.

235. *Id.* at 297.

236. *Id.* at 321.

237. *Id.* at 325.

238. *Id.* at 328.

239. A victim impact statement has been defined as follows: "Information or version of events filed voluntarily by the victim of a crime, appended to the presentence investigation report as a supplement for judicial consideration in sentencing the offender. Describes injuries to victims resulting from convicted offender's actions." A presentence (investigation) report has been defined as follows: "Report filed by probation or parole officer appointed by court containing background information relative to defendant. Facts in the case are included. Used to influence sentence imposed by judge and by parole board considering an inmate for early release." See Dean J. Champion, *Dictionary of American Criminal Justice* (Chicago: Fitzroy Dearborn Publishers, 1998), 127 and 97, respectively.

240. *Booth v. Maryland,* 482 U.S. 496 (1987) at 498.

241. *Id.*

242. *Id.* at 498–500.

243. *Id.* at 504–5.

244. *Id.* at 505.

245. *Id.* at 206.

246. *Id.*

247. See *Payne v. Tennessee,* 501 U.S. 808 (1991).

248. *Lowenfield v. Phelps,* 484 U.S. 231 (1988) at 233.

249. *Id.* at 234.

250. *Id.* at 235.

251. *Id.*

252. *Id.* at 240.

253. *Id.* at 243–44.

254. *Id.* at 244–45.

255. *Id.* at 246.

256. *Id.* at 247.

257. *Id.* at 259.

258. *Id.*

259. *Satterwhite v. Texas,* 486 U.S. 249 (1988) at 251.

260. *Id.* at 253.

261. *Id.*

262. *Id.*

263. *Id.* at 260.

264. *Maynard v. Cartwright,* 486 U.S. 356 (1988) at 358–59.

265. *Id.* at 359.

266. *Id.* at 361.

267. *Id.* at 361–62.

268. Oklahoma argued as well that the lower court identified two aggravating circumstances and that therefore the sentence should stand. White notes, however, that there was no statutory provision for determining what should be done in the event that an aggravating circumstance failed constitutional review. Accordingly, with one aggravating circumstance identified, the death penalty in this case cannot stand. See *Id.* at 365.

269. *Mills v. Maryland,* 486 U.S. 367 (1988) at 371.

270. *Id.* at 372.

271. *Id.*

272. *Id.* at 373–74.

273. *Id.* at 374.

274. *Id.* at 377–78.

275. *Id.* at 381.

276. *Id.* at 393.

277. *Id.* at 395.

278. See Victor L. Streib, *Death Penalty for Juveniles* (Bloomington: Indiana University Press, 1987).

279. *Thompson v. Oklahoma,* 487 U.S. 815 (1988) at 819.

280. *Id.* at 820 (my italics).

281. *Id.* at 823–24.

282. *Id.* at 836.

283. *Id.* at 836–38.

284. *Id.* at 860.

285. *South Carolina v. Gathers,* 490 U.S. 805 (1989) at 809.

286. *Id.* at 809–10.

287. *Id.* at 810.

288. See *Id.* at 810–12.

289. *Id.* at 817.

290. *Id.* at 818.

291. *Id.* at 820–21.

292. *Penry v. Lynaugh,* 492 U.S. 302 (1989) at 307.

293. *Id.* at 308.

294. *Id.* at 308–9.

295. *Id.* at 310.

296. *Id.* at 309–10.

297. *Id.* at 310.

298. *Id.* at 311.

299. *Id.*

300. *Id.* at 312.

301. *Id.* at 313.

302. *Id.* at 322.

303. *Id.* at 328.

304. *Id.* at 331.

305. *Id.* at 331–32.

306. *Id.*

307. *Id.* at 336.

308. *Id.* at 338–39.

309. *Id.* at 340.

310. *Id.* at 346.

311. *Id.* at 348.

312. *Penry v. Johnson,* No. 00–6677, slip op. at 10 (June 4, 2001) (references omitted).

313. *Id.* at 14.

314. *Stanford v. Kentucky,* 492 U.S. 361 (1989) at 368.

315. *Id.* at 369.

316. *Id.* at 370–71.

317. *Id.* at 373.

318. *Id.* at 374.

319. *Id.* at 374–75.

320. *Id.* at 380.

321. *Id.* at 387.

322. *Id.* at 393.

323. *Id.* at 394.

324. *Id.* at 396.

325. *Id.* at 402.

326. For Brennan's complete line of reasoning here, see *Id.* at 403–4.

327. *Id.* at 404.

328. *Blystone v. Pennsylvania,* 494 U.S. 299 (1990) at 305.

329. *Id.* at 306.

330. *Id.* at 306–7.

331. *Id.* at 307–8.

332. *Id.* at 323–24.

333. *McKoy v. North Carolina,* 494 U.S. 433 (1990) at 443.

334. *Id.* at 444.

335. *Id.* at 458–59.

336. *Clemons v. Mississippi,* 494 U.S. 738 (1990) at 741.

337. *Id.*

338. *Id.* at 745.

339. *Id.* at 748.

340. *Id.* at 748–49.

341. *Id.* at 749.

342. *Id.* at 751.

343. *Id.* at 754.

344. *Walton v. Arizona,* 497 U.S. 639 (1990) at 645.

345. *Id.*

346. *Id.*

347. *Id.* at 646.

348. *Id.*

349. *Walton* will be overturned in 2002 in *Ring v. Arizona,* No. 01–488. Argued April 22, 2002—Decided June 24, 2002.

350. *Id.* at 649.

351. *Id.* at 650.

352. *Id.* at 651–52.

353. *Id.* at 654–55.

354. *Id.* at 677.

355. *Id.* at 712–13.

356. See *Ring.*

357. *Lewis v. Jeffers,* 497 U.S. 764 (1990) at 777.

358. *Id.* at 793–95.

359. *Parker v. Dugger,* 498 U.S. 308 (1991) at 313–14.

360. *Id.* at 314.

361. *Id.* at 320.

362. *Id.* at 322.

363. *Id.* at 323.

364. *Id.* at 333.

365. This due process requirement, among others, can be compared with "informed consent" in medical care. Patients must be informed about the possible consequences of recommended surgery, medication, or treatment options if they are to evaluate meaningfully their options. In criminal law, informed consent as due process requires that defendants know what possible consequences await them if they are to evaluate meaningfully their defense strategies. Once again, "due process" is a moving target, as is in many ways informed consent. That reality should not be troublesome. Indeed, I would argue that the open-ended nature of these two concepts are strengths, not weaknesses.

366. *Lankford v. Ohio,* 500 U.S. 110 (1991) at 111.

367. *Id.* at 116.

368. *Id.* at 119.

369. *Id.* at 120.

370. *Id.* at 127.

371. *Id.* at 135.

372. *Payne v. Tennessee,* 501 U.S. 808 (1991) at 814.

373. *Id.* at 819.

374. *Id.* at 820–21.

375. *Id.* at 823–24.

376. *Id.* at 825.

377. *Id.*

378. *Id.* at 827.

379. *Id.* at 845–46.

380. *Id.* at 856.

381. *Id.* at 856–57. See his more specific concerns at 860–61.

382. We have reached a truly macabre point when we can say that there are "really bad" murders—perhaps the victim was tortured and mutilated—as opposed to "run-of-the-mill" murders in which the victim is *just* murdered. For all practical purposes, those guilty individuals who sit on death row sit there solely because they have committed a particularly gruesome (an "especially heinous, atrocious, or cruel") murder.

383. See the previous discussion of *Clemons* and *Maynard.*

384. The precise wording of this particular aggravating circumstance is not essential for it to be unconstitutionally vague. In *Godfrey* the aggravating circumstance "outrageously, wantonly vile and inhuman" was declared unconstitutionally vague as well.

385. *Stringer v. Black,* 503 U.S. 222 (1992) at 230.

386. *Id.*

387. *Id.* at 236.

388. *Clemons* and *Maynard* were decided several years after Stringer's conviction and sentence.

389. *Stringer v. Black,* 503 U.S. 222 (1992) at 243–48.

390. *Morgan v. Illinois,* 504 U.S. 719 (1992) at 721.

391. *Id.* at 723.

392. *Id.*

393. *Id.*

394. *Id.* 733–34.

395. See especially *id.* at 736–39.

396. *Id.* at 742.

397. *Id.* at 741.

398. *Id.* at 750.

399. *Id.*

400. *Herrera v. Collins,* 506 U.S. 390 (1993) at 394–95: "The evidence showed that Herrera's Social Security card had been found alongside Rucker's patrol car on the night he was killed. Splatters of blood on the car identified as the vehicle involved in the shootings, and on petitioner's blue jeans and wallet were identified as type A blood—the same type which Rucker had. (Herrera has type O blood.) Similar evidence with respect to strands of hair found in the car indicated that the hair was Rucker's, and not Herrera's. A handwritten letter was also found on the person of petitioner when he was arrested, which strongly implied that he had killed Rucker."

401. *Id.* at 399.

402. *Id.* at 403.

403. *Id.* at 405. Rehnquist notes here that Herrera does not claim "that some error was made in imposing a capital sentence upon him, but that a fundamental error was made in finding him guilty of the underlying murder in the first place." That being the case, Rehnquist writes that it "would be a rather strange jurispru-

dence, in these circumstances, which held under our Constitution [Herrera] could not be executed, but that he could spend the rest of his life in prison."

404. For example, Rehnquist writes that "[t]he early federal cases adhere to the common law rule that a new trial may be granted only during the term of court in which the final judgment was rendered." *Id.* at 408. In general, see *id.* at 405–14.

405. *Id.* at 411.

406. *Id.*

407. *Id.* at 415.

408. *Id.*

409. *Id.* at 415–17.

410. *Id.* at 432.

411. *Id.* at 434.

412. *Id.* at 443.

413. *Id.* at 446.

414. *Romano v. Oklahoma,* 512 U.S. 1 (1994) at 3.

415. *Id.* at 4.

416. *Id.* at 6.

417. *Id.* at 10.

418. *Id.* at 15.

419. *Id.* at 17.

420. *Id.*

421. *Simmons v. South Carolina,* 512 U.S. 154 (1994) at 156.

422. *Id.*

423. *Id.* at 157.

424. *Id.*

425. *Id.* at 180–81.

426. *Harris v. Alabama,* 513 U.S. 504 (1995) at 505.

427. *Id.* at 509.

428. *Id.* at 510.

429. *Id.* at 515–16.

430. *Id.* at 520.

431. *Id.* at 526.

432. *Buchanan v. Angelone,* 522 U.S. 269 (1998) at 271.

433. *Id.* at 273.

434. *Id.*

435. *Id.* at 275.

436. *Id.* at 276.

437. *Id.*

438. *Id.* at 278–79.

439. *Id.* at 279.

440. *Id.* at 281.

441. See Justice O'Connor's dissenting opinion in *Ring v. Arizona,* No. 01—488. Argued April 22, 2002—Decided June 24, 2002, at 2).

442. See http://www.deathpenaltyinfo.org. Search DPIC under U.S. Supreme Court: *Ring v. Arizona*; click on "U.S. Supreme Court: Ring v. Arizona."

443. *Ring v. Arizona,* No. 01–488. Argued April 22, 2002—Decided June 24, 2002, Justice Ginsberg at 1–2.

444. *Id.* at 1.

445. *Id.* at 10–11.

446. *Hildwin v. Florida,* 490 U.S. 638 (1989).

447. A *per curiam* opinion is "an opinion 'by the court,' which expresses its decision in the case but who author is not identified." Gifis, *Law Dictionary,* 352.

448. See discussion of *Walton.*

449. *Ring* at 23.

450. *Ring v. Arizona,* No. 01–488, slip op. at 3 (Scalia, J., concurring) (italics in original).

451. *Id.,* slip op. at 1 (Breyer, J., concurring).

452. *Id.* at 2.

453. *Id.* at 2–3.

454. *Id.* at 3.

455. *Id.*

456. *Id.* at 6.

457. *Id.,* slip op. at 3 (O'Connor, J., dissenting)

CHAPTER 5

1. David Gottlieb, "The Death Penalty in the Legislature: Some Thoughts about Money, Myth, and Morality," 39 *U. Kan. L. Rev.* 443 (1989), 470.

2. U.S. Const. amend. XIV, § 1.

3. *The New Oxford Annotated Bible* (New York: Oxford University Press); Exodus 21: 22–25.

4. *Id.,* Genesis 9: 6.

5. Matthew Silverstein, "COMMENT: Sentencing Coker v. Georgia to Death: Capital Child Rape Statutes Provide the Supreme Court an Opportunity to Return Meaning to the Eighth Amendment," *37 Gonz. L. Rev. 121* (2001/2002).

6. *Zant,* 462 U.S. at 877.

7. *Godfrey,* 446 U.S. at 422.

8. *Id.* at 428.

9. *Id.* at 433.

10. Chief Justice Burger's dissent has been summarized in chapter 4.

11. *Godfrey,* 466 U.S. at 449.

12. *Barclay v. Florida,* 463 U.S. 939 (1983).

13. *Id.* at 949.

14. *Id.* at 950–51.

15. *Poland v. Arizona,* 476 U.S. 147 (1986).

16. *Id.* at 154.

17. *Maynard v. Cartwright,* 486 U.S. 356 (1988).

18. *Id.* at 358.

19. *Id.* at 364–65.

20. *Walton v. Arizona,* 497 U.S. 639 (1990).

21. *Id.* at 655.

22. *Stringer v. Black,* 503 U.S. 222 (1992).

23. See the previous discussion of *Clemons* and *Maynard.*

24. The precise wording of this particular aggravating circumstance is not essential for it to be unconstitutionally vague. In *Godfrey,* the aggravating circum-

stance "outrageously, wantonly vile and inhuman" was declared unconstitutionally vague as well.

25. *Stringer*, 503 U.S. 222 (1992) at 230.

26. *Id.*

27. *Id.* at 236.

28. *Sochor v. Florida*, 504 U.S. 527 (1992).

29. *Id.* at 530.

30. *Id.* at 540–41.

31. *Id.* at 542.

32. *Id.*

33. *Richmond v. Lewis*, 506 U.S. 40 (1992).

34. *Id.* at 46.

35. *Id.* at 52.

36. *Arave v. Creech*, 507 U.S. 463 (1993).

37. *Id.* at 467.

38. *Id.* at 468.

39. *Id.* at 469.

40. *Id.* at 465.

41. *Id.* at 471.

42. *Id.* at 471–72.

43. *Id.* at 475–76.

44. *Id.* at 478.

45. *Id.* at 479.

46. *Id.* at 480.

47. *Id.* at 480–81.

48. *Id.* at 488.

49. James R. Acker and Charles S. Lanier, *Beyond Human Ability? The Rise and Fall of Death Penalty Legislation,* in *America's Experiment with Capital Punishment,* ed. James R. Acker, Robert M. Bohm and Charles S. Lanier (Durham, N.C.: Carolina Academic Press, 1998), 77–115.

50. Ibid., 101.

51. Ibid.,101–2.

52. Ibid., 102.

53. Steven B. Bright, "Elected Judges and the Death Penalty in Texas: Why Full Habeas Corpus Review by Independent Federal Judges Is Indispensable to Protecting Constitutional Rights," *Texas Law Review* 78, no. 7 (June 2000): 1805–37, 1826.

54. Ibid. at 1811.

55. David D. Langfitt and Billy H. Nolas, "Ineffective Assistance of Counsel in Death Penalty Cases," *Litigation* 26, no. 4 (summer 2000): 6–13 and 70–71.

56. Ibid., 13.

57. Ibid.

58. Ibid., 71.

59. Ibid.

60. Bright, "Elected Judges," 1813.

61. Langfitt and Nolas, "Ineffective Assistance," 6.

62. Ibid., 12.

63. Ibid., 71.

64. Bright, "Elected Judges," 1836.

65. Ibid., 1809.

66. Ibid., 1808.

67. *Wainwright v. Witt*, 469 U.S. at 439.

68. *Id.* at 460.

69. *Id.* at 463.

70. Joseph L. Hoffman, "How American Juries Decide Death Penalty Cases: The Capital Jury Project" in *The Death Penalty in America,* ed. Hugo Adam Bedau (New York: Oxford University Press, 1997), 333–43.

71. Ibid., 338.

72. Ibid., 338–39.

73. Stephen R. McAllister, "The Problem of Implementing a Constitutional System of Capital Punishment," *Kan. L. Rev,* Vol. 43, No. 5 (1995), 1040.

74. *Id.*, 1100–1101.

75. *Id.*, 1100.

76. Amy K. Phillips, "Thou Shalt Not Kill Nice People: The Problem of Victim Impact Statements in Capital Sentencing," *American Criminal Law Review* 35, no. 1 (fall 1997): 93–118.

77. Ibid., 105.

78. Ibid.

79. Ibid., 118.

80. Ibid.

81. Ibid.

82. Joshua D. Greenberg, "Is Payne Defensible?: The Constitutionality of Admitting Victim-Impact Evidence at Capital Sentencing Hearings," *Ind. L. J.,* Vol. 75, No. 4, Fall (2000), 1342–82.

83. *Id.*, 1350.

84. *Id.*, 1382.

85. Wayne A. Logan, "Through the Past Darkly: A Survey of the Uses and Abuses of Victim Impact Evidence in Capital Trials," 41 *Ariz. L. Rev.* 143, Spring (1999), 190.

86. Austin Sarat, *When the State Kills* (Princeton, N.J.: Princeton University Press, 2001). See especially chapter 2, pp. 33–59.

87. Ibid., 53.

88. Immanuel Kant, *Kant's Political Writings,* ed. with an Introduction and notes by Hans Reiss, trans. by H.B. Nisbet (Cambridge: Cambridge University Press, 1970), 155.

89. Anthony Neddo, "Comment: Prosecutorial Discretion in Charging the Death Penalty: Opening the Doors to Arbitrary Decisionmaking in New York Capital Cases," 60 *Alb. L. Rev.* 1949 (1997), 1949.

CHAPTER 6

1. As of June 2001, more than 3,800 convicted capital defendants sit on death row. The Supreme Court hears approximately 200 cases each year, only a handful of which concern capital punishment. Because some 300 death sentences are handed down each year, what the justices do not hear could be more important than what they do hear.

2. C. Ronald Huff, Arye Rattner, and Edward Sagarin, *Convicted but Innocent* (Thousand Oaks, Calif.: Sage Publications, 1996).

3. Geoffrey Abbott, *The Book of Execution: An Encyclopedia of Methods of Judicial Execution* (London: Headline Book Publishing, 1994), 156.

4. Ibid.

5. For even more exciting punishment options, see Abbott, *The Book of Execution*.

6. William J. Bowers and Glenn L. Pierce, "Deterrence or Brutalization: What Is the Effect of Executions?" reprinted in Victor L. Streib, *A Capital Punishment Anthology* (Cincinnati, Ohio: Anderson Publishing Company, 1993), 84.

7. I read the following newspaper accounts that appeared on June 12, 2001: *Philadelphia Inquirer, New York Times, USA Today,* and the *New York Daily News.*

8. Countless writers have identified capital punishment costs. For some quick insight into capital punishment costs, see the following: John Kaplan, "The Problem of Capital Punishment,"in *A Capital Punishment Anthology* ed. by Victor L. Streib (Cincinnati, Ohio: Anderson Publishing Company, 1933), 8–11; Mark Costanzo, *Just Revenge* (New York: St. Martin's Press, 1997), 59–69; Sister Helen Prejean, *Dead Man Walking* (New York: Vintage Books, 1994), 129–30.

9. Richard Sisk, "Legal Tab's $15M, and Counting," *New York Daily News,* June 12, 2001, national ed., 4.

10. *Baldwin v. Alabama,* 472 U.S. 372 (1985) at 374–75.

11. *Callins v. Collins,* 510 U.S. 1141 (1994) at 1142–43.

12. See, for example, Bob Weinstein and Jim Bessent, *Death Row Confidential* (New York: Harper Paperbacks, 1996); Jan Arriens, ed., *Welcome to Hell: Letters and Writings from Death Row* (Boston, Mass.: Northeastern University Press, 1997); and David von Drehle, *Among the Lowest of the Dead* (New York: Random House, 1995).

13. Contrary to some authors, I continue to maintain that there is a substantive difference between retribution and revenge or vengeance.

14. See, for example, Jeffrie G. Murphy, *Getting Even: The Role of the Victim,* in *Punishment and Rehabilitation,* 3d ed., ed. Jeffrey G. Murphy (Belmont, Calif.: Wadsworth Publishing, 1995).

15. John Locke, *Second Treatise of Government,* ed., with an Introduction by C. B. Macpherson (Indianapolis, Ind.: Hackett Publishing Company, 1980), 9.

16. Ibid., 12.

17. I do not base my position on the possibility that an innocent person will be executed for several reasons, one of which is that I believe that one day there will be foolproof means to guarantee that no innocent person will be convicted, much less executed. At that point I will continue to maintain that errorless sentences of death do not comport with the Eighth Amendment.

18. *Herrera v. Collins,* 506 U.S. at 430.

19. *Id.* at 430–31.

20. Willard Gaylin, *The Killing of Bonnie Garland* (New York: Simon and Schuster, 1982), 316.

21. Ibid., 327–28.

22. Ibid., 328.

23. There are numerous books available on both prison in general and death row in particular. The following are particularly good: Pete Early, *The Hot House: Life Inside Leavenworth Prison* (New York: Bantam Books, 1992); Wilbert Rideau and

Ron Wikberg, *Life Sentences: Rage and Survival Behind Bars* (New York: Times Books, 1992); Jan Arriens, ed., *Welcome to Hell: Letters and Writings from Death Row* (Boston, Mass.: Northeastern University Press, 1997); David Von Drehle, *Among the Lowest of the Dead* (New York: Random House, 1995); Donald A. Cabana, *Death at Midnight: The Confession of an Executioner* (Boston, Mass.: Northeastern University Press, 1996); and Stephen Trombley, *The Execution Protocol* (New York: Anchor Books, 1992).

24. John Stuart Mill, "In Support of Capital Punishment," in *Philosophical Essays on Punishment,* ed. Gertrude Ezorsky (Albany, N.Y.: State University of New York Press, 1972).

25. One such group is Murder Victims' Families for Reconciliation (MVFR). Mark Costanzo, *Just Revenge: Costs and Consequences of the Death Penalty* (New York: St. Martin's Press, 1997), 144–45.

26. Willie Francis's case is examined in chapter 2.

27. For example, Stuart A. Creque has argued that nitrogen asphyxiation offers a painless and inexpensive means of carrying out executions. See Stuart A. Creque, "Killing with Kindness," *National Review,* September 11, 1995.

28. This possibility develops creatively in the excellent "speculative" and futuristic novel by James Halperin. James Halperin, *The Truth Machine* (New York: Ballantine Books, 1996).

29. Arthur S. Miller and Jeffrey H. Bowman, *Death by Installments* (New York: Greenwood Press, 1988), 144–46.

30. The idea of using organs of executed inmates for transplant purposes is not new. Since there will soon be over 4,000 death row inmates, there are a plethora of organs to harvest. If we must have a death penalty, should we not maximize whatever good can come from it? Of course, the use of executed murderers' organs could result in charges of a mini-holocaust inasmuch as most murderers on death row are poor and/or uneducated. In essence, such a benevolent sounding program could quickly escalate into a pogrom directed against the poor and the illiterate. In addition, I would be willing to wager, since organ demand exceeds organ supply, that even more capital defendants will be found guilty and sentenced to death. From an economic perspective, the program (or pogrom, depending on your perspective) makes sense. But a society that can so easily discard its poorest and most illiterates hardly constitutes a society in which I want to live. It is at that point that we not forget the frequently cited observation of Fyodor Dostoyevsky, namely, "'A society should be judged not by how it treats its outstanding citizens but by how it treats its worst criminals.'" Costanzo, *Just Revenge,* 58. On the use of executed murderers' organs, see Louis J. Palmer, "Capital Punishment: A Utilitarian Proposal for Recycling Transplantable Organs as Part of a Capital Felon's Death Sentence," *U. West L.A. L. Rev.,* Vol. 29, 1998, 2–41.

Bibliography

Abbott, Geoffrey. *The Book of Execution: An Encyclopedia of Methods of Judicial Execution.* London: Headline Book Publishing, 1994.

Abraham, Henry J., and Barbara A. Perry. *Freedom and the Court: Civil Rights and Liberties in the United States.* 7th ed. New York: Oxford University Press, 1998.

Acker, James R., and Charles S. Lanier. "Beyond Human Ability? The Rise and Fall of Death Penalty Legislation." In *America's Experiment with Capital Punishment,* edited by James R. Acker, Robert M. Bohm, and Charles S. Lanier, 77–115. Durham, N.C.: Carolina Academic Press, 1998.

Adams, Randall, with William Hoffer and Marilyn Mona Hoffer. *Adams v. Texas.* New York: St. Martin's Press, 1991.

Alderman, Ellen, and Caroline Kennedy. *In Our Defense: The Bill of Rights in Action.* New York: William Morrow and Company, Inc., 1991.

Arriens, Jan, ed. *Welcome to Hell: Letters and Writings from Death Row.* Boston, Mass.: Northeastern University Press, 1997.

Baldus, David C., George Woodworth, and Charles A. Pulaski Jr. *Equal Justice and the Death Penalty.* Boston, Mass.: Northeastern University Press, 1990.

Barnes, Patricia G. *Desk Reference on American Criminal Justice.* Washington, D.C.: CQ Press, 2001.

Bedau, Hugo Adam, ed. *The Death Penalty in America.* New York: Oxford University Press, 1997.

Bentham, Jeremy. *The Principles of Morals and Legislation.* Amherst, N.Y.: Prometheus Books, 1988.

Berger, Raoul. *Death Penalties.* Cambridge, Mass.: Harvard University Press, 1982.

Bigel, Alan I. *Justices William J. Brennan, Jr. and Thurgood Marshall on Capital Punishment.* Lanham, Md.: University Press of America, 1997.

Biskupic, Joan, and Elder Witt. *The Supreme Court and the Powers of the American Government.* Washington, D.C.: Congressional Quarterly, Inc., 1997.

Black's Law Dictionary. 7th ed. St. Paul, Minn.: West Publishing, 1999.

Bowers, William J., and Glenn L. Pierce. "Deterrence or Brutalization: What Is the Effect of Executions?" In *A Capital Punishment Anthology,* edited by Victor Streib, 82–88. Cincinnati, Ohio: Anderson Publishing, 1993.

Bright, Stephen B. "Elected Judges and the Death Penalty in Texas: Why Full Habeas Corpus Review by Independent Federal Judges Is Indispensable to Protecting Constitutional Rights." *Texas Law Review* 78, no. 7 (June 2000): 1805–37.

Cabana, Donald A. *Death at Midnight: The Confession of an Executioner.* Boston, Mass.: Northeastern University Press, 1996.

Cardozo, Benjamin N. *The Nature of the Judicial Process.* New Haven, Conn.: Yale University Press, 1921.

Carter, Dan T. *Scottsboro: A Tragedy of the American South.* Revised edition. Baton Rouge: Louisiana State University Press, 1979.

Champion, Dean J. *Dictionary of American Criminal Justice: Key Terms and Major Supreme Court Cases.* Chicago: Fitzroy Dearborn Publishers, 1998.

Clapp, James E. *Random House Webster's Dictionary of the Law.* New York: Random House, 2000.

Costanzo, Mark. *Just Revenge: Costs and Consequences of the Death Penalty.* New York: St. Martin's Press, 1997.

Creque, Stuart A. "Killing with Kindness." *National Review,* September 11, 1995: 51.

Earley, Pete. *The Hot House: Life Inside Leavenworth Prison.* New York: Bantam Books, 1992.

Frost-Knappman, Elizabeth, and David S. Shrader, with the assistance of Scarlet Riley. *The Quotable Lawyer.* Revised edition. New York: Facts on File, Inc., 1998.

Gaylin, Willard. *The Killing of Bonnie Garland.* New York: Simon & Schuster, 1982.

Gifis, Steven H. *Law Dictionary.* 3rd ed. Hauppauge, N.Y.: Barron's Educational Series, 1991.

Goldberg, Arthur J., and Alan M. Dershowitz. "Declaring the Death Penalty Unconstitutional." 83 *Harvard Law Review* 1773 (1970).

Gottlieb, David. "The Death Penalty in the Legislature: Some Thoughts about Money, Myth, and Morality," 39 *University of Kansas Law Review* 443 (1989).

Greenberg, Joshua D. "Is Payne Defensible?: The Constitutionality of Admitting Victim-Impact Evidence at Capital Sentencing Hearings." *Indiana Law Journal* 75, no. 4 (fall 2000): 1342–82.

Greenley, Mark B. "Faith on the Bench: The Role of Religious Belief in the Criminal Sentencing of Judges." *Dayton Law Review* 26, no. 1, 2–41.

Halperin, James. *The Truth Machine.* New York: Ballantine Books, 1996.

Hoffman, Joseph L. "How American Juries Decide Death Penalty Cases: The Capital Jury Project." In *The Death Penalty in America,* edited by Hugo Adam Bedau, 333–43. New York: Oxford University Press, 1997.

Huff, C. Ronald, Arye Rattner, and Edward Sagarin. *Convicted but Innocent.* Thousand Oaks, Calif.: Sage Publications, Inc., 1996.

Jacoby, Susan. *Wild Justice: The Evolution of Revenge.* New York: Harper & Row, 1983.

Kant, Immanuel. *Lectures on Ethics.* Translated by Louis Infield. Indianapolis, Ind.: Hackett Publishing, 1963.

Kant, Immanuel. *Ethical Philosophy.* 2nd ed. Translated by James Ellington. Indianapolis, Ind.: Hackett Publishing, 1994.

Kaplan, John. "The Problem of Capital Punishment." In *A Capital Punishment Anthology,* edited by Victor Streib, 1–12. Cincinnati, Ohio: Anderson Publishing, 1993.

Langfitt, David D., and Billy H. Nolas. "Ineffective Assistance of Counsel in Death Penalty Cases." *Litigation* 26, no. 4 (summer 2000): 6–13, 70–71.

Lieberman, Jethro K. *A Practical Companion to the Constitution.* Berkeley: University of California Press, 1999.

Locke, John. *Two Treatises of Government.* Cambridge: Cambridge University Press, 1988.

Logan, Wayne A. "Through the Past Darkly: A Survey of the Uses and Abuses of Victim Impact Evidence in Capital Trials." 41 *Arizona Law Review* 143 (spring 1999): 143–92.

Lyons, David. *Ethics and the Rule of Law.* New York: Cambridge University Press, 1984.

May, Herbert G., and Bruce M. Metzger, eds. *The New Oxford Annotated Bible.* New York: Oxford University Press, 1973.

McAllister, Stephen R. "The Problem of Implementing a Constitutional System of Capital Punishment." *Kansas Law Review* 43, no. 5 (1995): 1039–101.

Meltsner, Michael. *Cruel and Unusual.* New York: Random House, 1973.

Menninger, Karl. *The Crime of Punishment.* New York: Viking Press, 1968.

Mill, John Stuart. "In Support of Capital Punishment." In *Philosophical Essays on Punishment,* edited by Gertrude Ezorsky, 271–78. Albany: State University of New York Press, 1972.

Miller, Arthur S., and Jeffrey H. Bowman. *Death by Installments.* New York: Greenwood Press, 1988.

Miller, Kent S., and Michael L. Radelet. *Executing the Mentally Ill.* Newbury Park, Calif.: Sage Publications, 1993.

Murphy, Jeffrie G. "Getting Even: The Role of the Victim." In *Punishment and Rehabilitation,* 3rd ed., edited by Jeffrey G. Murphy, 132–51. Belmont, Calif.: Wadsworth Publishing, 1995.

Neddo, Anthony. "Comment: Prosecutorial Discretion in Charging the Death Penalty: Opening the Doors to Arbitrary Decisionmaking in New York Capital Cases." 60 *Albany Law Review* 1949 (1997), 1949–83.

Packer, Herbert. *The Limits of the Criminal Sanction.* Stanford, Calif.: Stanford University Press, 1968.

Palmer, Louis J. "Capital Punishment: A Utilitarian Proposal for Recycling Transplantable Organs as Part of a Capital Felon's Death Sentence." *University of West Los Angeles Law Review* 29 (1998): 2–41.

Phillips, Amy K. Phillips. "Thou Shalt Not Kill Nice People: The Problem of Victim Impact Statements in Capital Sentencing." *American Criminal Law Review* 35, no. 1 (fall 1997): 93–118.

Prejean, Sister Helen. *Dead Man Walking.* New York: Vintage Books, 1993.

Rawls, John. "Two Concepts of Rules." In *The Philosophy of Punishment,* edited by H.B. Acton, 105–14. London: Macmillan and Co. Ltd., 1969.

Reiss, Hans, ed. *Kant's Political Writings.* London: Cambridge University Press, 1970.

Rideau, Wilbert, and Ron Wikberg. *Life Sentences: Rage and Survival behind Bars.* New York: Times Books, 1992.

Rooner, Amy D. "When Judges Impose the Death Penalty after the Jury Recommendations of Life: *Harris v. Alabama* as the Excision of the Tympanic Membrane in an Augmentedly Death-Biased Procedure." *Hastings Const. L. Q.* 23, no. 1 (fall 1995): 217–69.

Sarat, Austin. *When the State Kills.* Princeton, N.J.: Princeton University Press, 2001.

Sarat, Austin, and Neil Vidmar. "Public Opinion, the Death Penalty, and the Eighth Amendment: Testing the Marshall Hypothesis." In *A Capital Punishment Anthology,* edited and with comments by Victor L. Streib, 88–91. Cincinnati, Ohio: Anderson Publishing, 1993.

Sisk, Richard. "Legal Tab's $15M, and Counting." *New York Daily News.* June 12, 2001, national edition, 4.

Stangerup, Henrik. *The Man Who Wanted to Be Guilty.* New York: Marion Boyars, 1982.

Streib, Victor, ed. *A Capital Punishment Anthology.* Cincinnati, Ohio: Anderson Publishing, 1993.

Streib, Victor L. *Death Penalty for Juveniles.* Bloomington: Indiana University Press, 1987.

Szasz, Thomas S. *The Myth of Mental Illness.* Revised edition. New York: Harper & Row Publishers, 1974.

Thorne, Samuel E., William H. Dunham Jr., Philip B. Kurland, and Sir Ivor Jennings. *The Great Charter: Four Essays on Magna Carta and the History of Our Liberty.* New York: Pantheon Books, 1965.

Trombley, Stephen. *The Execution Protocol: Inside America's Capital Punishment Industry.* New York: Anchor Books, 1992.

United States Supreme Court. *U.S. Reports.*

van den Haag, Ernest. "The Death Penalty Once More." In *A Capital Punishment Anthology,* edited by Victor Streib, 1–12. Cincinnati, Ohio: Anderson Publishing, 1993.

Vila, Bryan and Cynthia Morris, eds. *Capital Punishment in the United States.* Westport, Conn.: Greenwood Press, 1997.

"Virginia Declaration of Rights." In *The Annals of America.* Vol. 2, 1775–1783. Chicago: Encyclopaedia Britannica, 1976.

Von Drehle, David. *Among the Lowest of the Dead: The Culture of Death Row.* New York: Times Books, 1995.

Weinstein, Bob, and Jim Bessent. *Death Row Confidential.* New York: Harper, 1996.

Table of Cases

Index

About the Author

MICHAEL A. FOLEY is Full Professor and Chair of the Philosophy Department, Marywood University, Scranton, Pennsylvania. His primary academic interests are philosophical perspectives on constitutional issues.